CARICATURE DRAWING MADE EASY

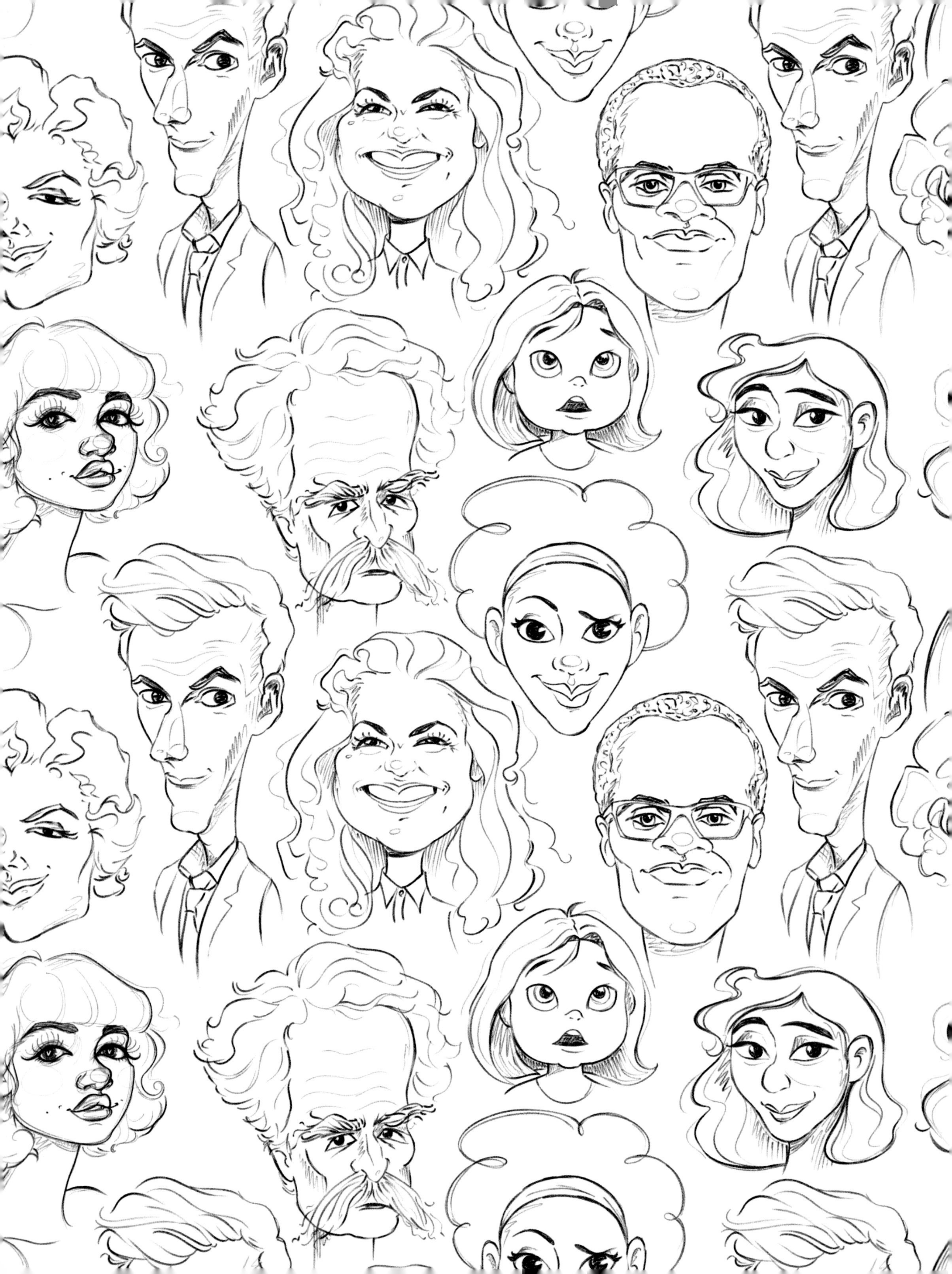

CARICATURE DRAWING MADE EASY

A STEP-BY-STEP GUIDE TO CREATING CARTOONS, CHARACTERS, AND FAN ART

MELISSA LEE

DAVID & CHARLES
— PUBLISHING —

www.davidandcharles.com

CONTENTS

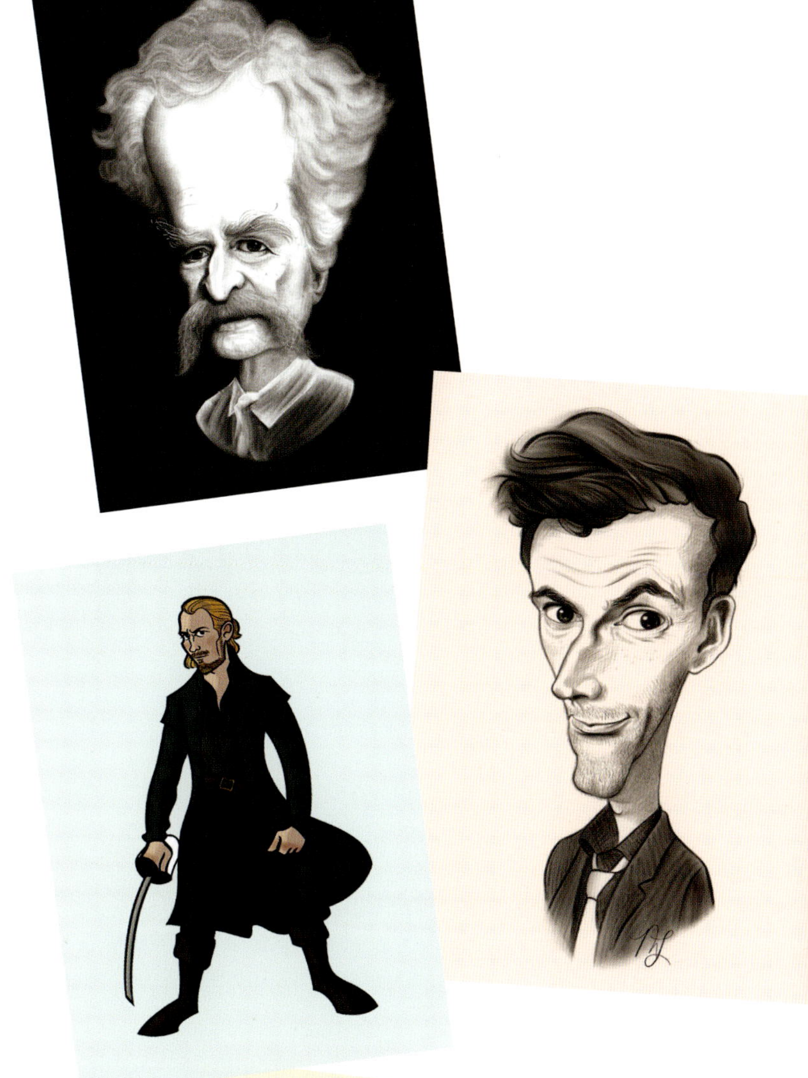

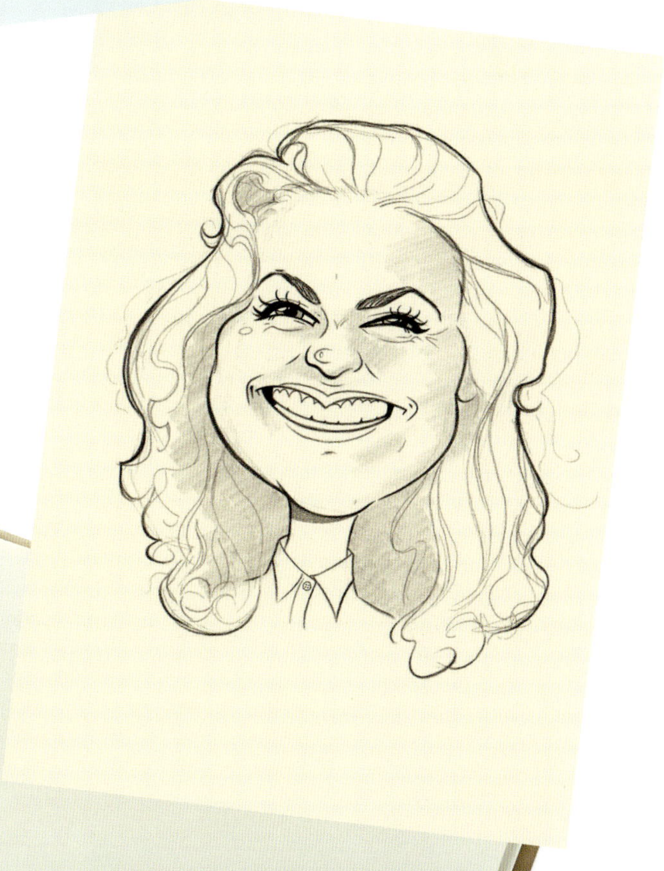

WELCOME

Hi there! Thank you from the bottom of my heart for choosing my book; I'm so honored that you're here. My name is Melissa Lee, and I'm a professional illustrator and online art teacher from Northern California. Over the years, I've had the privilege of teaching tens of thousands of students across various art subjects, with caricature and character design being particularly close to my heart.

You may be wondering about my credentials for teaching caricature. And the truth is, I don't claim to be a world-renowned expert—just someone with an immense passion for this art form and a desire to share what I've learned. My journey has involved studying and learning from the greats of caricature drawing; developing my own approaches through careful observation and trial and error; and, most importantly, lots of practice!

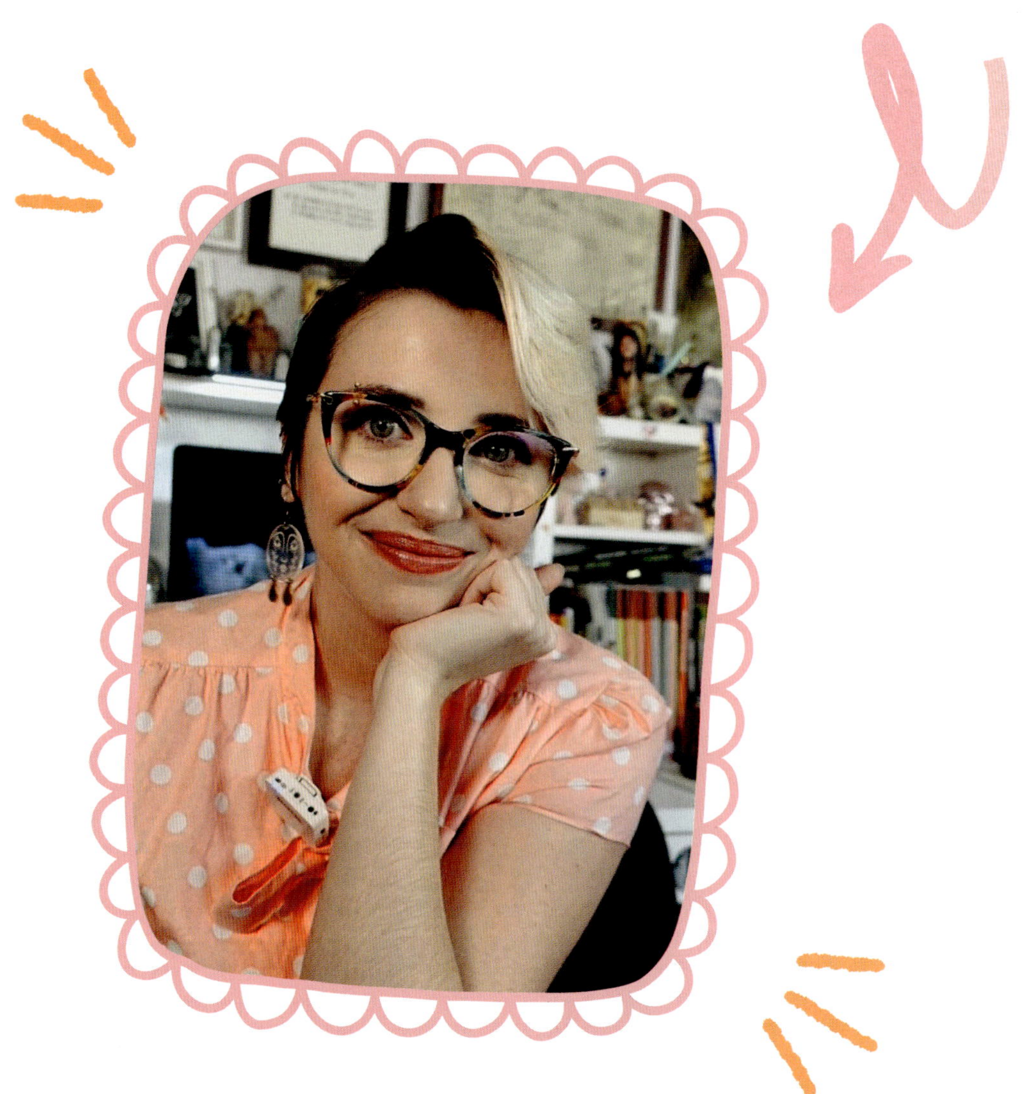

WHAT WILL YOU LEARN?

We'll begin by exploring the foundations of caricature: understanding facial proportions; identifying defining features; and mastering the art of exaggeration. As you progress through the book, you'll learn both simplified "cute-icature" techniques for creating charming, stylized portraits, and traditional methods for developing highly-rendered, detailed caricatures. I'll share some of my favorite historical and contemporary caricature artists and I'll explain how caricature and cartooning go hand-in-hand. I'll also teach you how to infuse personality into your drawings, and even how to transform beloved live-action fictional characters into cartoons!

Whether you're interested in designing original characters, creating fan art, or capturing the essence of friends and family in a funny and playful way, this book provides the step-by-step guidance you need and a solid foundation to build upon.

My hope is that by the end of our journey together through these pages, you'll not only have improved your technical skills but also begun to develop your own unique caricature and cartooning style. I see myself as a fellow traveler on this artistic path, and I invite you to join me as we improve our caricature skills together.

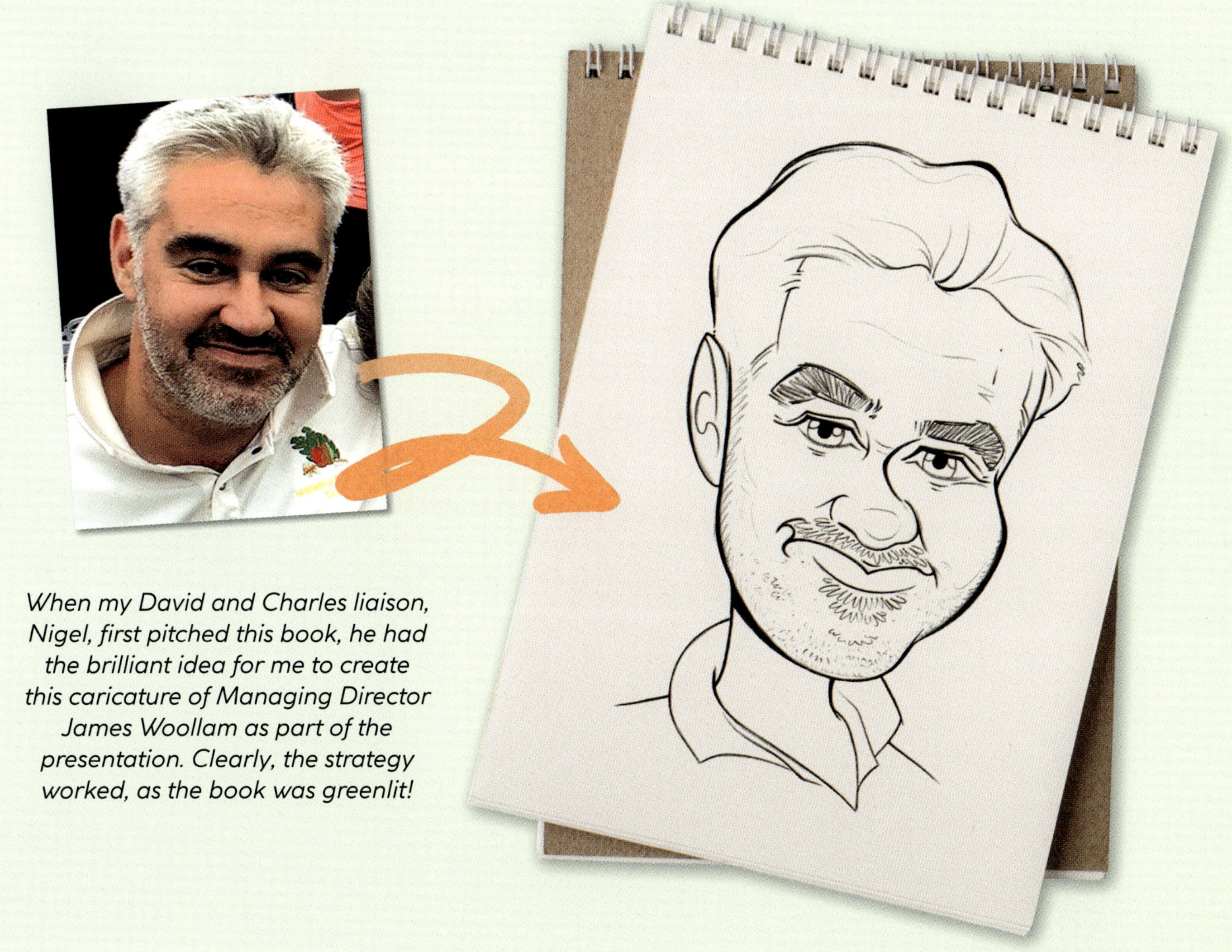

When my David and Charles liaison, Nigel, first pitched this book, he had the brilliant idea for me to create this caricature of Managing Director James Woollam as part of the presentation. Clearly, the strategy worked, as the book was greenlit!

FOUNDATIONS

In this chapter, we'll explore the fundamentals of caricature and touch on its relationship to character design. These core principles will help you to create caricatures that are bold, expressive, and full of life. We'll also work through several approachable warm-up exercises to help ease you into an art form that many find quite challenging.

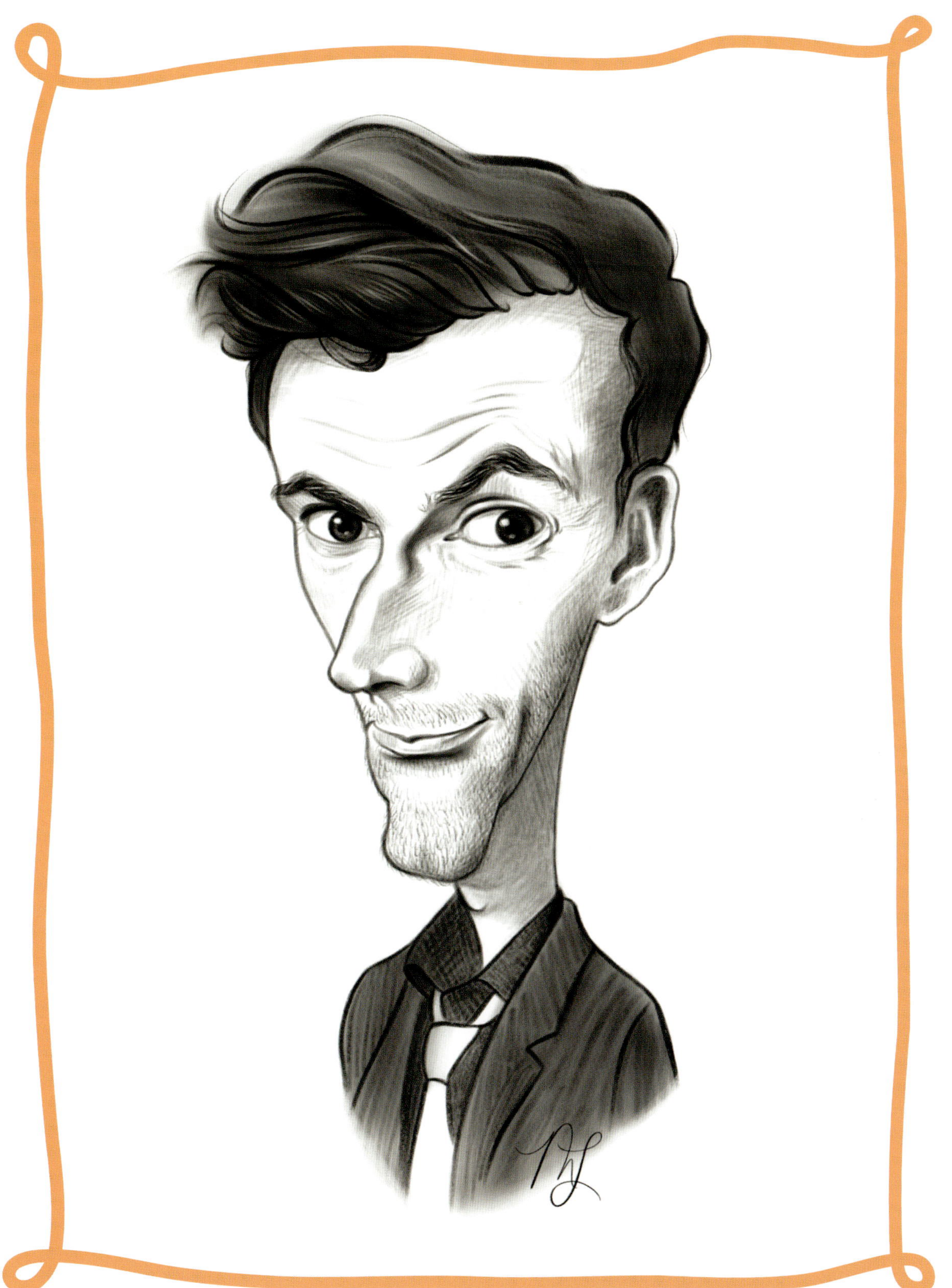

WHAT IS CARICATURE?

OK, so what is caricature? And what does it have to do with character design?

The dictionary definition of caricature is as follows:

CARICATURE · NOUN

cari.ca.ture

1: exaggeration by means of often ludicrous distortion of parts or characteristics.

"CARICATURE IS A PORTRAIT WHERE THE PROPORTIONS ARE CHANGED TO HIGHLIGHT WHAT MAKES A PERSON DIFFERENT FROM EVERYONE ELSE (OR THE AVERAGE)."

Court Jones

But I like this definition by caricature artist Court Jones as well.

CARICATURE EXAMPLE

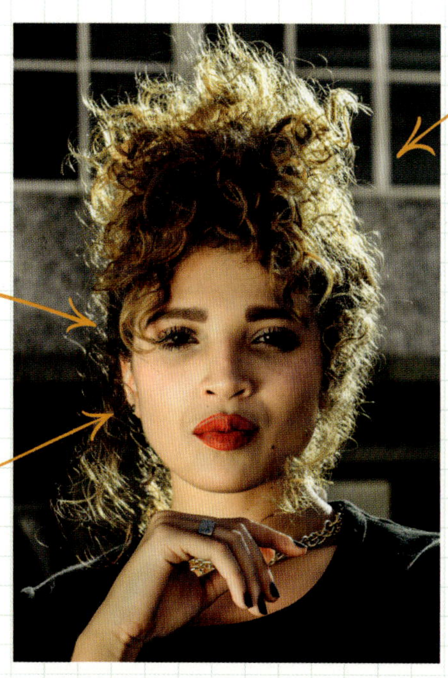

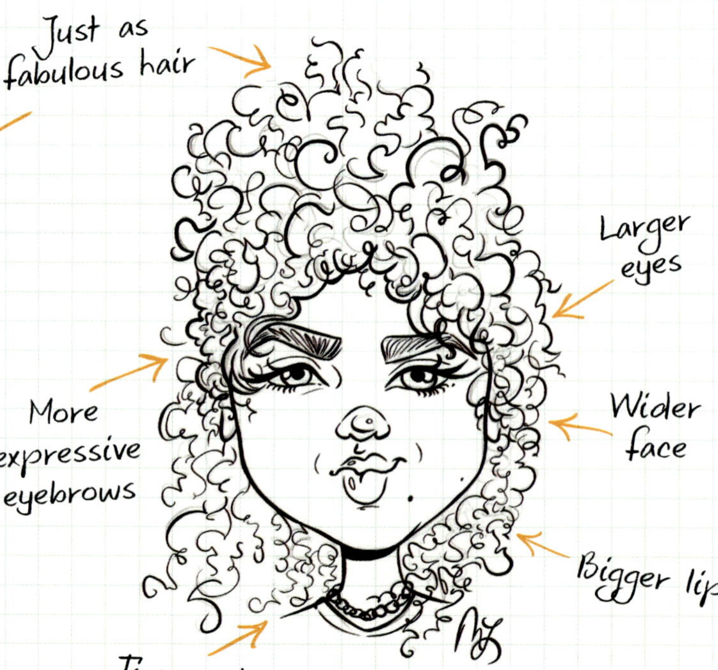

WHAT IS EXAGGERATION?

Exaggeration is essentially a deviation from the norm. When you push a design beyond the constraints of reality, you are exaggerating that form.

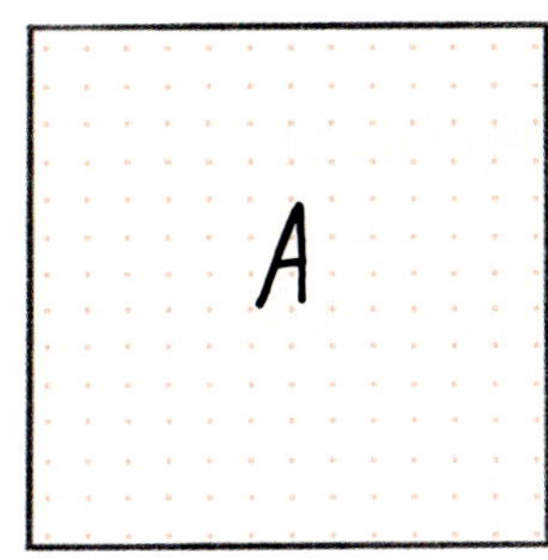

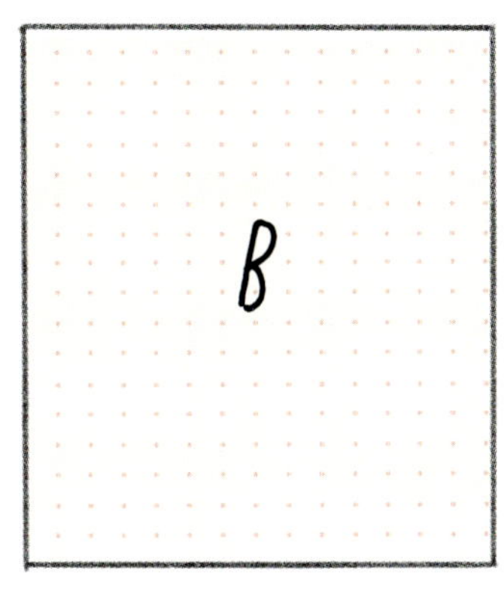

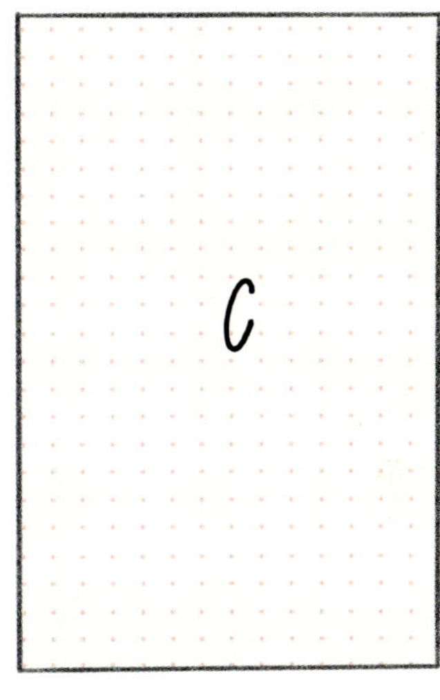

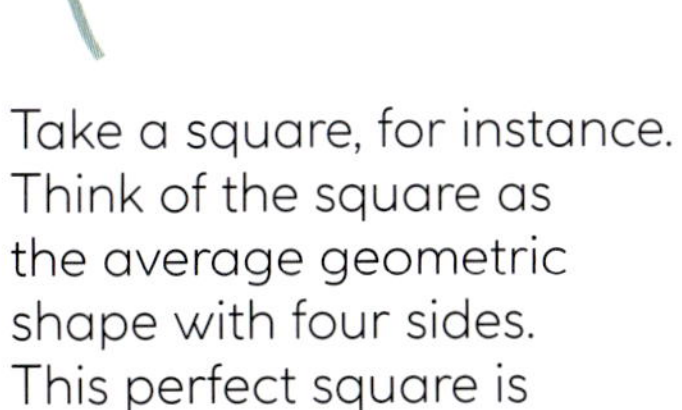

Caricature of B

Take a square, for instance. Think of the square as the average geometric shape with four sides. This perfect square is labeled "A" for "Average."

If I were to draw a caricature of shape B, I would need to observe how it differs from the average shape, which is our square. We can see that B is slightly taller, or longer, than the average. So in order to caricature it, I'm exaggerating how it differs from the square by making it even taller.

Shape C, with its stretched proportions, is a caricature of shape B.

This concept is a lot more complex when applied to a human face, of course, as faces have much more going on in them than simple rectangles do, but the ideas behind it are the same.

Caricature is all about careful observation. When you're looking at a face that you want to caricature, study all of the subtle and often unsubtle ways in which that particular face deviates from the average.

EXAMPLES OF EXAGGERATION

Let's look at some faces with obvious variations on the average and some with not-so-obvious variations.

Abraham Lincoln had protruding ears and a large-ish nose, so in his caricature, Court Jones exaggerated those features even further.

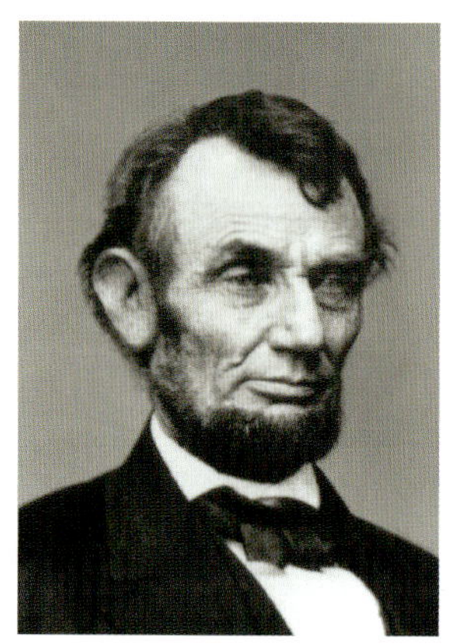

Library of Congress, LC-DIG-pga-03412 (digital file from original print)

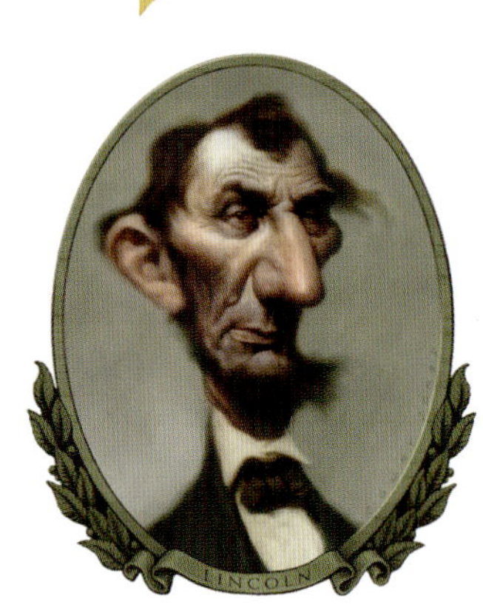

© Court Jones

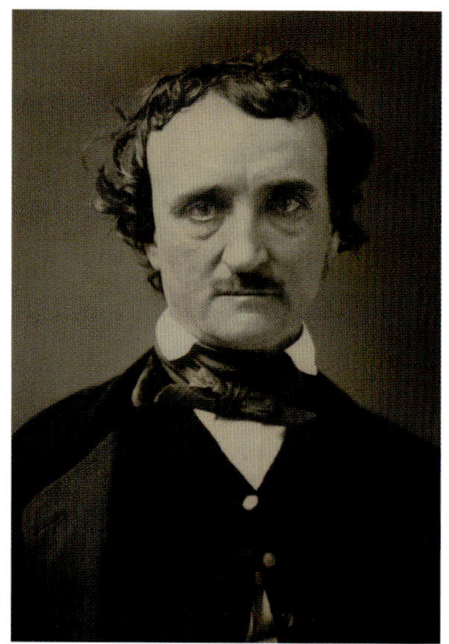

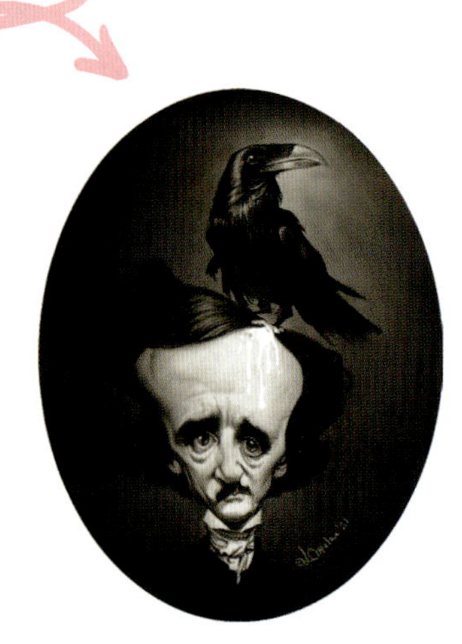

Title: Poe, Date: June 2021, Artist: Loopydave

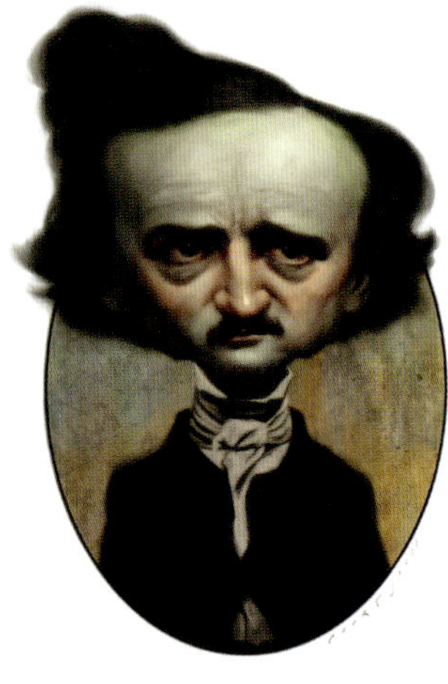

© Court Jones

Edgar Allen Poe had a larger-than-average forehead, so in his caricatures by Court Jones and David Dunstan, his forehead becomes even larger. In addition to focusing on physical traits, it is important to consider behavioral and personality traits as well.

Poe, for example, had hooded eyes and often wore a morose expression, features that both artists emphasized in their drawings.

Lastly, we have Marilyn Monroe. The physical traits that set her apart from the average are a little less obvious. I purposefully chose Marilyn to caricature for this book (see Rendered Caricature: Marilyn Monroe) because she is conventionally beautiful, with a fairly symmetrical, proportionate face. None of her features vary significantly from the norm. I find handsome or average-looking people more difficult to caricature for this reason. (This goes for all genders, not just women!)

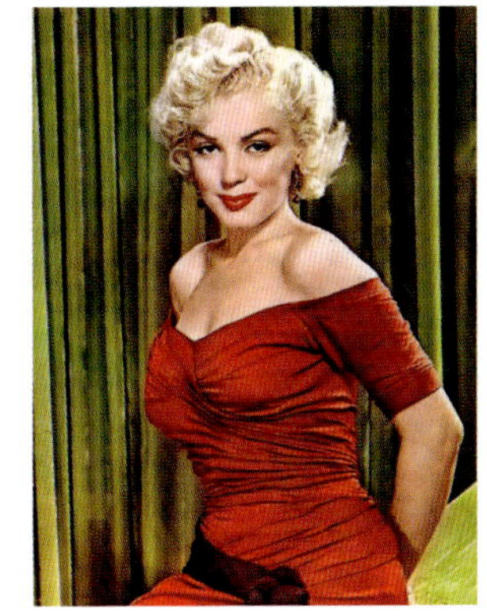

In these cases, instead of focusing on larger-than-average or unusually shaped features, pay attention to expressions and, in the case of well-known figures like Marilyn Monroe, iconic traits such as her signature blonde hair, makeup, and beauty mark. David Cowles drew on (pun intended!) these characteristics in his caricature of her.

It's clear that a lot of observation of form, expression, and personality went into all of these designs.

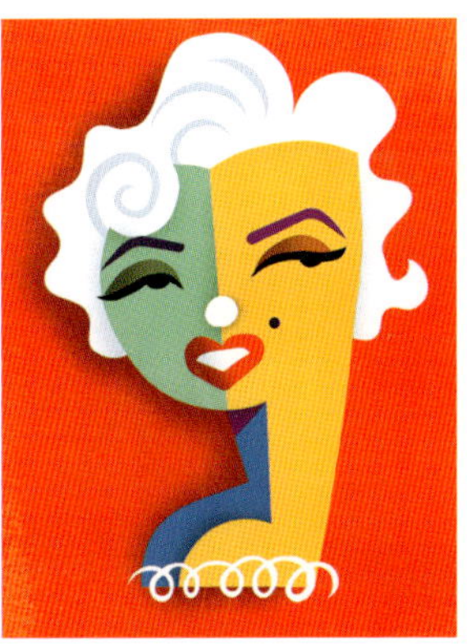

© David Cowles

FUN OBSERVATION EXERCISE!

Search online for caricatures of famous people, as well as photos of said people. Compare and analyze how each artist has caricatured their features. Take note of the artistic choices they made and consider why they might have chosen to portray the subjects in that particular way. Ryan Gosling, for example, has inspired some interesting caricatures over the years!

SHAPE & PROPORTION

You may have figured out by now that to understand how to caricature, you need to understand the proportions of an average head first. You won't know how to exaggerate with intention unless you're already familiar with the average.

"IF YOU CHANGE THE PROPORTIONS INCORRECTLY, WITHOUT INTENTION, YOU'LL LOSE THE LIKENESS. BUT WHEN IT'S DONE CORRECTLY AND INTENTIONALLY ... THE LIKENESS WILL BE EVEN STRONGER THAN THE PHOTO."

Court Jones

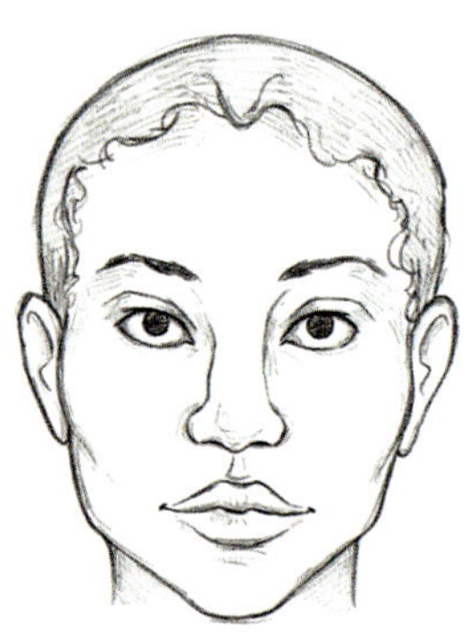

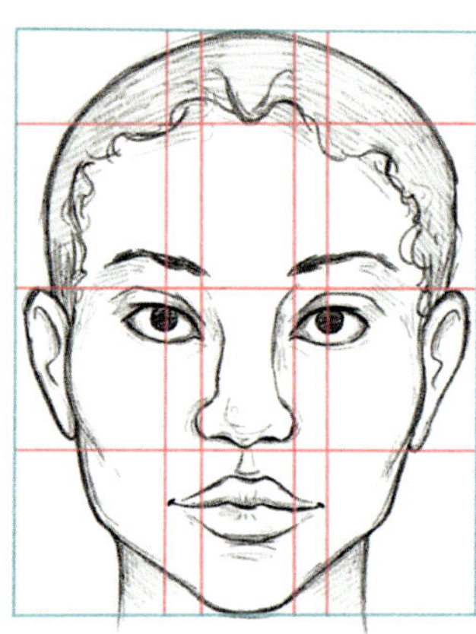

The diagrams on the right illustrate the standard proportions of an average adult head. A proportionate face is divided into three nearly equal sections: from the hairline to the top of the eyes; from the eyes to the bottom of the nose; and from the bottom of the nose to the chin.

The tops of the ears line up with the tops of the eyes, and the bottoms of the ears line up with the bottom of the nose. The inner corners of the eyes line up with the sides of the nostrils. The outer corners of the mouth line up with the centers of the eyes. In other words, when a person is looking straight ahead, the middle of the pupil should line up with the outer corners of the mouth. Lastly, the space between the eyes is about the same size as the width of one eye.

As you can see in the profile view, the middle of the eye still lines up with the corner of the mouth.

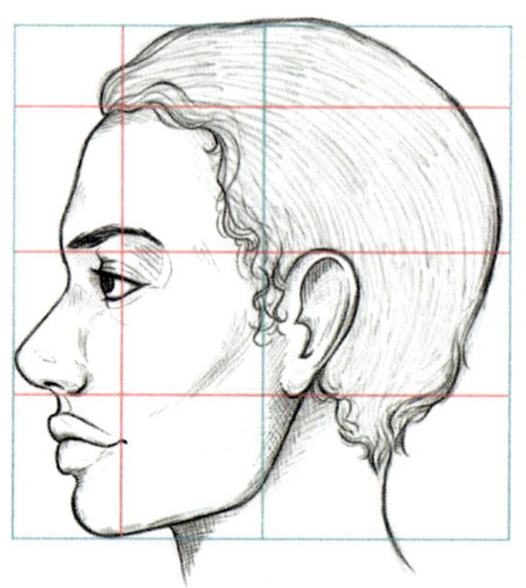

It's also important to have a basic understanding of skull structure and key facial muscle groups (more on muscle groups later on).

In profile, the contours of the skull are more pronounced, making it easier to see how the bone structure supports and defines the face, and can help artists more accurately place features. Familiarity with the average enhances your ability to identify the unique angles and variations that give each face its distinct character.

Everything can be built up using basic shapes to start. I started with simple squares and circles, added a trapezoid for the lower jaw, and a triangle to represent the cheekbone. Pay attention to the way these shapes align with one another. Using this as a blueprint, I was able to relatively easily add more detail to draw out the more organic shape of the skull.

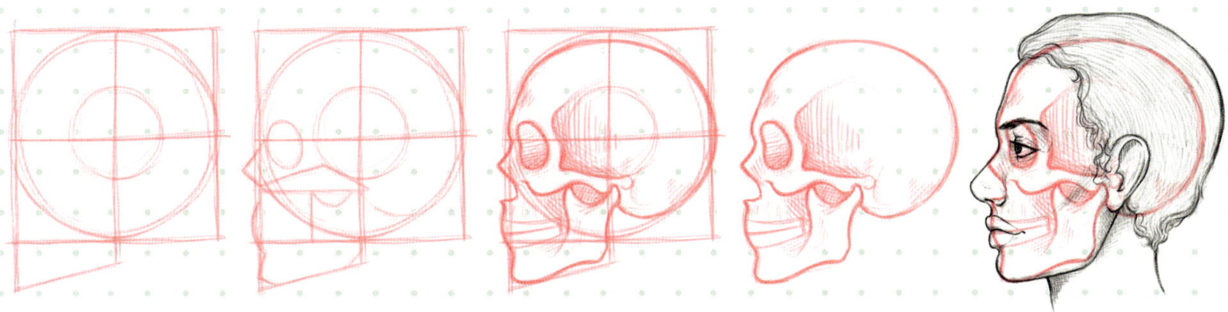

ARTIST INSIGHT

If you haven't figured it out yet, you'll soon understand that so much of drawing involves layering. The more you draw something, the more familiar you'll become with its building blocks and the more muscle memory you'll develop. As a result, over time, you'll find that you need to rely less and less on drawing all of those building blocks, but utilizing these shapes is essential for developing that skill in the first place.

The muscle groups of the face affect the pull and stretch of the features. This, in particular, informs how you draw expressions and provides valuable insights for effective caricature exaggeration. The cheek bands—shown in purple—are the most helpful muscle group to focus on. Careful observation of these muscles is key to understanding where to draw wrinkles, jowls, smile lines, laugh lines, and dimples.

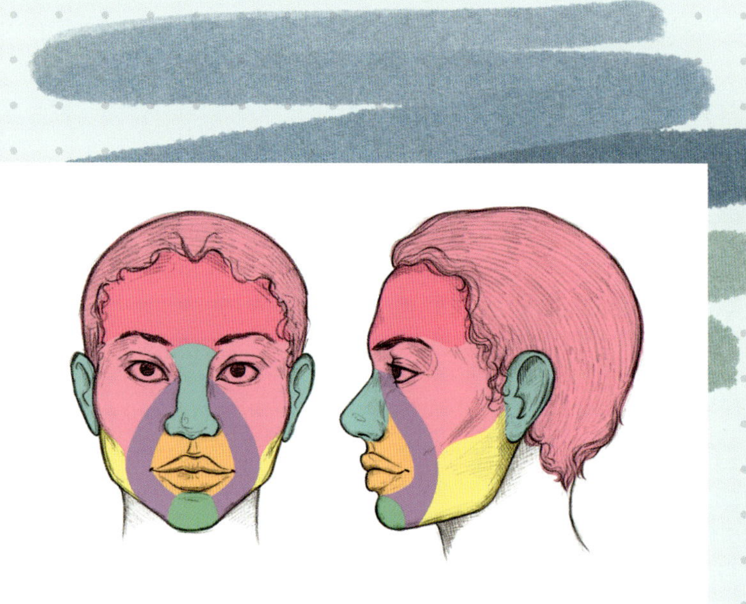

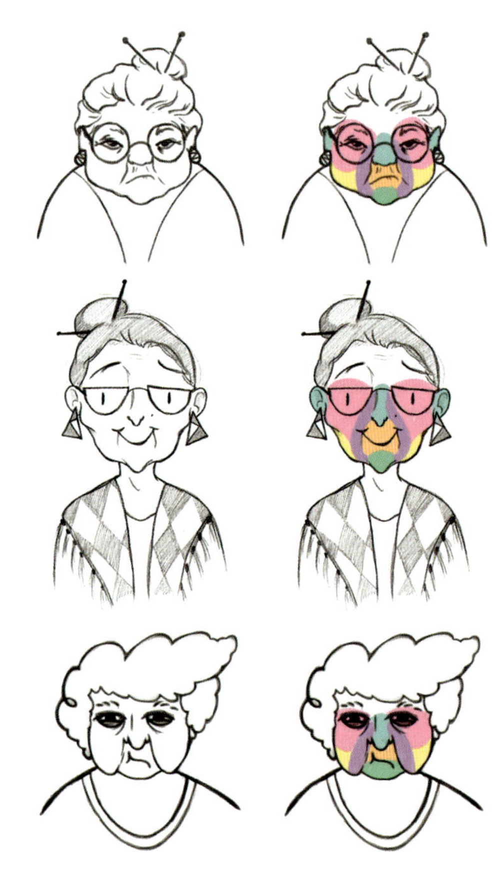

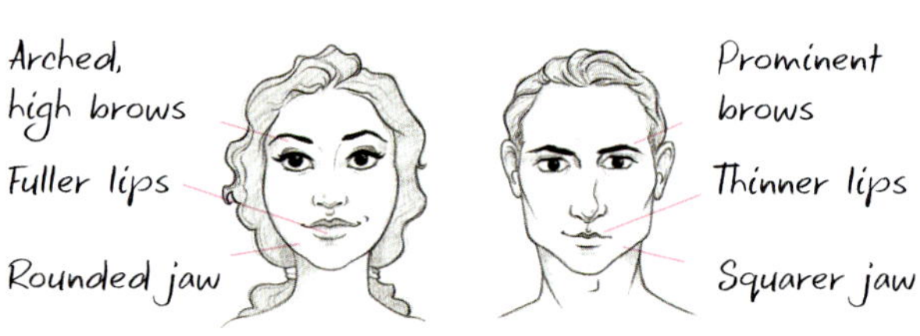

Keep in mind that the average proportions of details like the eyes, nose, and lips may differ somewhat, depending on where in the world you're from and what the dominant facial type is there. Additionally, there are differences between typically masculine and typically feminine features and head shapes, but the overall proportions are going to be about the same for all facial types.

To the right are some examples of faces that show how "typical" features do not apply to everyone. You can create masculine characters with fuller lips and feminine characters with sharp, square jaws. Or play with these features to create androgynous and/or non-binary folks. No two faces are exactly the same and that makes us all so much more interesting, don't you think?

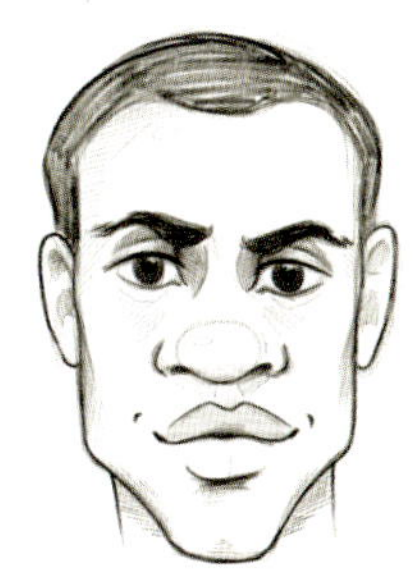

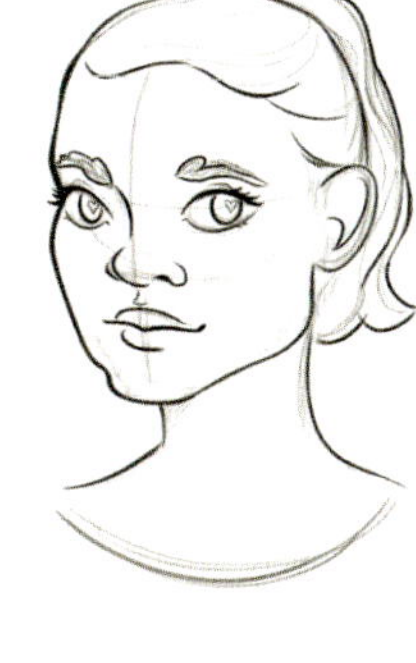

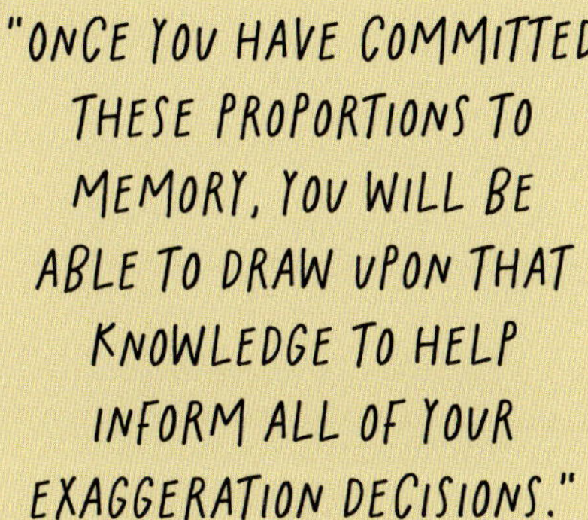

"ONCE YOU HAVE COMMITTED THESE PROPORTIONS TO MEMORY, YOU WILL BE ABLE TO DRAW UPON THAT KNOWLEDGE TO HELP INFORM ALL OF YOUR EXAGGERATION DECISIONS."

Court Jones

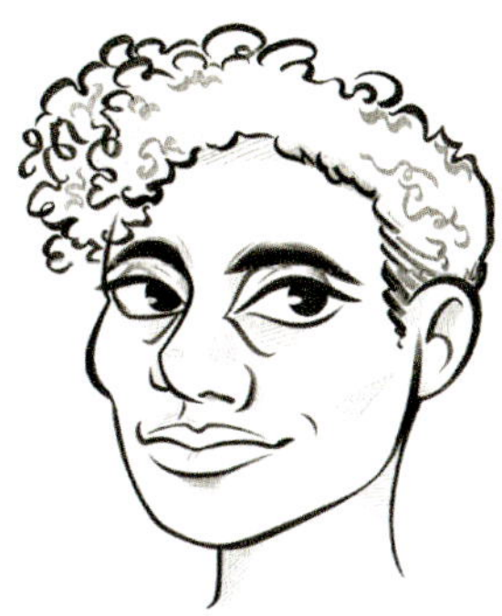

When cartooning or caricaturing, you can and will bend and break the rules of proportion, but they will still inform and guide those choices.

There are about a thousand different ways you can caricature people, maintain their likeness, and create something that's fun and interesting. But the more you understand this, the better you'll be at drawing this.

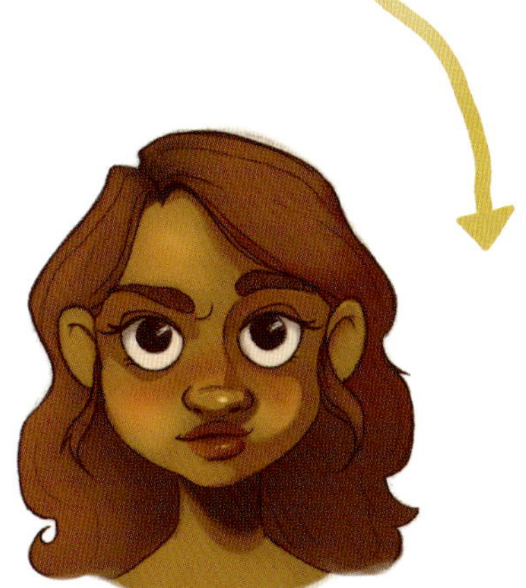

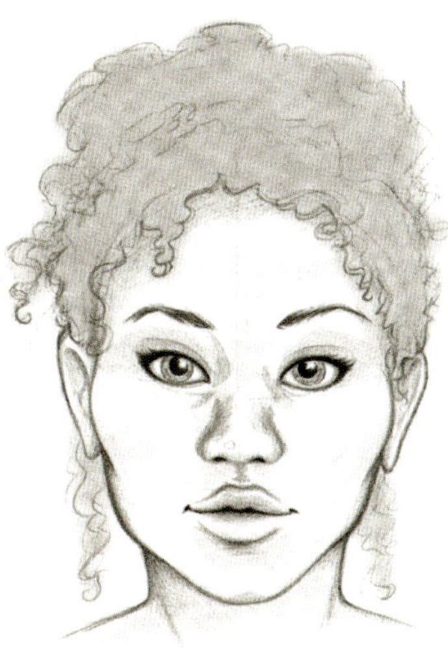

HOW DO CARICATURE & CHARACTER DESIGN RELATE?

Caricature and cartooning go hand-in-hand because both involve careful observation and varying levels of stylization, simplification, and exaggeration of proportions. However, one key difference is where the focus of the exaggeration is.

In traditional caricature, the focus is on taking a person's real face and exaggerating or pushing their features while still maintaining the likeness of that person. Whereas in character design, it's less about maintaining a specific likeness and more about emphasizing the traits of a character that you have created from scratch through exaggeration and stylization.

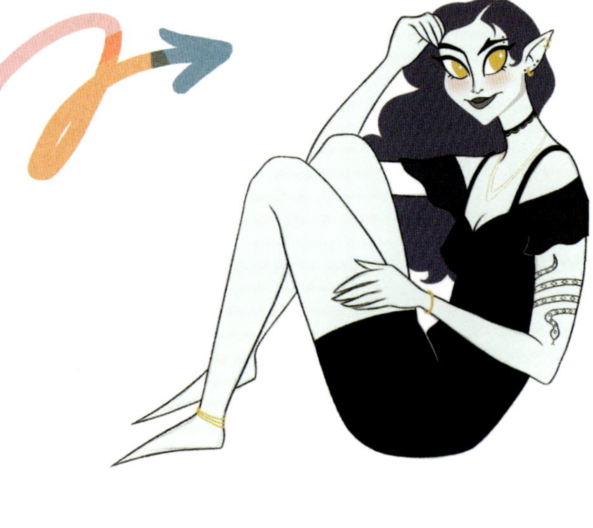

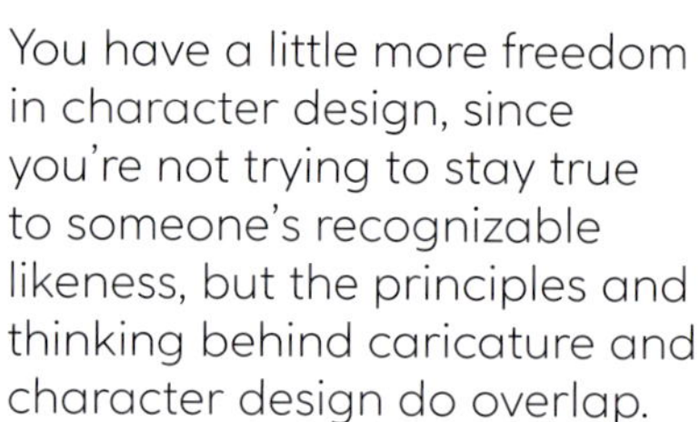

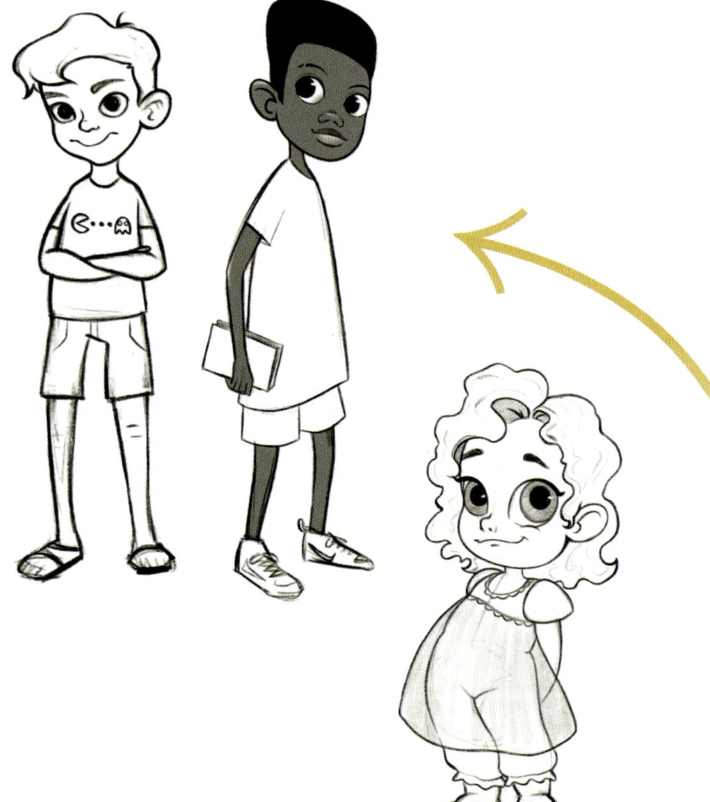

You have a little more freedom in character design, since you're not trying to stay true to someone's recognizable likeness, but the principles and thinking behind caricature and character design do overlap.

For example, there are certain features I enjoy exaggerating in my cartooning. I love drawing big, stylized dramatic eyes, but my overall shape language tends to lean closer to the realistic side of the proportions scale.

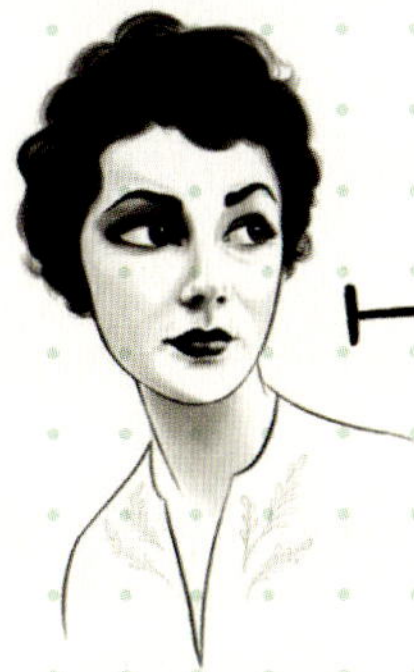

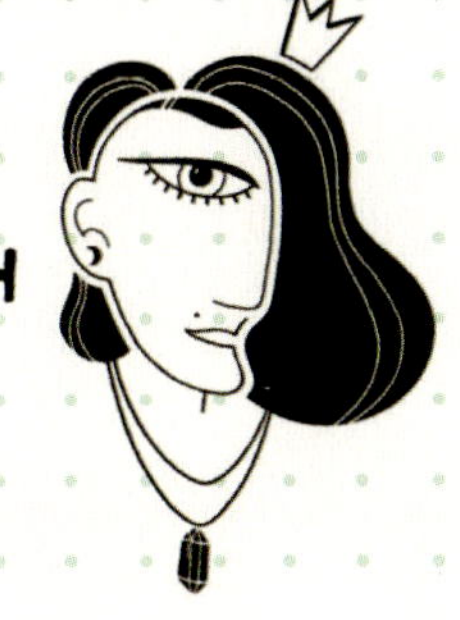

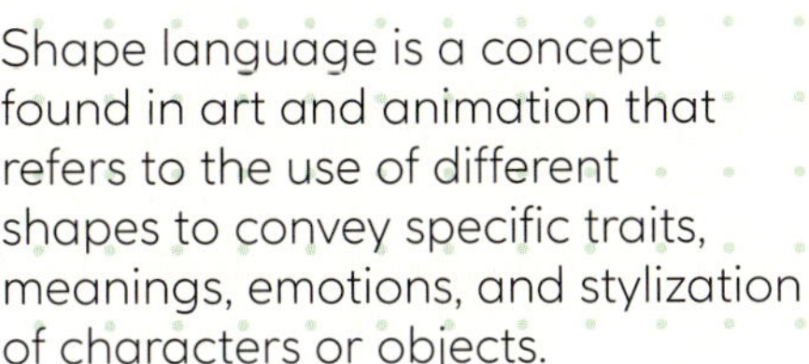

Shape language is a concept found in art and animation that refers to the use of different shapes to convey specific traits, meanings, emotions, and stylization of characters or objects.

When I'm caricaturing someone, my exaggeration choices are influenced by that specific person's features. If my subject didn't have particularly big eyes, I wouldn't draw them very big, despite how fun it is. Instead, I would most likely focus on pushing another feature, whether it's the shape of their head, an impossibly wide smile, or some other distinctive characteristic.

Once you understand how to exaggerate someone's features while maintaining their likeness, making stylization and exaggeration choices in cartooning becomes much easier. In short, if you understand caricature, you are a character designer.

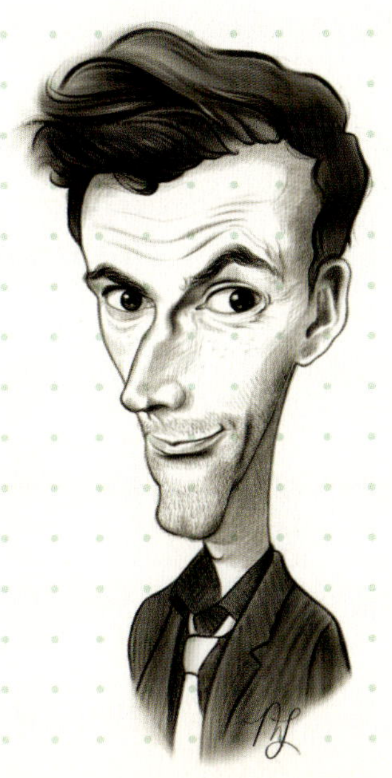

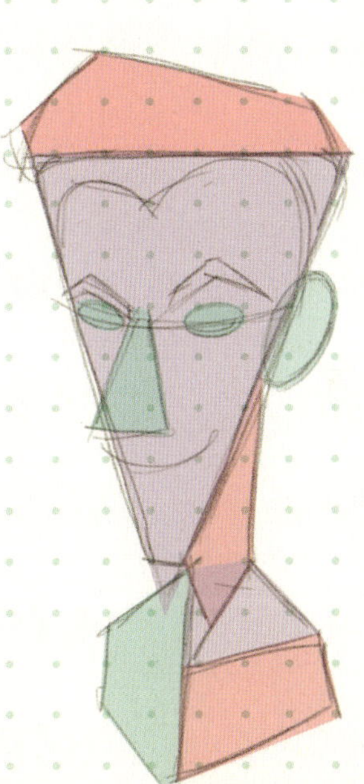

ARTIST INSIGHT

Obviously, the actor David Tennant doesn't have such a long, triangle-shaped head; he's a handsome guy. However, I think I did a pretty good job of capturing his likeness.

I tend to draw a lot of aesthetically pleasing faces, which may seem a little counterintuitive because I draw caricatures, but I believe that caricature drawing has made me a much stronger character artist. The point is, you really can't have character design without caricature.

MY GREATEST INFLUENCES

The two people from whom I've learned the most about caricature are Stephen Silver and Court Jones, both of whom are professional caricature artists. Technically, Stephen Silver is primarily a character designer, but he began his career as a caricaturist at amusement parks and continues to use those principles regularly in his current work.

Their respective styles are on the opposite ends of the spectrum. Silver's work is more simplified, very stylized and, for lack of a better word, cartoony, while Jones's work leans toward the hyperrealistic and super-rendered side of the spectrum. In a sense, this is more in line with what most people typically think of when they hear the word "caricature."

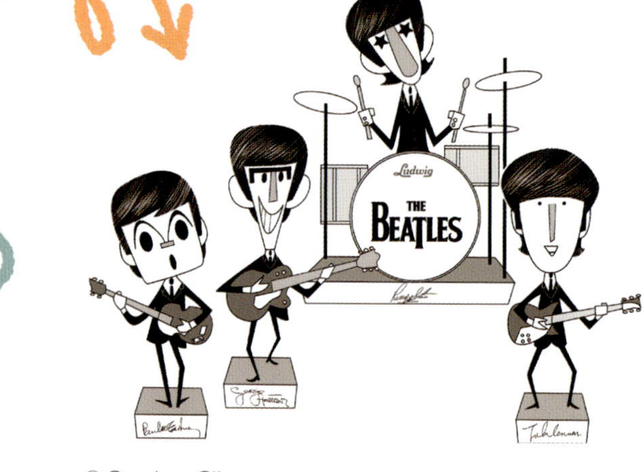

© Stephen Silver

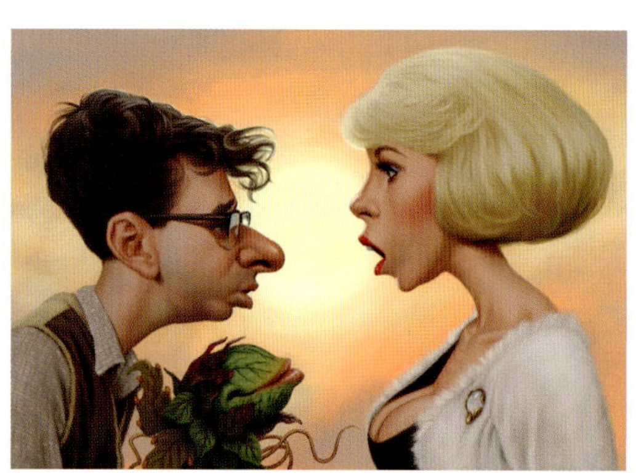

© Court Jones

I think it's important to study multiple styles in order to become a well-rounded caricaturist. Much of what I've learned over the years has come not only from taking these artists' respective courses but also from observing their work and the unique approaches they take to their craft.

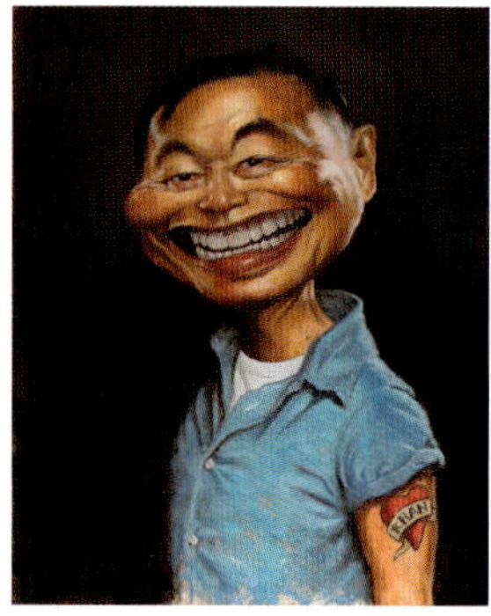

© Court Jones

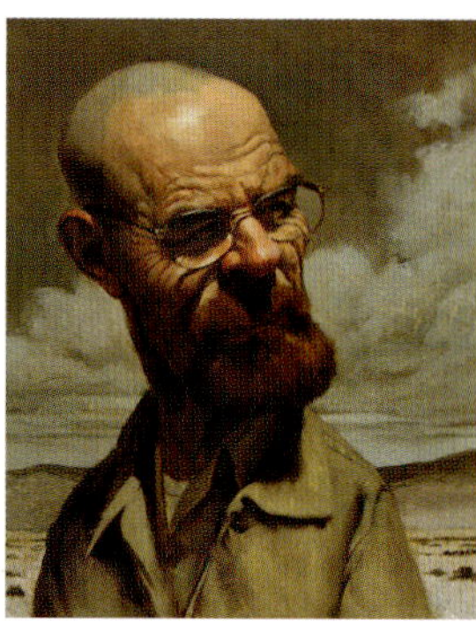

© Court Jones

SHAPE, SPACING, & PLACEMENT

The key factors to consider when you are caricaturing someone are shape, spacing, placement, and proportion. Caricature is the result of manipulating these elements, and a successful caricature exaggerates **shape**, **spacing**, **placement, and proportion** in such a way that the likeness of the person is still there.

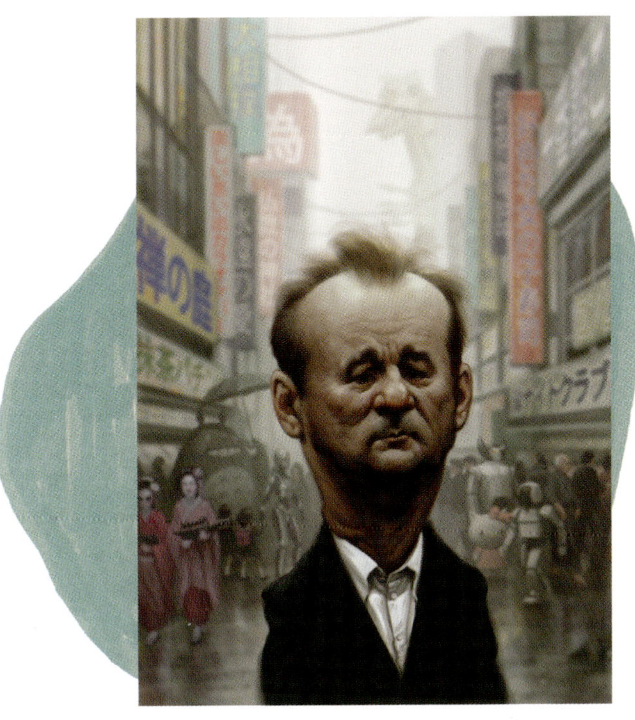

© Court Jones

A great caricature can appear highly realistic and dimensional, can be done with simple black and white line work, or even be more abstract

The main goal is to capture the likeness of whoever you're caricaturing in a fun and eye-catching way. In the Masters of Caricature chapter, I've included more awesome artists for you to check out and be inspired by, but first, let's get to some fun warm-up drawing exercises.

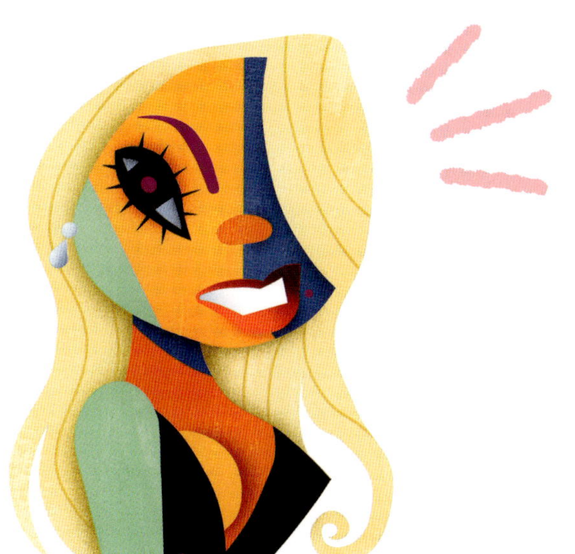

© David Cowles

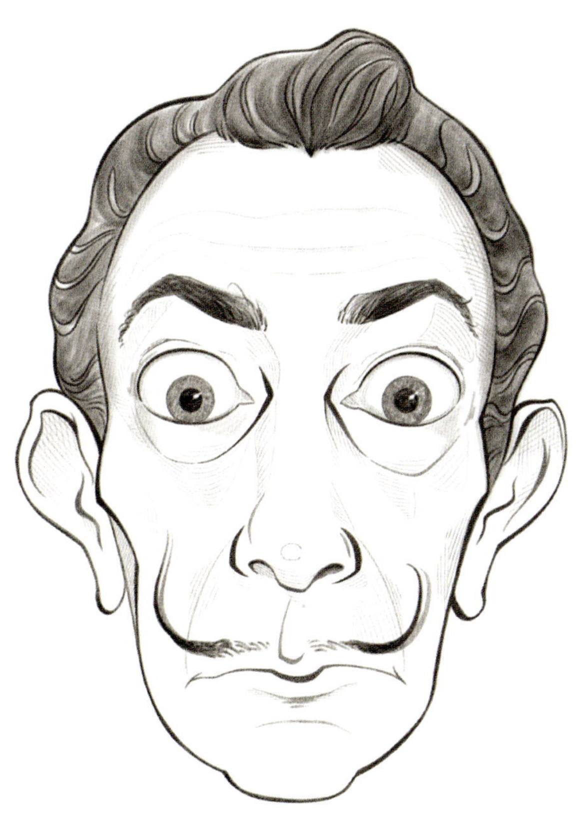

SHAPE & PROPORTION EXERCISES

You won't know how to exaggerate with intention unless you're already familiar with the average, so let's get started on some exercises you can use to familiarize yourself with standard proportions.

WARM UP!

If you haven't done any drawing today, I suggest warming up first. Start by picking up your pencil and practicing drawing a few straight and curved lines, varying the length.

Next, try drawing some simple shapes, such as circles, ellipses, and cubes. You could also experiment with loose shapes like figure eights. Play around with different sizes and adjust the pressure of your pencil as you go. And remember, there's no right or wrong way to do this, it's just a warm-up!

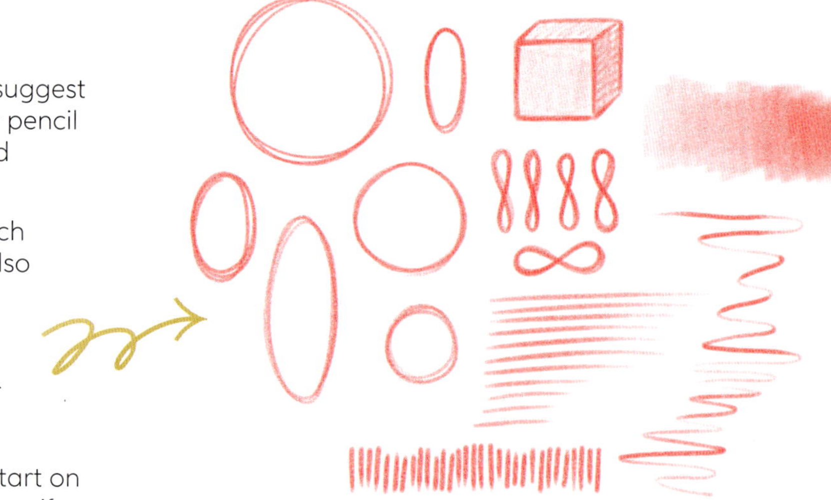

This helps me loosen up and get a jump start on my muscle memory in a low-stress way. Plus, if you start with really simple shapes, you can build on top of them to make more detailed designs.

EMBRACING THE "BAD ART"

I almost always start a new drawing with a little fear. Even though, at this point in my practice, I know that eventually, things will start to flow because they always do, I always seem to forget that part. Or I'm simply unable to see past the fear, regardless.

So to help combat that, something that I've found extremely helpful for any project—whether it's a caricature, a pattern collection, a logo, or whatever—is to decide that the first few pages of sketches are going to be "bad."

Embracing the fact that the first round of thumbnails won't be great makes it so much easier to start and frees you up to make the mistakes that you need to make to improve your skills and get to your final designs. Learning to recognize and appreciate the value of your "bad art" is crucial for fostering progress and developing skills.

Another helpful warm-up involves starting with simple shapes, marks, and lines to explore cartoon faces. Below, you'll see how simple circles, ovals, and geometric shapes serve as the underlying structure for faces with different expressions and characteristics. From there, you can either build on top of these shapes to create more detailed designs or keep it simple, depending on what style you're going for. This approach is a great, low-stress way to practice cartooning

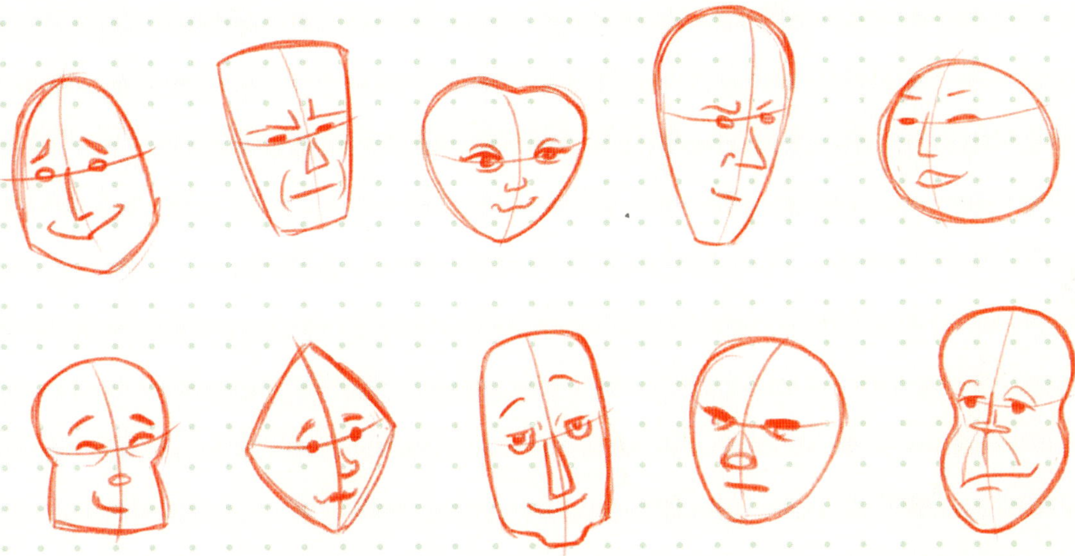

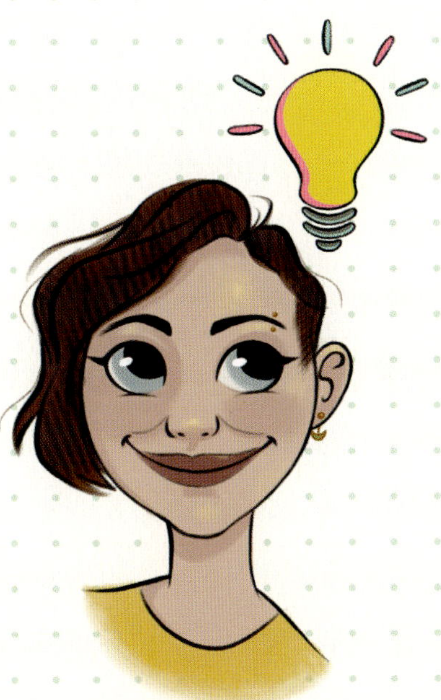

ARTIST INSIGHT

If you feel reluctant to "mess up" a beautiful sketchbook, consider dedicating a separate sketchbook to warm-ups. That way, your Instagram-ready sketchbook can remain pristine, and you'll feel far less precious about marking up your warm-up sketchbook. It's a win-win!

ANCHOR MEASUREMENTS

One way to practice drawing proportionally is to use an anchor measurement. Select one key line or shape in your reference as a baseline for measuring the other parts. Measure your pencil with your finger or thumb against your chosen measurement and use it to compare sizes. Try to choose a measurement that's easy to work with—not too small or too large. Once you have your anchor, measure it against another section of the reference. For example, in the image (left) below, I'm using the bottom of the nose as my anchor and measuring it against the mouth (right). This comparison shows that the bottom of the nose is about two-thirds the length of the mouth.

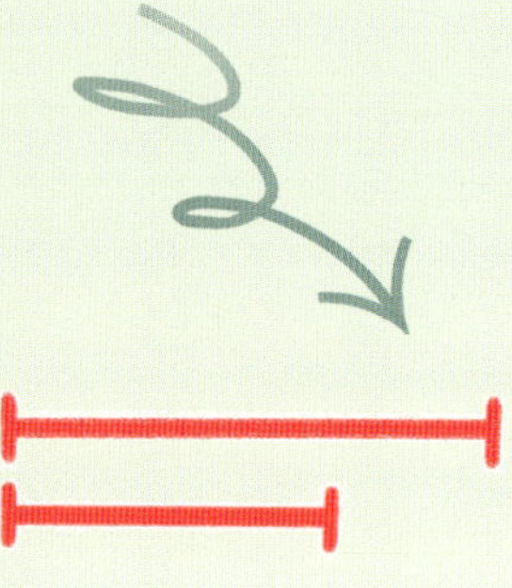

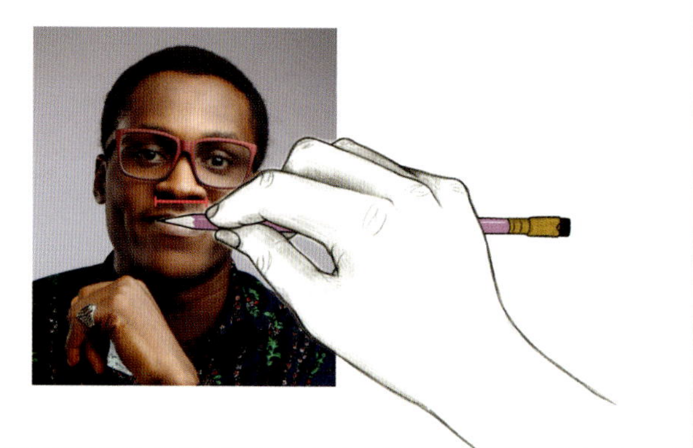

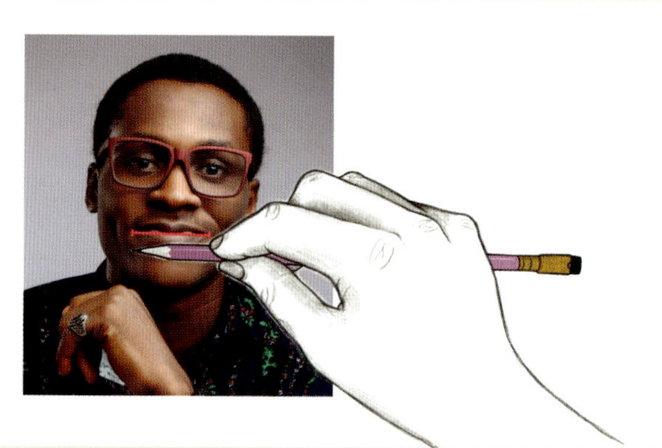

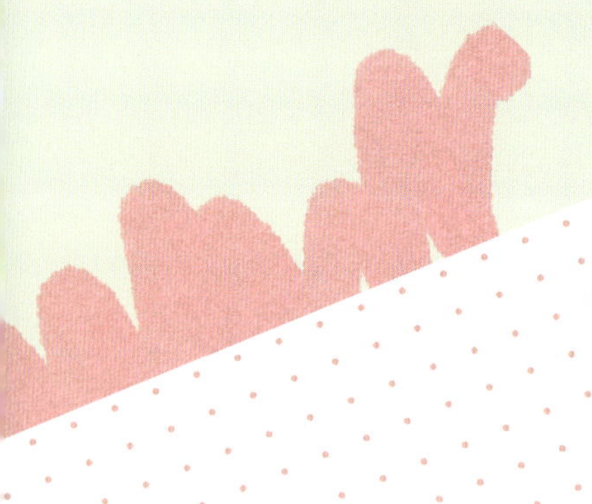

We don't usually want to draw something at the exact same size as it appears in the reference so remember to use an anchor to compare sizes, not to transfer measurements from your reference image to your canvas. Using the same anchor measurement throughout the drawing will help maintain consistency.

With time and practice, you'll build the observational skills needed to consistently and accurately gauge proportions by eye without relying on physical measurements.

TURN YOUR REFERENCE UPSIDE DOWN

The verbal side of our brain is often linked to the part of our brain that can make drawing more challenging. Flipping an image upside down makes it easier to interpret the forms of your reference as simple lines and shapes because it disrupts the brain's tendency to identify objects more literally. This confusion can cause the verbal side of your brain to disengage, allowing the visual and artistic side to take over.

Remember that if you find these exercises difficult or struggle to get them right on the first try, that's actually a good sign! It means you're literally forming new neural pathways in your brain and strengthening your drawing skills. While it might feel frustrating at times, it's proof that you're making progress!

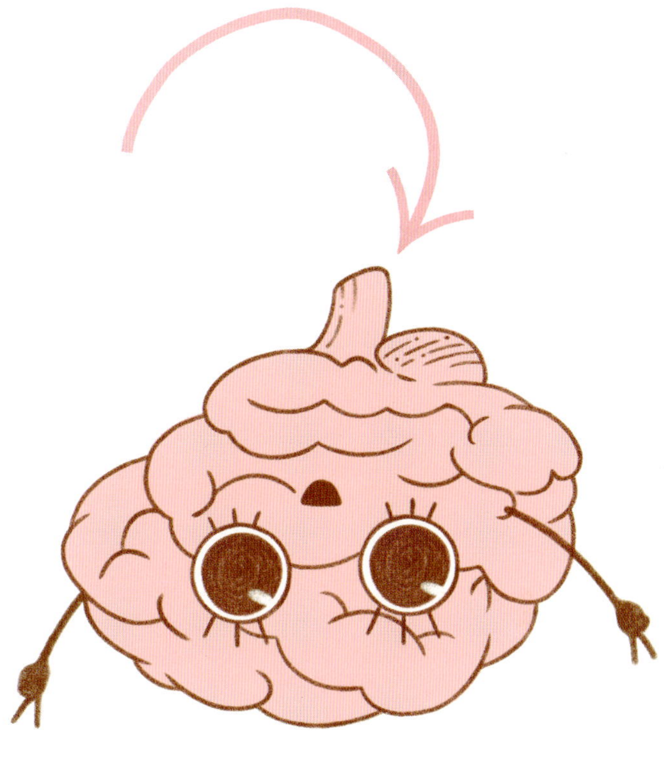

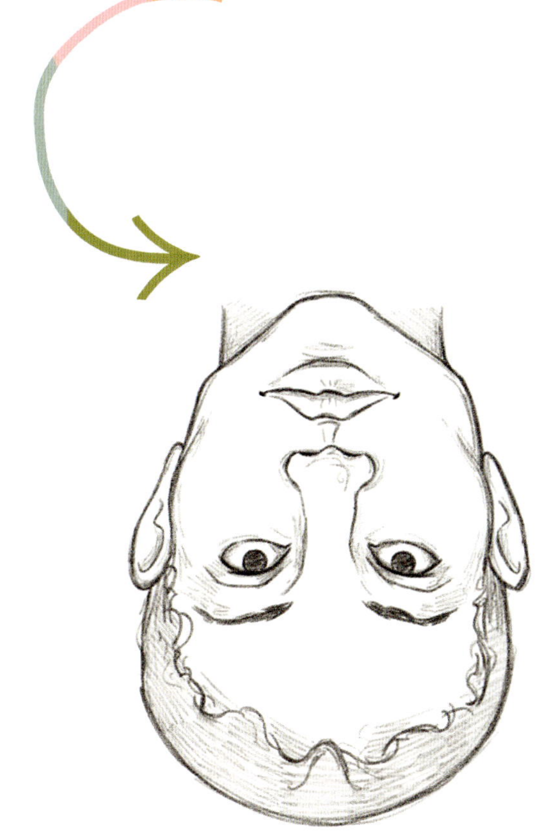

ARTIST INSIGHT

If you find yourself naming an object or body part, try to stop and think of it as a shape, NOT an "eye" or a "nose."

EXPERIMENT WITH SHAPES

You can also experiment with contrasting shapes to see what designs you can come up with. Start with really basic, contrasting shapes and use them as a guide.

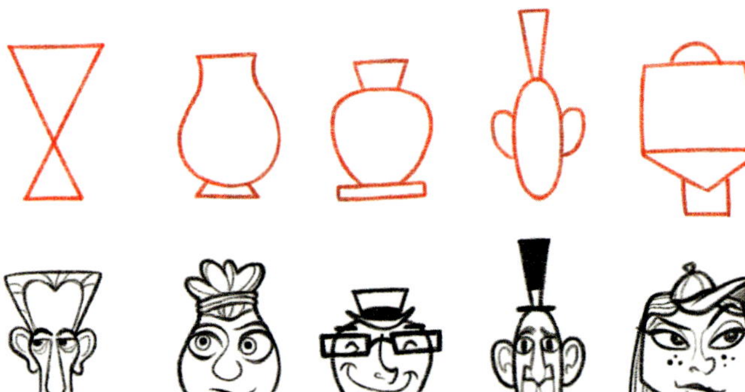

Or you can try using actual objects for shape inspiration. Challenge yourself to stay as close to the original shape as possible.

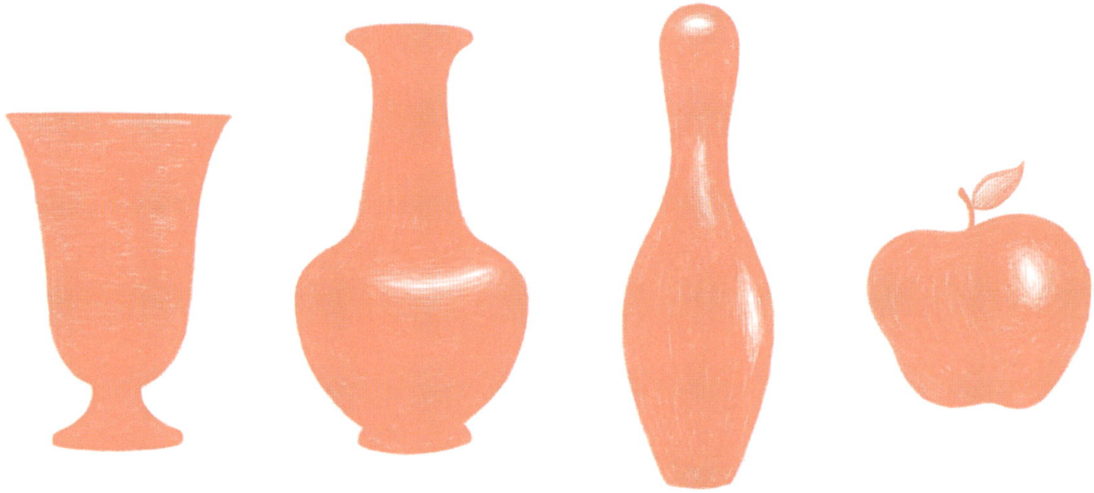

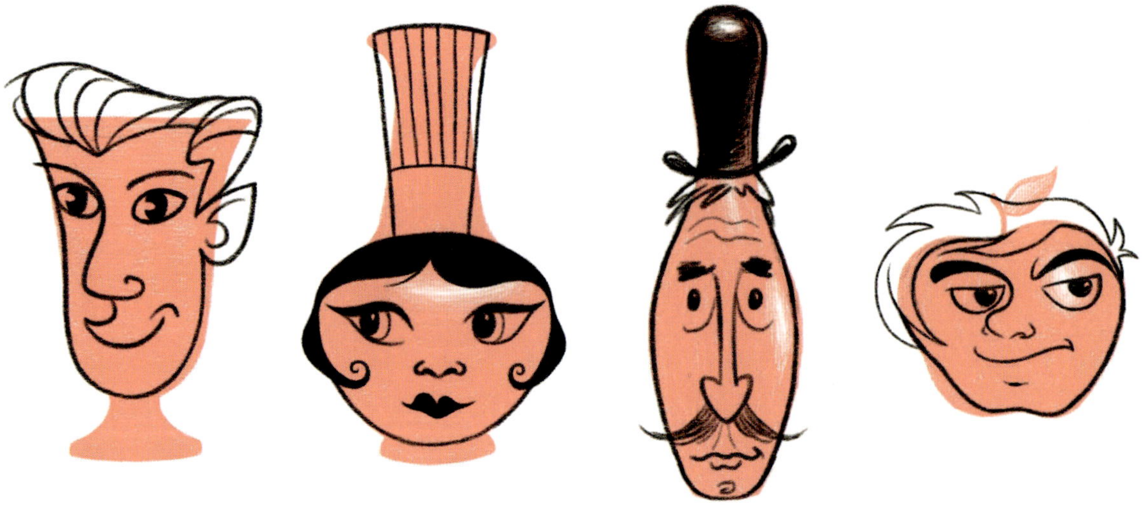

USE THE T-SHAPE!

One of my favorite tips is to use the T-shape in the face to help guide the exaggeration of the features. I find this really helpful when I'm trying to come up with multiple designs for the same character and I feel stuck.

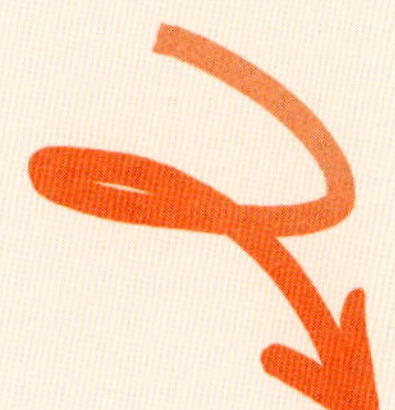

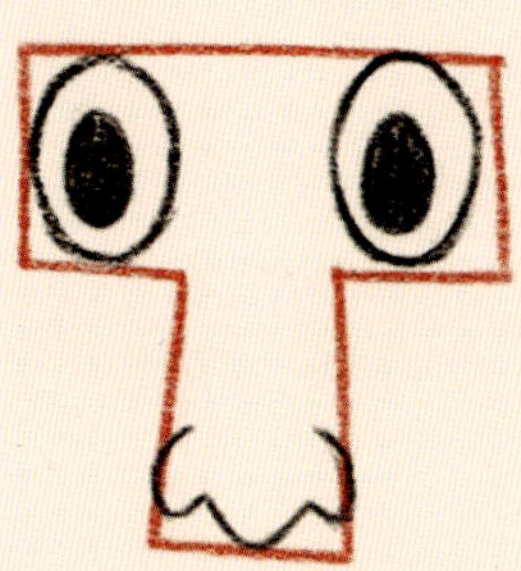

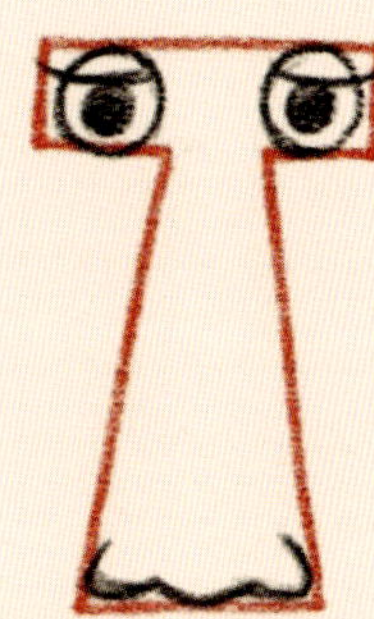

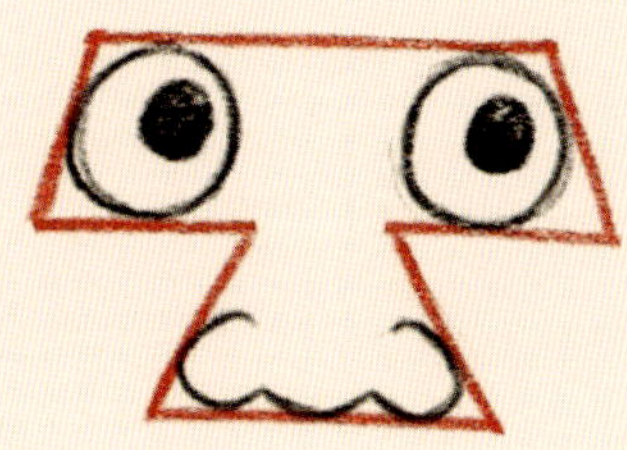

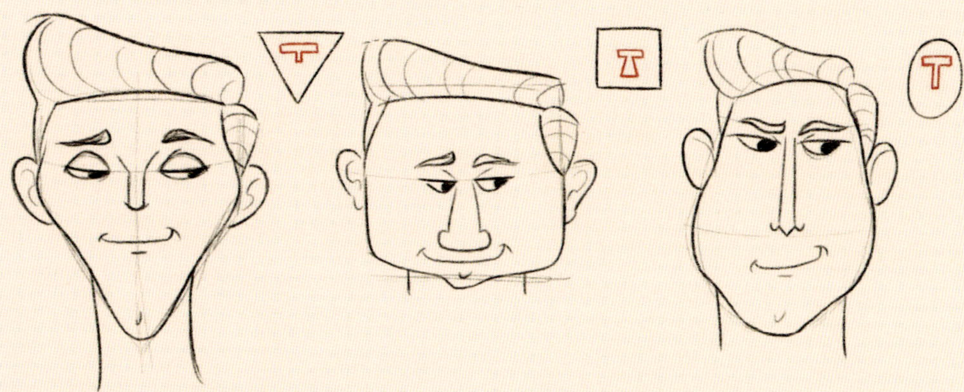

SPACING & PLACEMENT EXERCISE

A less intimidating way to approach caricature is to focus solely on changing the position of the eye, nose, and mouth lines.

It can be difficult for beginners to identify which exaggeration choices will best capture the essence of the subject they are drawing. By adjusting the eye, nose, and mouth lines, you can explore different caricature options in a more structured way and work from there to determine which exaggerations are right for the subject you're caricaturing.

I'll show you what I mean...

I'm using the artist Salvador Dali for this example, and I've marked on his face the spacing that you need to get into the habit of paying attention to. It can be helpful to draw your subject first, without trying to caricature them, so that you can get a feel for the realistic proportions and spacing of their face. To start, I marked faint lines where the eyes, nose, and mouth line up on his face in reality.

To reiterate, the main things you need to consider when you're caricaturing someone are shape, spacing, placement, and proportion. Caricature is the end result of playing around with these things, and a successful caricature exaggerates shape, spacing, placement, and proportion in such a way that the likeness of the person is still there. For this exercise, however, we're going to simplify things and focus solely on spacing and placement.

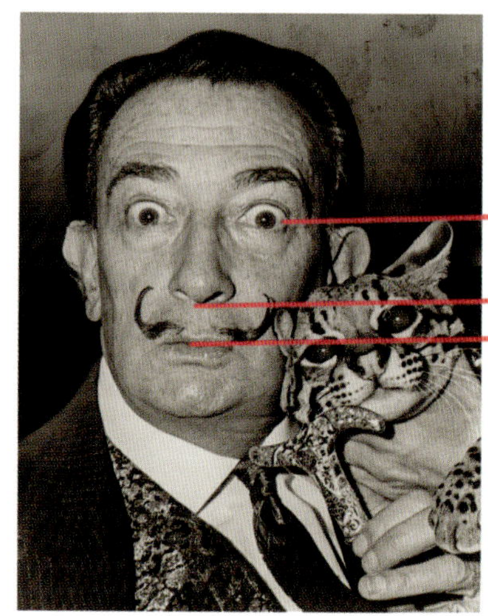

Library of Congress, LC-USZ62-114985 (b&w film copy neg.)

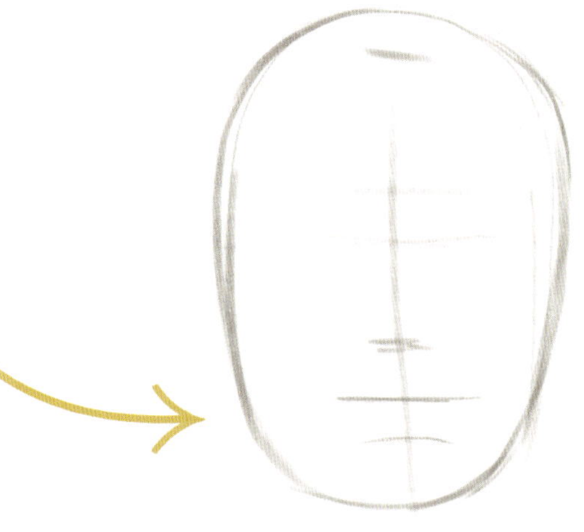

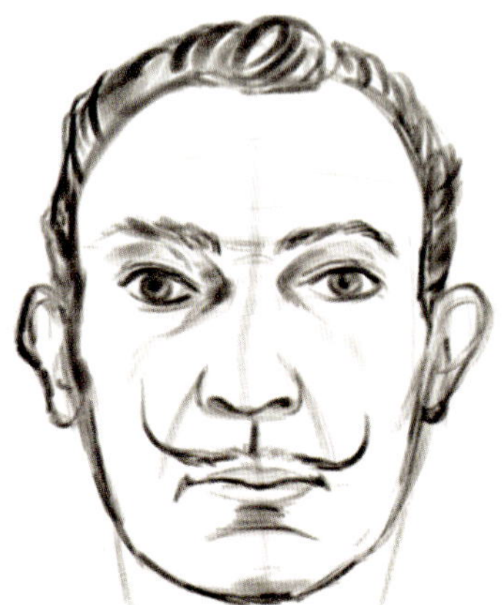

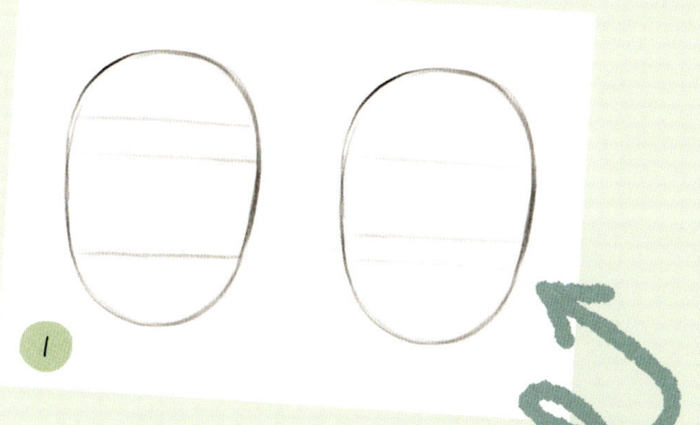

1. It's important to identify the basic head shape first. So for the first two examples, I haven't really exaggerated his head shape at all because that's not what I want you to focus on yet.

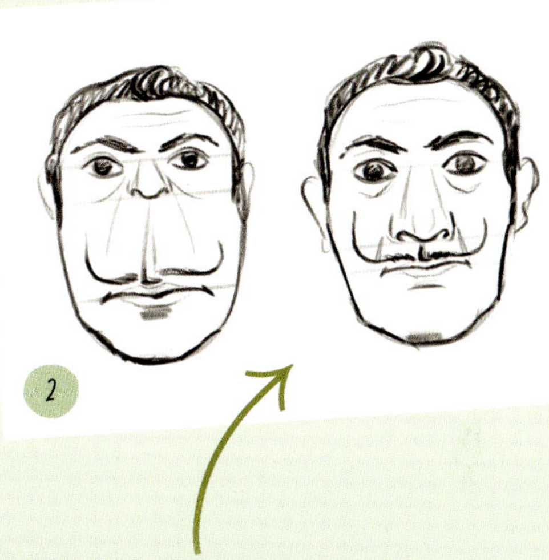

2. Space the eye, nose, and mouth lines differently for each example, and follow them accordingly, doing your best to draw his features as you see them. When I initially drew these feature placement lines, I wasn't thinking about what positioning would work best for him specifically; I placed them randomly, because I wanted to start drawing without analyzing too much. Plus, I wanted to explore spacing options that I might not usually try. Try to keep each sketch under five minutes. These aren't meant to be beautiful finished pieces. Think of them more as exploratory thumbnails.

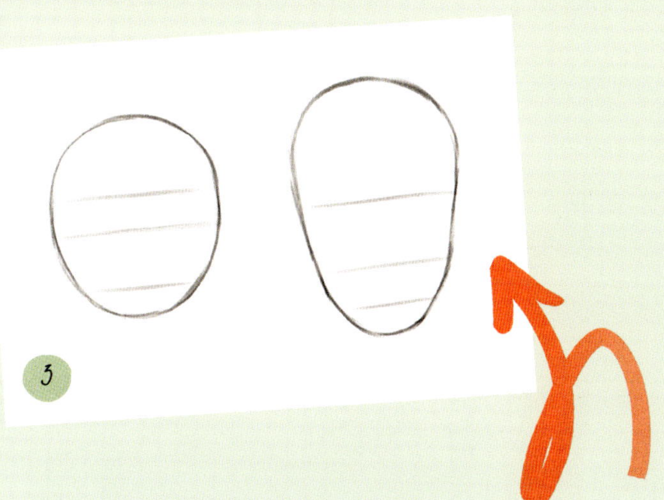

3. For the next two drawings, start with different head shapes. I chose to draw one significantly shortened and rounded and one lengthened. From there, I randomly placed the eye, nose, and mouth lines. I purposefully placed the eye line low down on the face in one shape because I wanted to see what he would look like with a lengthened forehead.

TIME TO ANALYZE!

4. Unsurprisingly, the smaller, rounder head (Fig 3) doesn't work for Dali. You can easily lose likeness by changing the fundamental shape of someone's head. In the case of Dali, I think this shows that the overall shape should be oval or rectangular rather than square or circular. As far as likeness goes, I think two and four are more successful, and part of that is due to the length of the heads. In two, though, I didn't actually exaggerate much, which I didn't mean to do; I just accidentally spaced the features fairly accurately, so it's not really all that helpful for me.

   One and three show me that shortening the nose takes away from his likeness quite a lot. I wouldn't say his nose dominates his face, but that's only because all of his facial features are quite large. He has wide eyes that are very wide set and a fairly large mouth, and then a mid-sized philtrum (the space between the nose and mouth) with an indent.

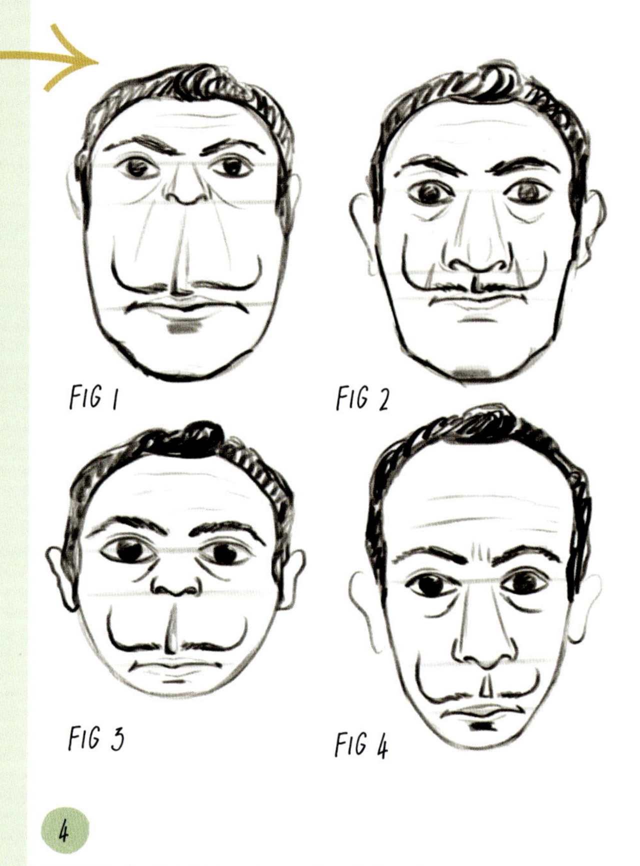

4

5. Take what you learned from this exercise (I learned that I shouldn't shorten his nose and I should lengthen and exaggerate all of his larger features) and draw your subject one more time.

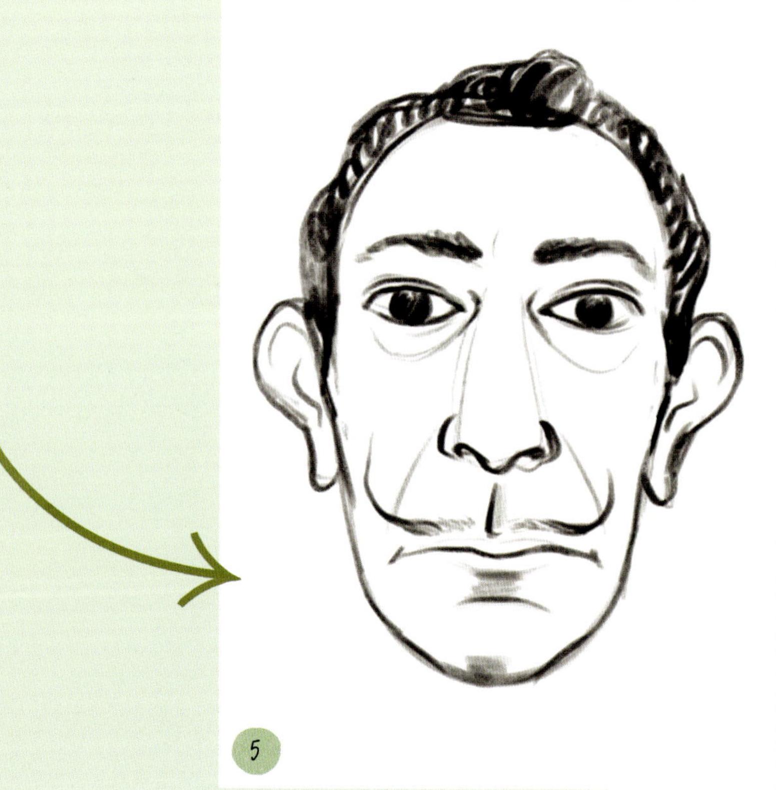
5

6. Interestingly, I think that the final drawing captures Dali's likeness even better than my original attempt, when I wasn't trying to caricature him. It's certainly more interesting to look at! From here, I could choose to push the exaggeration further if I wanted to, but the important thing is that I now have a better understanding of how I can go about doing that. This has helped me to figure out how to exaggerate his features by identifying the sections of the face that I can modify effectively, all while preserving his likeness.

This sort of analysis and careful observation can be applied to any face, though the specifics may vary. And I've hopefully started to train your brain on how to analyze and observe a person's face more effectively.

I also hope this exercise will not feel daunting and will provide a starting point if you're hesitant to jump directly into creating thumbnails.

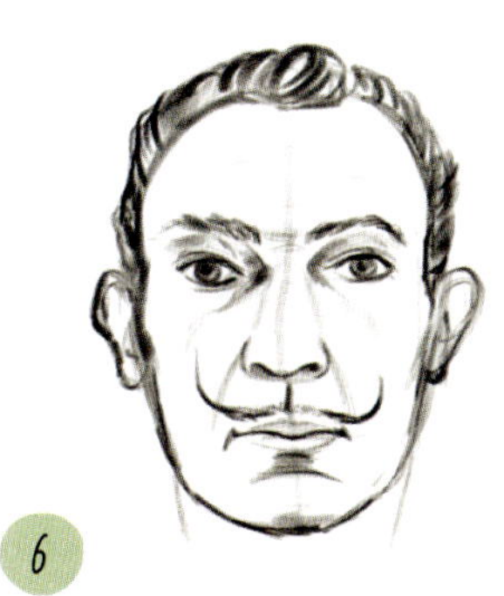

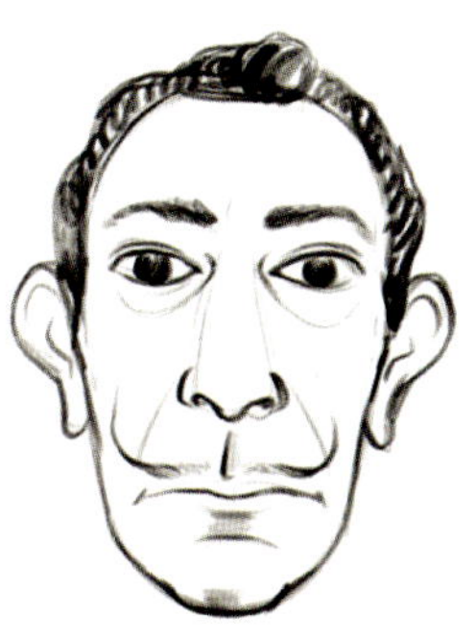

6

ARTIST INSIGHT

For any digital artists out there: use the transform, liquefy, and/or warp tools to manipulate your drawings and push the exaggeration further. Here, I used Transform to stretch the length of his face.

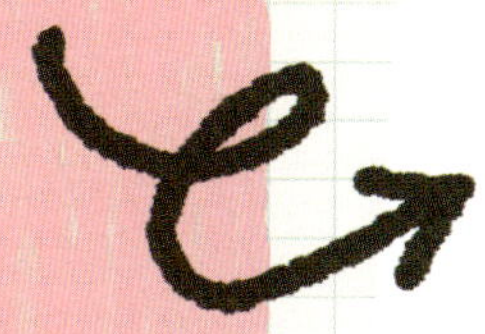

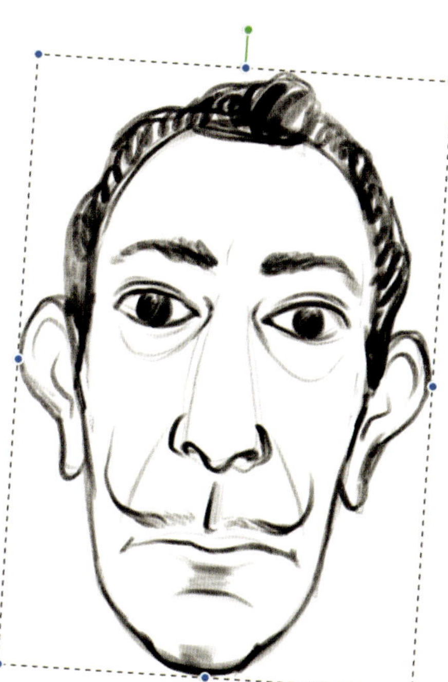

LET'S COMBINE A COUPLE OF TECHNIQUES!

I started by making a drawing based on a reference image. Then, using contrasting shapes, I made different designs of the same character. I also changed the spacing of the different sections of the face. In other words, I put the eye, nose, and mouth lines in different spots on each "face."

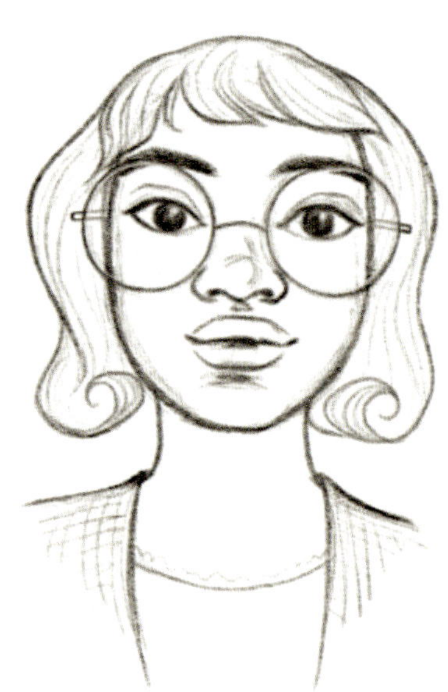

Make it a point to push the variations as much as possible. Variation in shape, spacing, and size is essential for creating visual interest. One key lesson I learned from Stephen Silver is to "avoid the ladder," meaning that when everything is parallel, equidistant, and the same size, quite frankly, it's boring to look at.

The bottom line is to experiment. Some techniques will resonate with you, while others may not, and that's OK. Learn to embrace your less-than-perfect drawings, as they are all leading you to create better drawings in the future. Try to stay loose and relaxed, have fun, and don't stress the details too much as you explore.

TRY IT YOURSELF

1. Make a drawing based on a reference image.

2. Use contrasting shapes to make different designs of the same character.

3. Change the spacing of the different sections of the face (eye, nose, and mouth lines).

PUSHING YOUR DESIGN

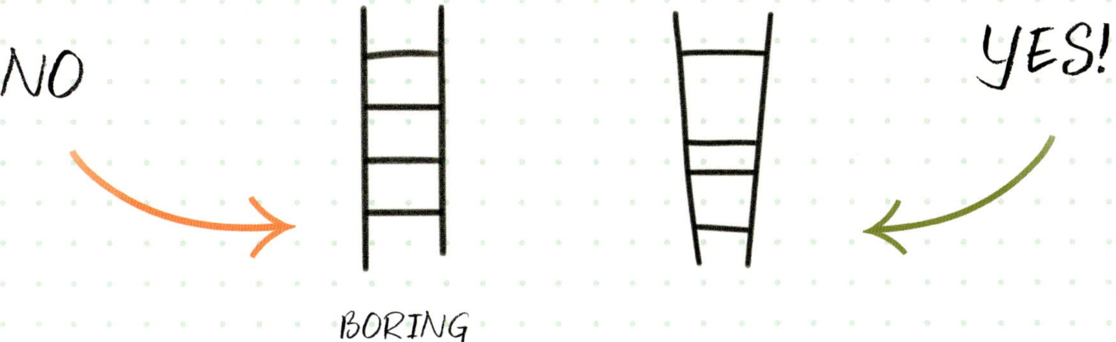

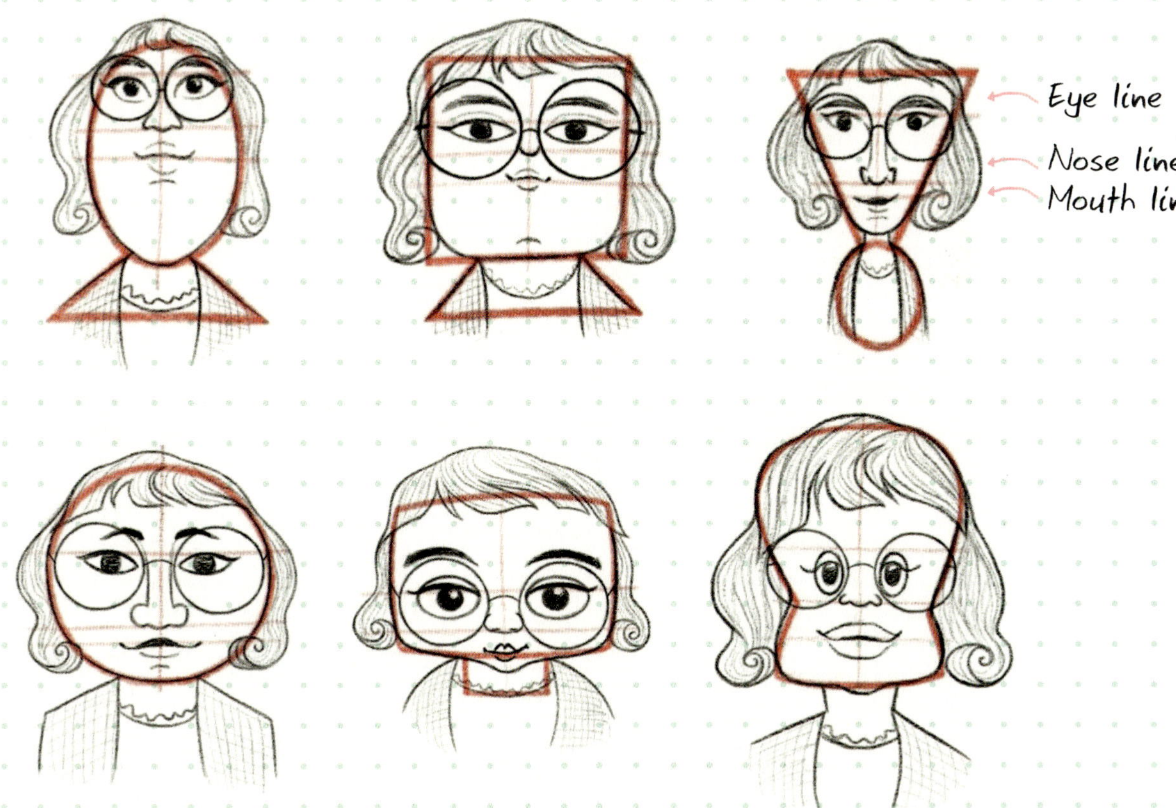

Push design with contrasting shapes

See how many different versions you can create!

MASTERS OF CARICATURE

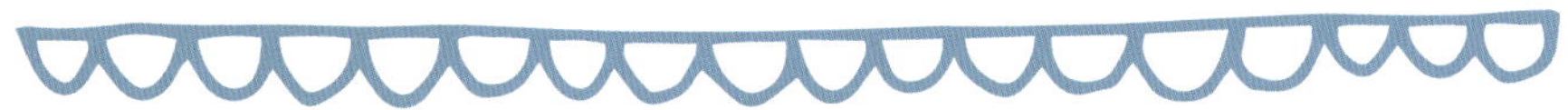

For most people, the word caricature probably brings to mind images of street artists in amusement parks or on board walks (promenades), quickly sketching humorous portraits of visitors, much to the amusement or annoyance of their subjects. But the realm of caricature encompasses far more than just that. Over the years, I've looked at the work of many different artists, including caricature artists. I take what I observe and see how I can apply it to my own work. I liken this process to the research one would undertake when writing a book. Broadening your research will enable you to develop a unique way of representing your subjects. In addition to being a bit of a history lesson, this chapter highlights some incredible artists that I think you'll enjoy checking out.

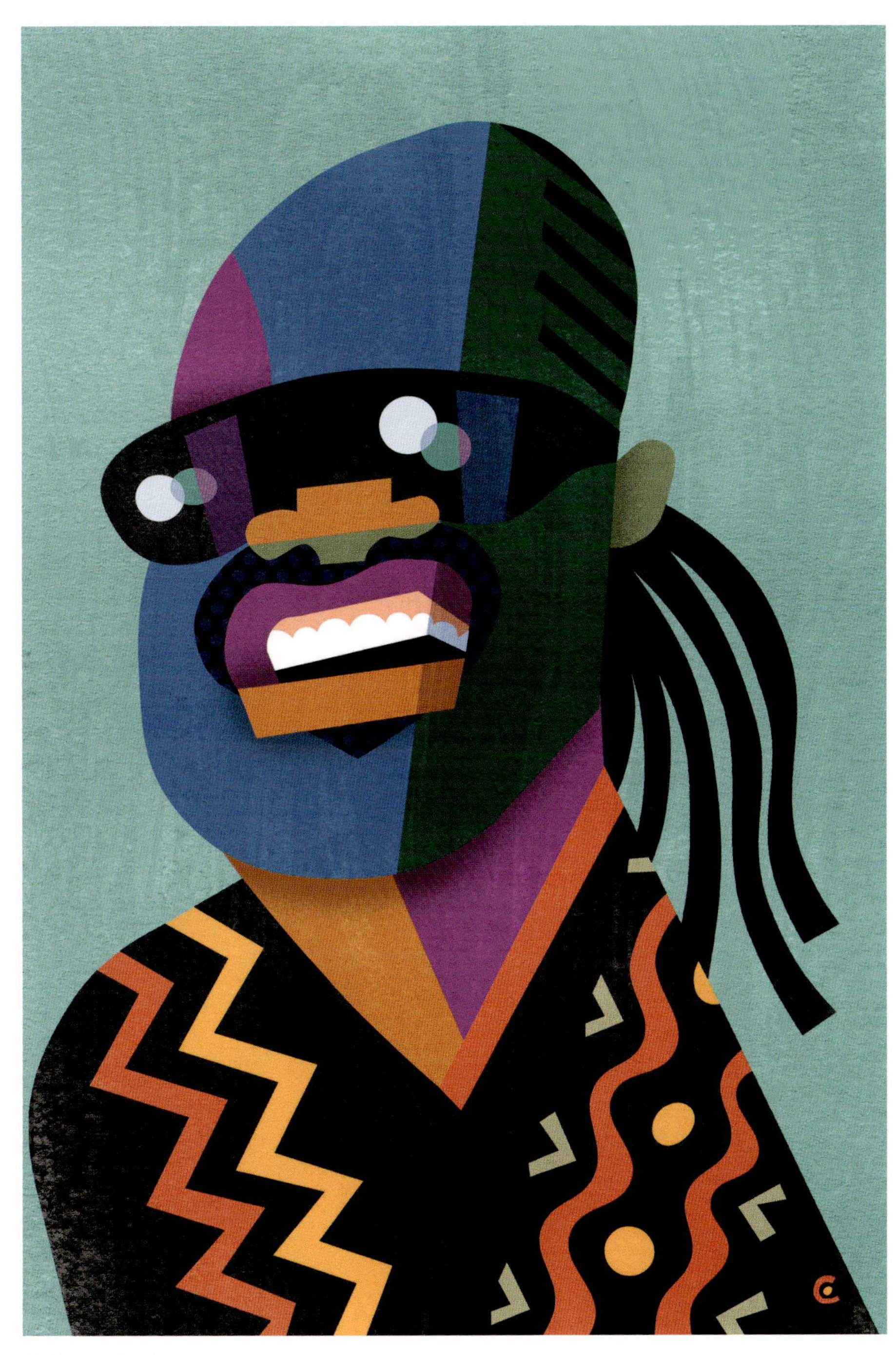

STEPHEN SILVER

This is one of my favorite quotes about drawing. It was something of an eye-opener for me when I was first learning about character design. Essentially, what Silver means is that it's important to study the styles of other artists. Study how they bend and break the rules of construction. Analyze their stylistic choices and what makes their style consistent. Look for basic visual concepts that you can adapt to your own work, such as how they draw eyes, hair, or hands, and so on.

"IF YOU WANT TO LEARN HOW TO PLAY AN INSTRUMENT, YOU HAVE TO LEARN TO PLAY ANOTHER MUSICIAN'S SONG. IF YOU WANT TO LEARN HOW TO DRAW, YOU HAVE TO DRAW ANOTHER ARTIST'S PICTURE."

Stephen Silver

It's important to be influenced by multiple artists to prevent your work from resembling the style of just one artist too closely. Additionally, this approach also helps you develop greater versatility in your art and a style that's unique to you. That being said, keep in mind that if you're interested in a career in animation, being able to mimic different drawing styles is a valuable, even essential, skill.

In summary, it's perfectly OK—and even desirable—to seek inspiration from other artists whenever you need it. Reference is necessary for growth as an artist, and you'll continue to use it throughout your life. While you may find yourself relying less and less on reference for certain aspects as you practice, you will never stop using it entirely.

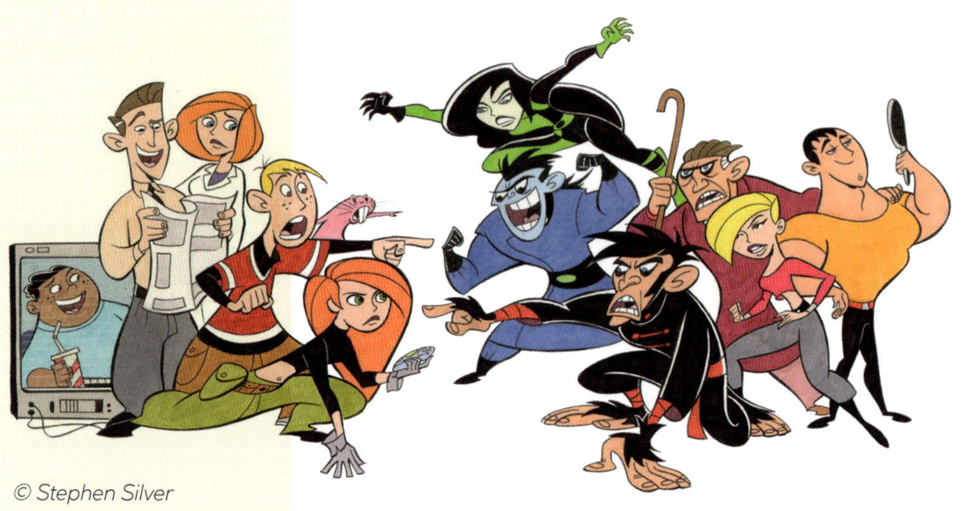

© Stephen Silver

In addition to being a great teacher and an incredibly talented artist, Silver is also a genuinely nice person. I had the pleasure of meeting him at a character design workshop he taught years ago, and it was an awesome experience. You might recognize his work from shows like *Kim Possible* or *Danny Phantom*.

His work has an incredibly distinctive, clean, and smooth shape language that he's able to apply to caricature in a way that's so fun and appealing. I love how his super cartoony characters look so much like the actors they're based on.

In these *Stranger Things* and *The Office* prints, Silver has designed cartoon versions of each of the live-action characters by caricaturing each actor.

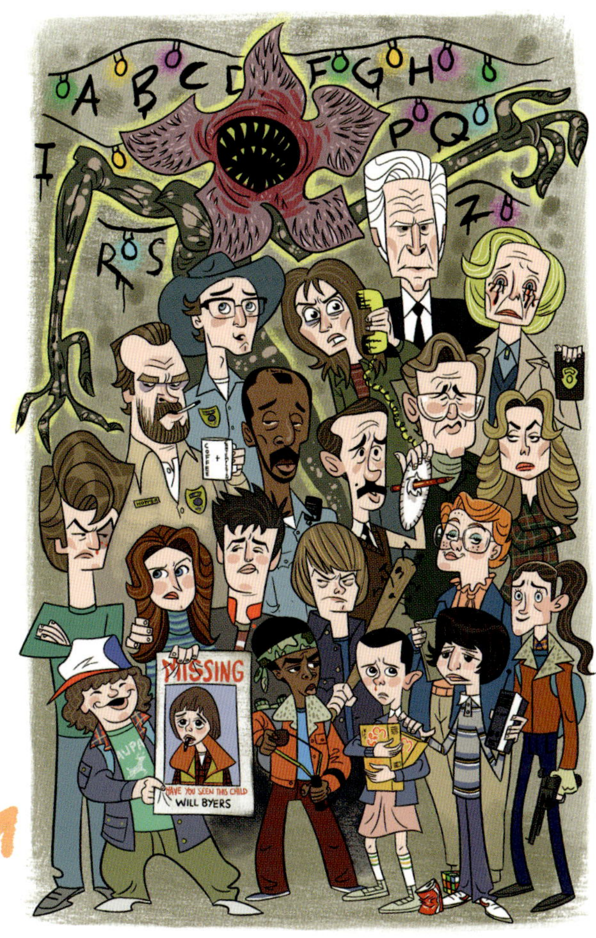

© Stephen Silver

FUN OBSERVATION EXERCISE!

Go online and search for images of the live-action characters from one of the prints on the right. Compare and analyze how Silver caricatured their features. Pay close attention to what he chose to exaggerate, how he simplified forms, and how he used the expressions and unique characteristics of each actor and character.

© Stephen Silver

COURT JONES

Court Jones is a freelance illustrator and caricature artist who began his career working as a caricature artist in theme parks. He has since won multiple awards, including the title of Master Caricature Artist of the Year at the annual International Society of Caricature Artists (ISCA) convention. Jones also has an incredible course on caricature art, which can be found online.

Here's what Court has to say about his work: "I strive to design my caricatures with a foundation in reality. That means I like the faces to look correct anatomically, with a painterly sort of realism, even though they are pulled and stretched beyond realistic proportions.

The most important element to a caricature is the likeness, with humor being a close second. The artwork needs to look like the subject or it is not a caricature. If done really well, a caricature will look more like the person than they look like themselves, while making you laugh, or at least chuckle a little."

The way he's able to render exaggerated forms in such a realistic way is so cool to me!

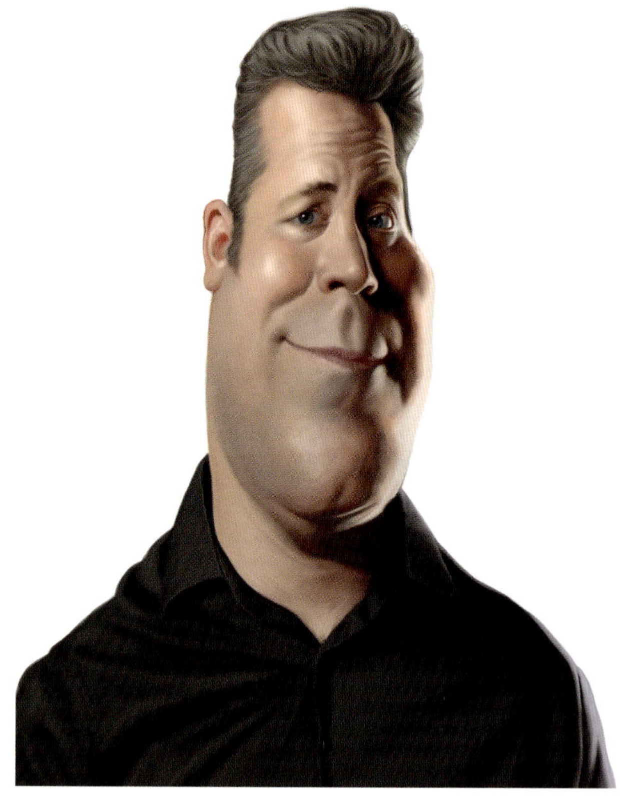

© Court Jones

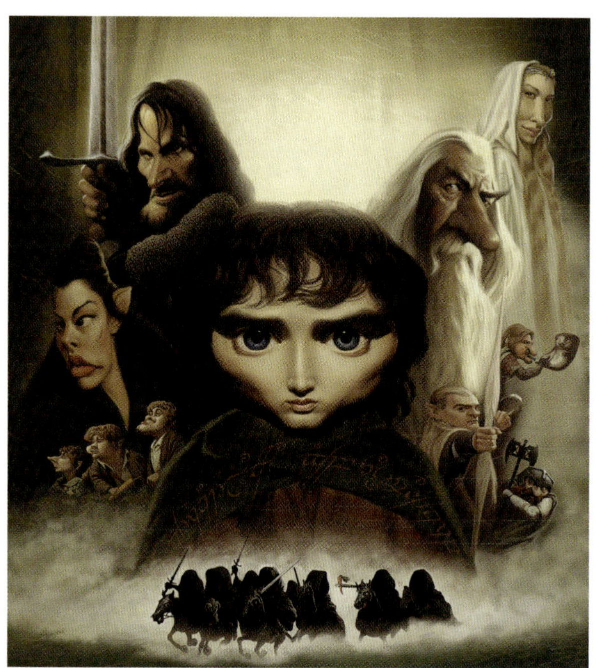

© Court Jones

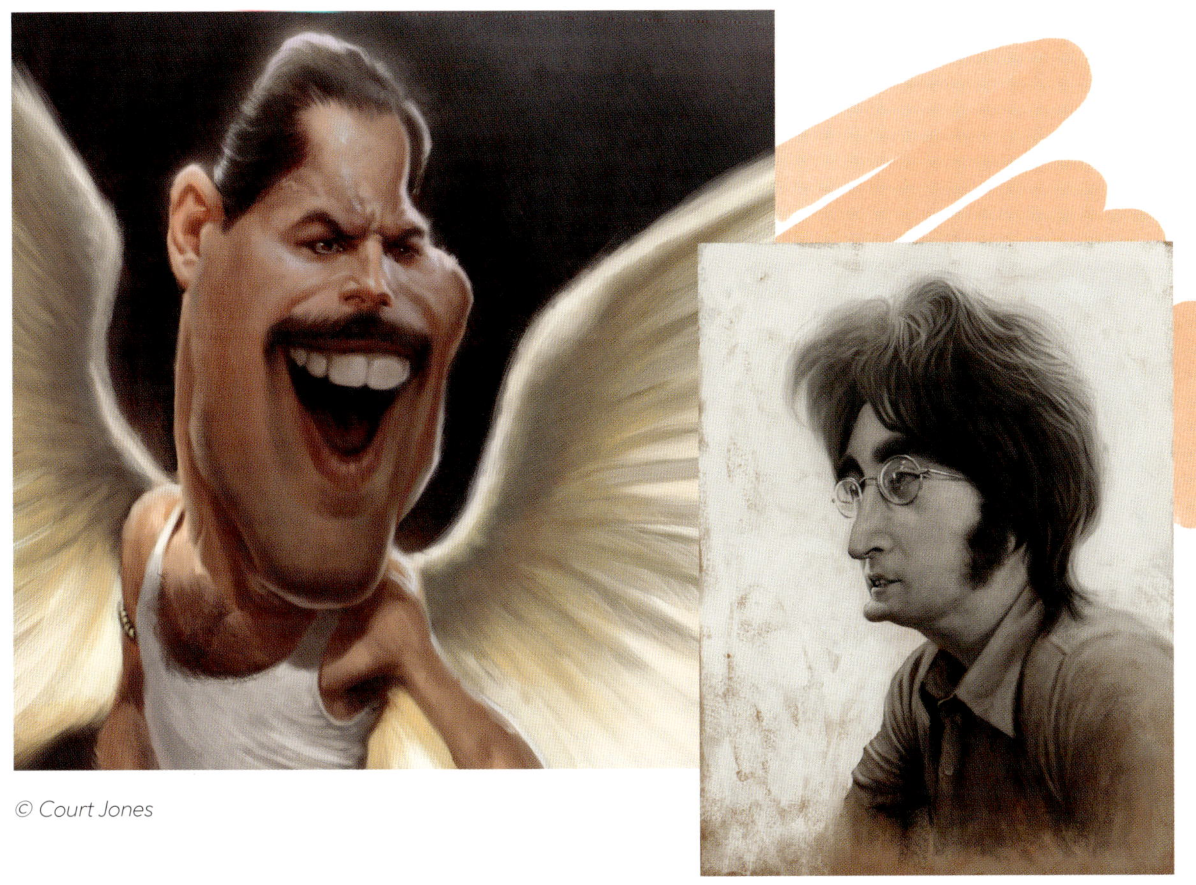

© Court Jones

© Court Jones

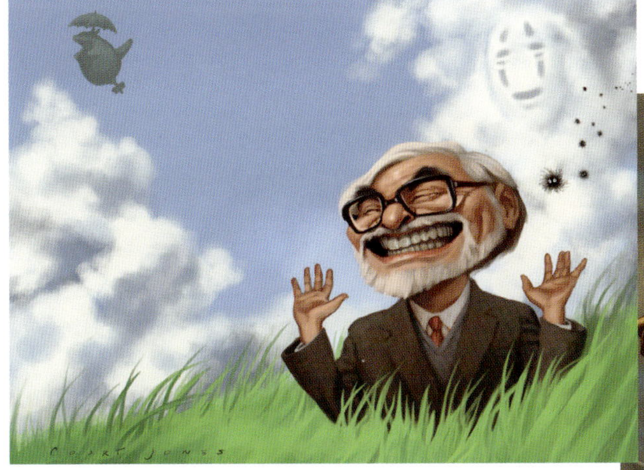

© Court Jones

© Court Jones

DAVID COWLES

Now, here is an artist who does something completely different.

David Cowles is one of my favorite abstract caricature artists. His work is highly textured and looks like paper cutouts. It amazes me how he manages to capture likeness despite the relative simplicity of his designs. I can pick out the things that support the likeness of each individual he caricatures, but at the same time, it still boggles my mind.

Cowles began his professional journey at the *Democrat and Chronicle* before launching his freelance career in the mid-1980s. His distinctive style has graced the pages of major publications including *Entertainment Weekly*, *Rolling Stone*, *Time*, *Newsweek*, *The New York Times*, and *Vanity Fair*, establishing him as one of the most recognizable voices in contemporary illustration. Beyond print work, Cowles has worked as a creator, writer, designer, storyboard artist, and director on animated projects for Disney, Sesame Street, and other major studios.

What sets him apart is his ability to distill complex facial features into geometric forms while maintaining recognizability. It really goes to show that you can do a lot with very little. He has a masterful understanding of how subtle differences in a face can convey a likeness. Amazing!

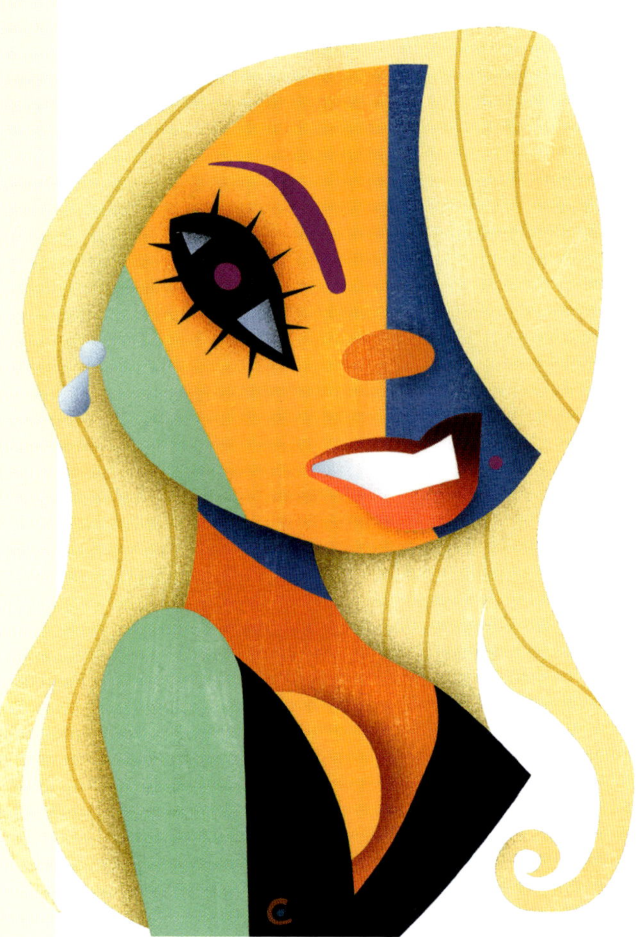

© David Cowles

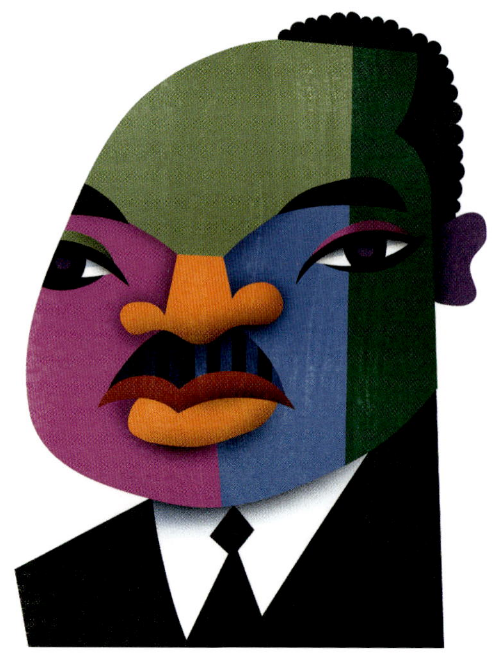

© David Cowles

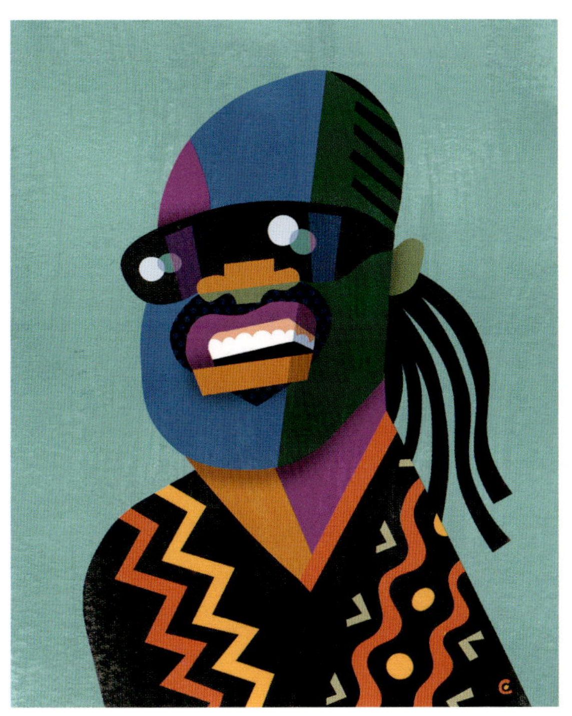

© David Cowles

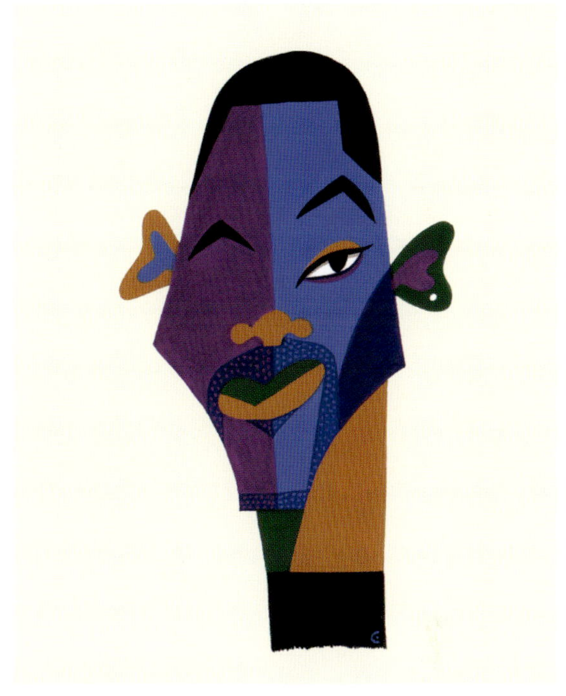

© David Cowles

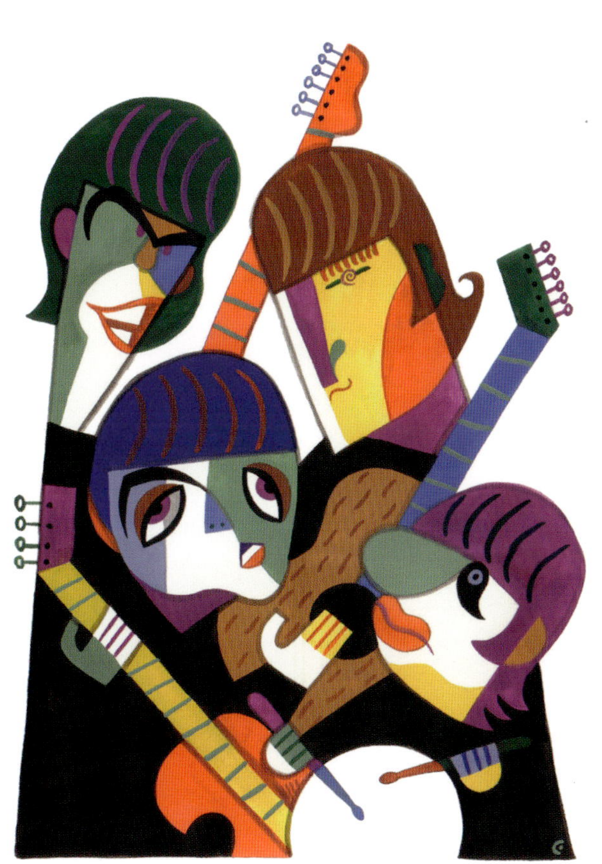

© David Cowles

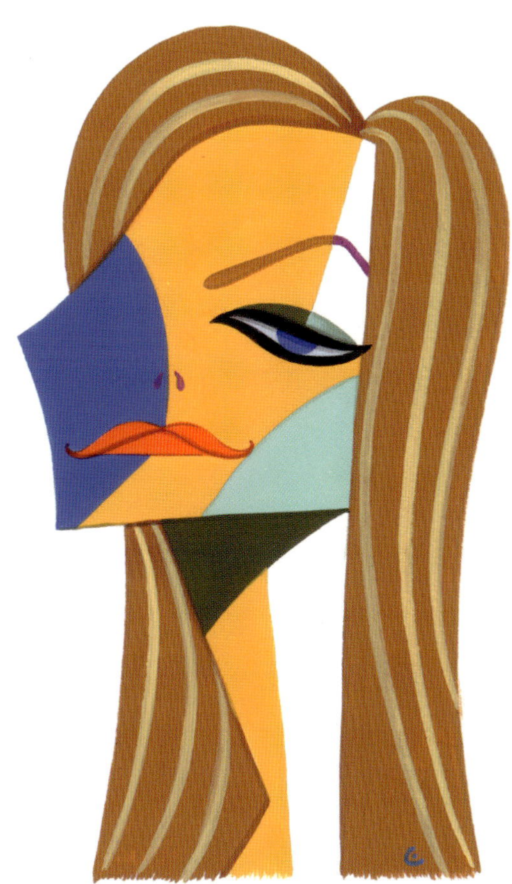

© David Cowles

DAVID DUNSTAN

Today's caricature scene is full of incredible talent.

One such talent is David Dunstan, known online as Loopydave. He's a prolific illustrator who's contributed to *MAD* magazine and *ImagineFX*, illustrated numerous children's books, done movie and DVD posters, and then some. I love the fluid quality of his shapes and line work.

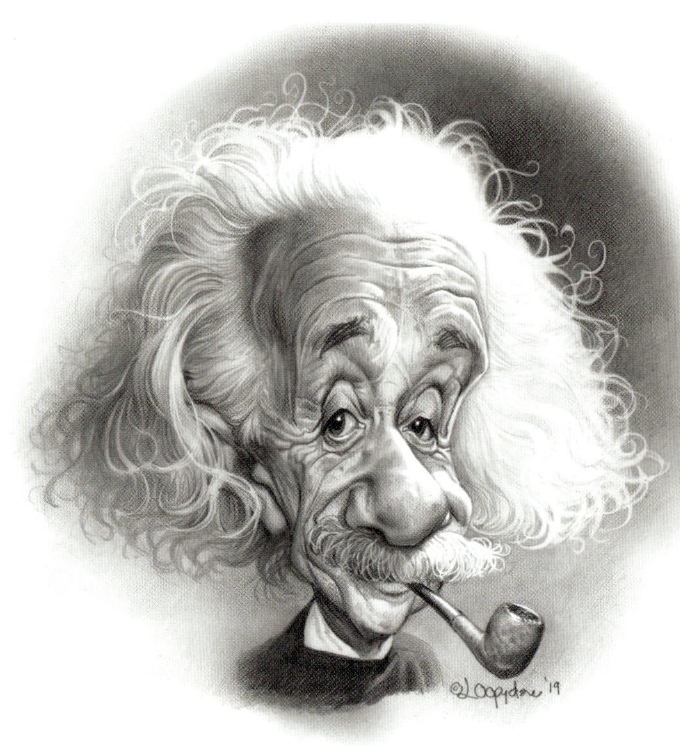

Title: Einstein, Date: September 2019, Artist: Loopydave

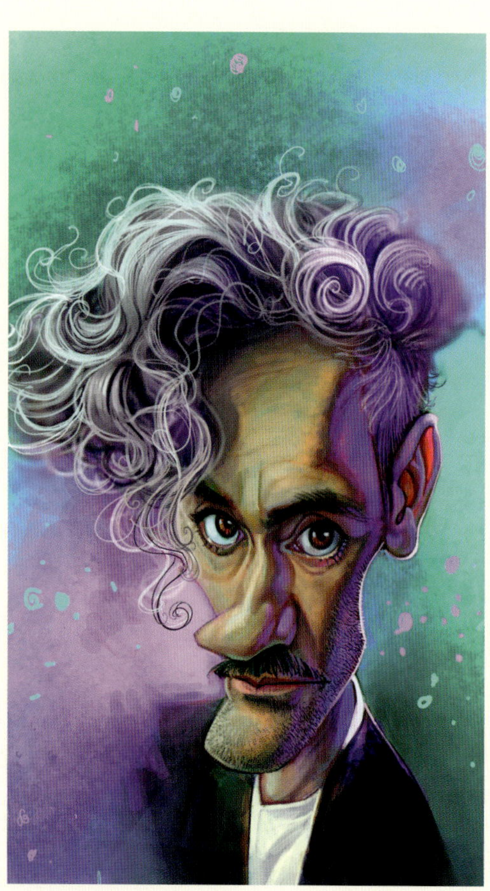

Title: Taika, Date: April 2021, Artist: Loopydave

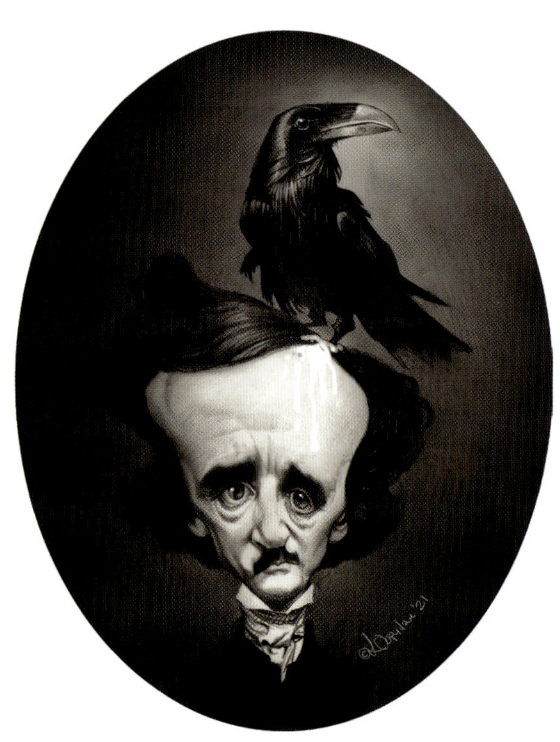

Title: Poe, Date: June 2021, Artist: Loopydave

ARTISTS OF MAD MAGAZINE

This satirical magazine has been, and still is, at the forefront of brilliant caricature.

No one is more synonymous with *MAD* than caricaturist and comics artist, Mort Drucker. Drucker was a contributor for over five decades, where he specialized in satires on feature films and television. Many caricature artists today site Drucker as a huge influence on their work, and it's no surprise as to why. Make sure you look up his work online. He's another incredible example of someone who knew how to manipulate and exaggerate faces with intention and style.

The magazine has been home to many legendary caricature artists beyond Drucker. Tom Richmond, Angelo Torres, Jack Davis, and Sam Viviano have all made significant contributions to the magazine's iconic visual style. These artists, along with Drucker, helped establish *MAD*'s distinctive approach to parody and social satire. Their work demonstrates how the best caricatures tell a story about their subject, celebrating what makes them unique or criticizing their actions, rather than simply poking fun at their appearance.

Caricatures certainly don't have to be mean-spirited. My personal goal is never to mock someone's appearance, but to make people smile or laugh.

MASTERS OF THE PAST

These two caricature artists helped define the art form.

Miguel Covarrubias was a Mexican painter, caricaturist, and art historian of the early to mid-20th century. His unique linear drawing style greatly influenced many other caricaturists, including the legendary Al Hirschfeld. Hirschfeld created some of the most recognizable illustrations in American art, using only black and white lines with minimal rendering. Take a look at their work online and you'll see how even the greatest artists build upon those who came before them.

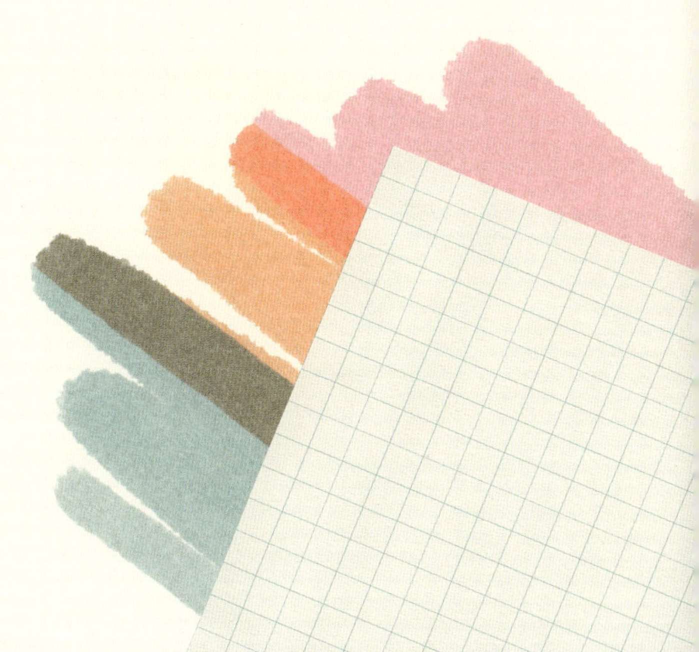

EARLY DAYS OF CARICATURE

Caricature has been around for a lot longer than many people assume! Long before it became a recognized art form, many famous historical artists experimented with exaggerated facial features (usually in their private sketchbooks), blending keen observation with playful distortion, and laying the groundwork for an entire artistic tradition.

This chapter is by no means a complete history of caricature, it isn't even a list of all of the artists I have admired over the years. Hundreds of artists, both throughout history and today, have used caricature as a means for political activism, storytelling, or to simply make people smile.

LEONARDO DA VINCI

Leonardo da Vinci does not tend to be associated with caricature, but he was among the first known artists to practice the art form in notebooks, where his wonderfully bizarre sketches of unusual faces and heads filled the pages. In fact, during the European Renaissance and the ensuing centuries of artistic development, nearly every artist had a caricature side project (if only in the margins of their sketchbooks) and some, like Leonardo, were widely known and appreciated for their skill in the art.

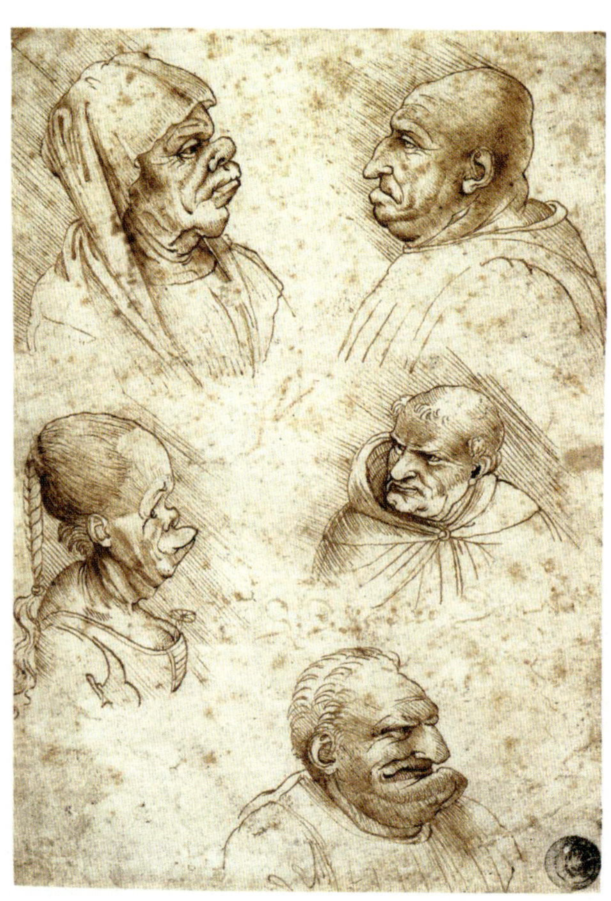

Art by Leonardo da Vinci

CLAUDE MONET

Another famous artist who is not typically recognized for his caricature art is Claude Monet. The critics of the late 19th century dismissed Impressionist artists, claiming they lacked the ability to draw before painting; however, this was actually a deliberate artistic choice. If these drawings don't clearly show that Monet knew how to draw, I don't know what would!

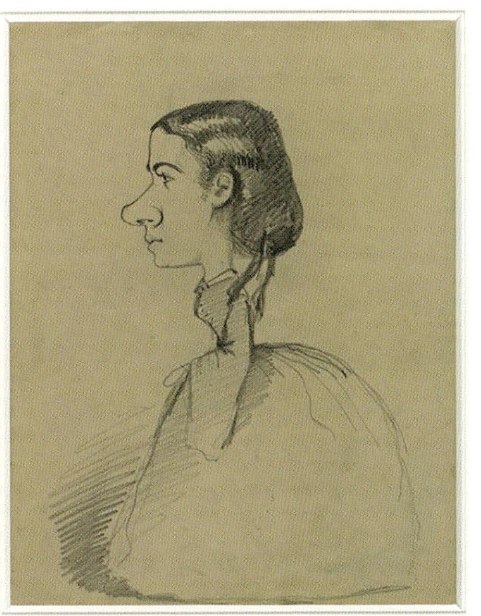

Art by Claude Monet

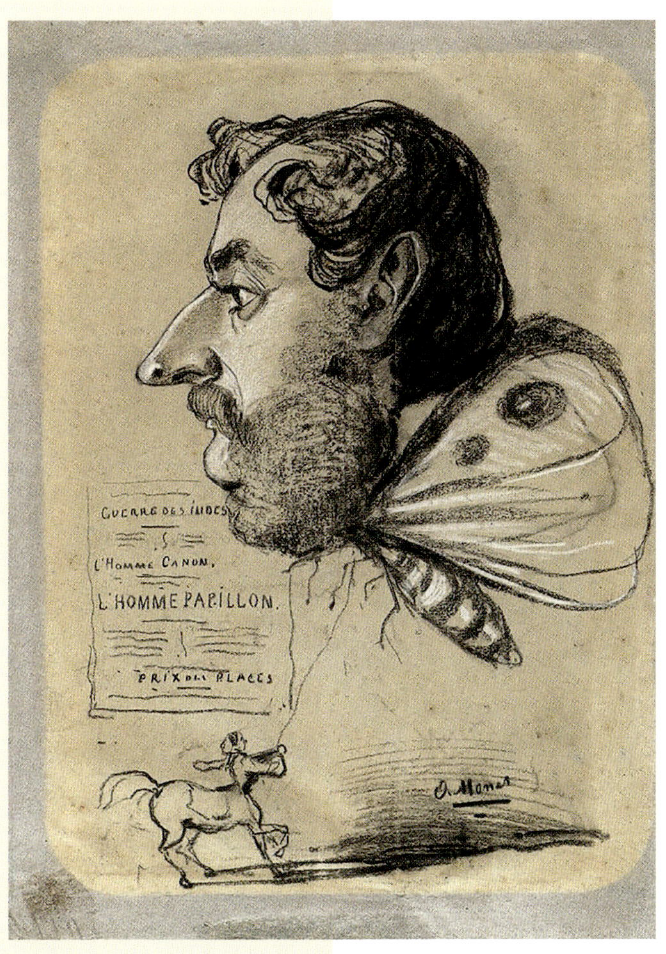

Art by Claude Monet

WOMEN IN CARICATURE

As a woman in a field historically dominated by men, it can sometimes feel a bit lonely; however, I'm far from alone!

A growing community of skilled professional women is breaking through the gender barrier with their awesome caricature art, and it would be remiss not to highlight their work here. The seven artists featured here represent just a small percentage of the female force transforming the industry.

THE ORGANIZATION

Women in Caricature is also the name of a group that, in their words, "aims to provide a safe space and community for the development of women in caricature." They are trans-inclusive and offer a variety of resources, including workshops, artist spotlights, community nights, and opportunities to connect with other women in caricature.

KELLY O'BRIEN

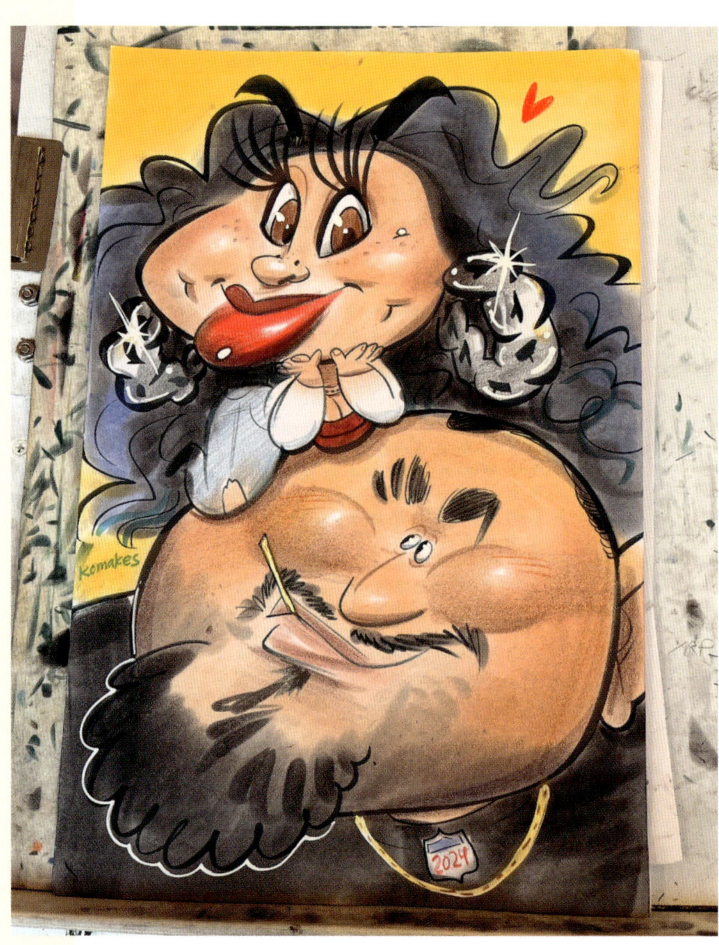

© Kelly O'Brien

SAM GORRIE

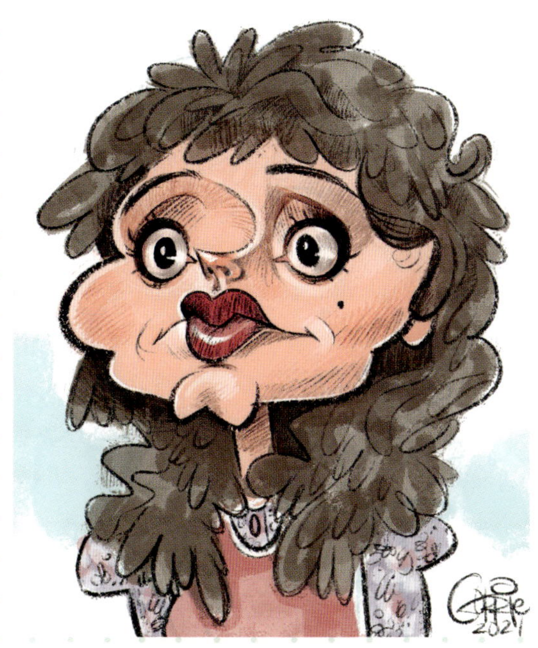
Geena Davis by Sam Gorrie

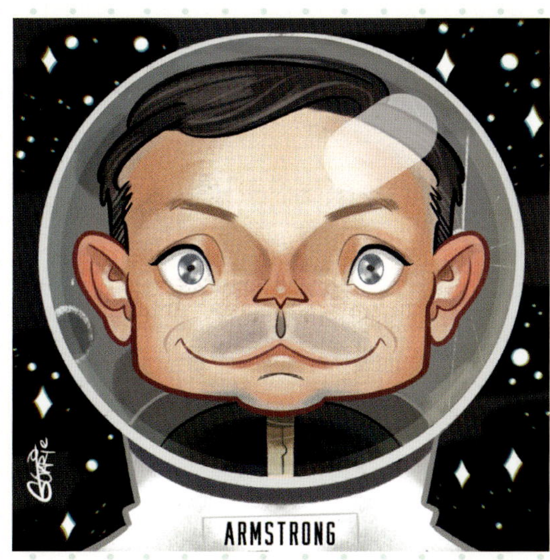

Neil Armstrong by Sam Gorrie

ASH STRYKER

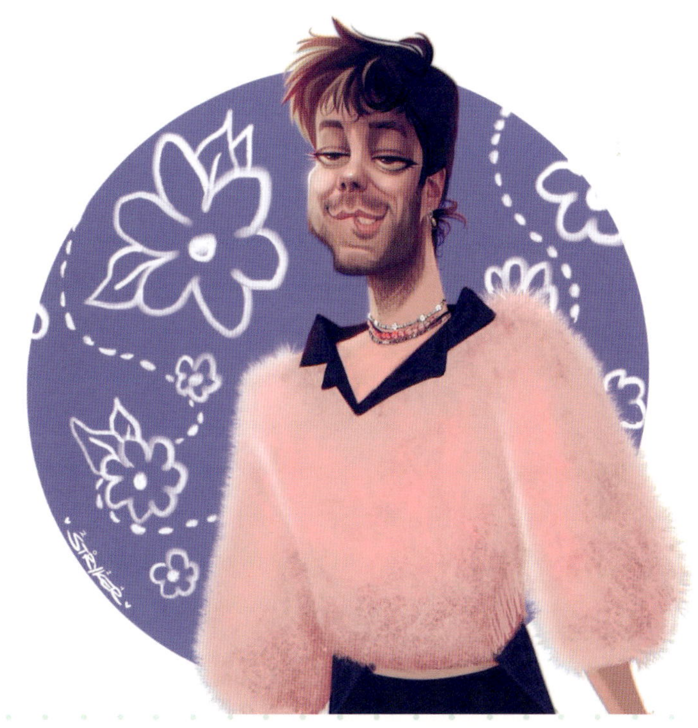
Andri, 2024 (Digital), by Ash Stryker

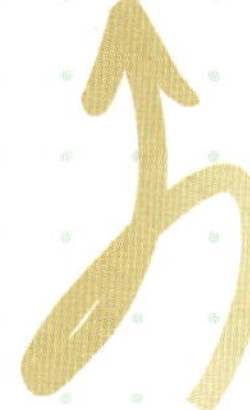

I love how Ash Stryker's base design is stylized and caricatured, but the rendering on top is very realistic and painterly.

MARIETTA WILLIAMS

Wildly cartoonish exaggeration does not always take away from likeness! I love how bold these choices are.

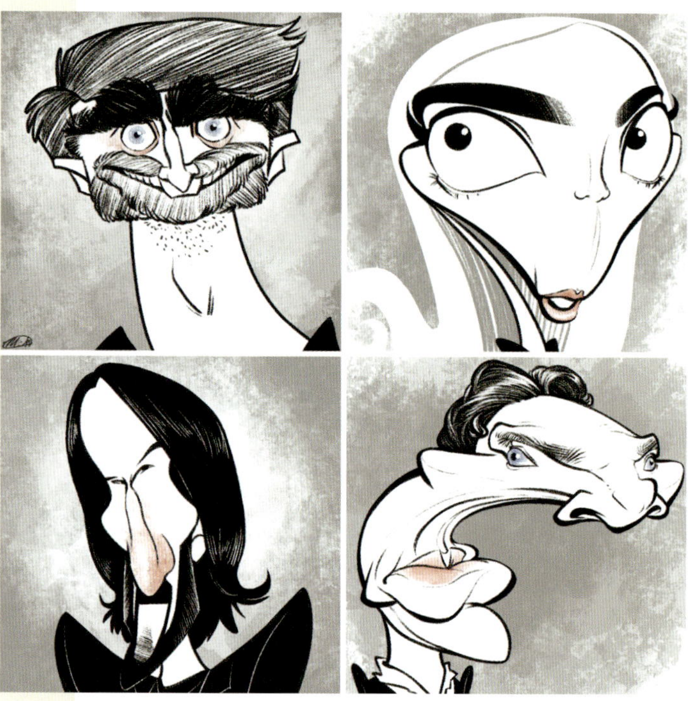

Celebrity Caricatures, 2022, by Marietta Williams

LINDSEY OLIVARES

Lindsey's exaggeration choices are strange and absurd but the subject is still recognizable.

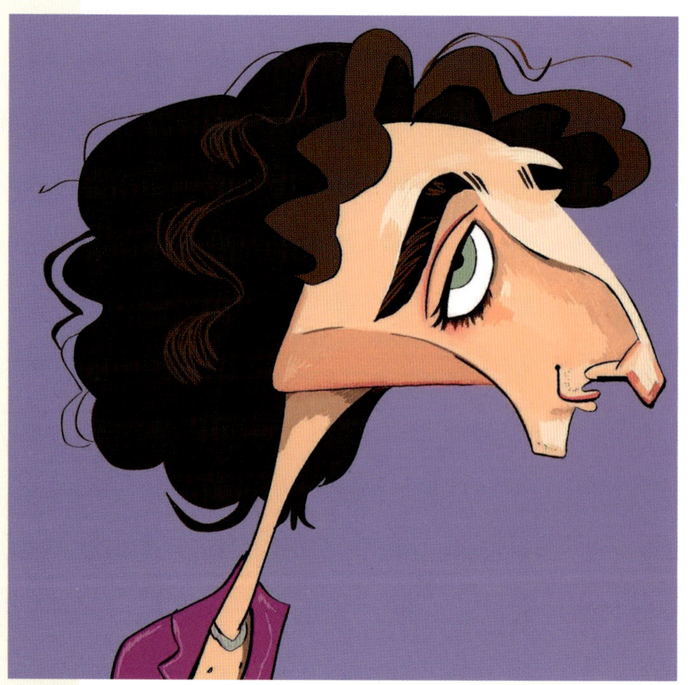

Timothée Chalamet by Lindsey Olivares

MARIA PICASSÓ PIQUER

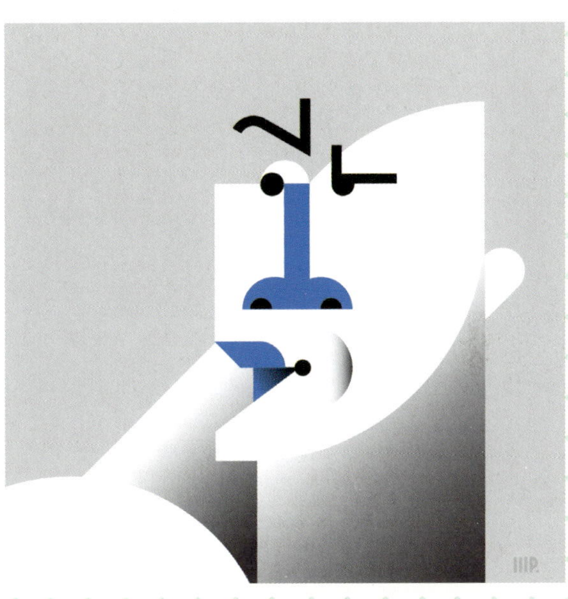

Dwayne "The Rock" Johnson by Maria Picassó Piquer

HITOMI ISHIHARA

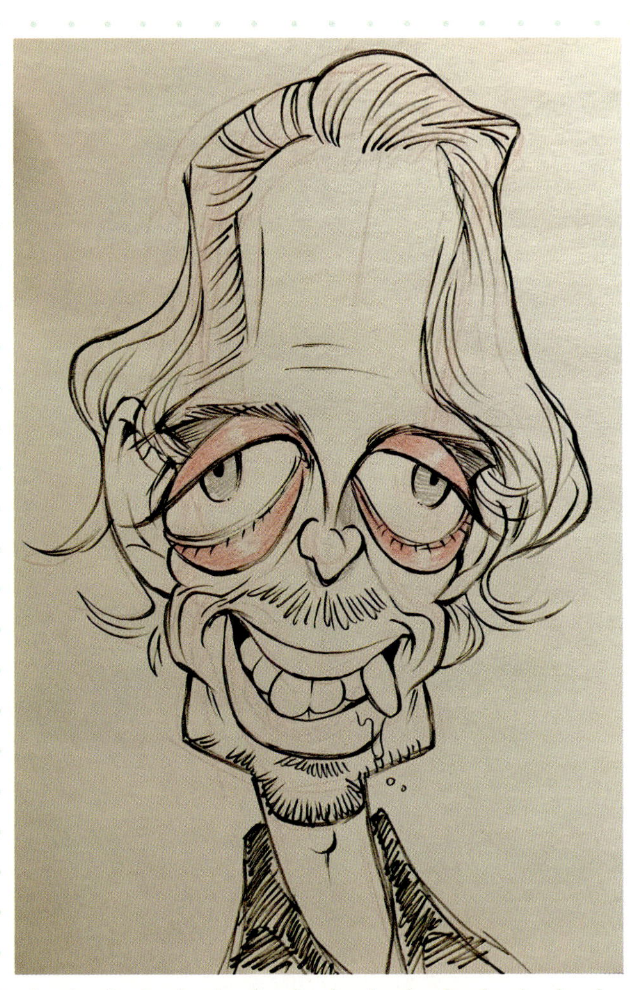

Image by Hitomi Ishihara (@hitomi.draws)

THE IMPORTANCE OF STUDYING A VARIETY OF STYLES

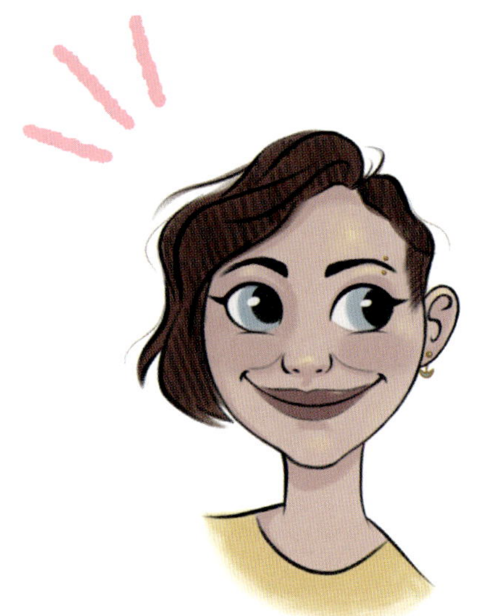

When people call something "original," they are often simply unaware of the references or the original sources it draws from.

I'd like to recommend a book—you may already be familiar with it—that's a must-read for every artist. It's called *Steal Like an Artist* by Austin Kleon. In it, Kleon discusses the idea that nothing is truly original.

There is a quote from the book that perfectly summarizes the concept:

"What a good artist understands is that nothing comes from nowhere. All creative work builds on what came before. Nothing is completely original.

Some people find this idea depressing, but it fills me with hope. As the French writer André Gide put it, 'Everything that needs to be said has already been said. But, since no one was listening, everything must be said again.'

If we're free from the burden of trying to be completely original, we can stop trying to make something out of nothing, and we can embrace influence instead of running away from it."

Kleon goes on to clarify that this, of course, doesn't mean you should literally plagiarize word for word, plot point for plot point, or trace someone else's drawing or photograph and claim it as your own, but that a healthy amount of influence from the creatives that you admire is normal and necessary. Even Picasso was influenced by the artists who came before him.

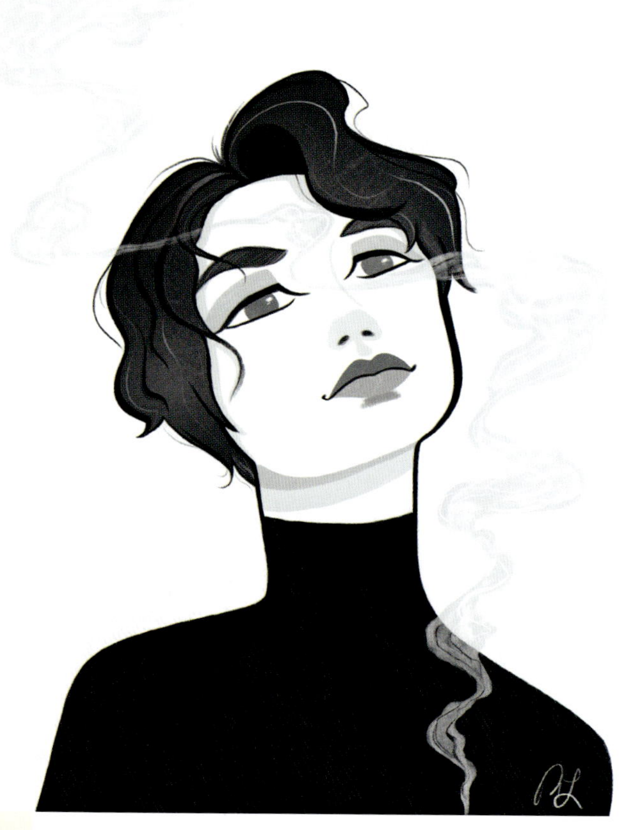

DEVELOPING A STYLE

I used to worry about finding my unique style, but what I've found is that my hand naturally draws in a way that is unique to me, regardless of what I'm drawing. Because I draw inspiration from many different artists, I don't emulate just one of them too closely. Your style (or styles) will develop organically over time through the joy of creating for its own sake, you'll begin to notice patterns and stylistic choices emerging naturally.

The point is that you shouldn't try to force your style; it will develop naturally through regular practice and careful observation.

"STYLE IS NOT ABOUT MIMICKING WHAT ANOTHER ARTIST DOES. IT'S ABOUT DEVELOPING A STYLE UNIQUE TO YOU WHILE TAKING INTO ACCOUNT UNIVERSAL CONCEPTS ABOUT WHAT MAKES APPEALING ART."

Brooke Glaser

SOME ENCOURAGEMENT

Here's the thing, caricature and cartooning is challenging. Just because an art form is simpler visually, does not mean that it is easier to do than something else. It is difficult and it takes a lot of trial and error and tons of practice to master. This is not meant to discourage you! Really, it's meant to do the opposite. My hope is that this book will help to ease the learning process for you; however, I still want you to manage your expectations. We're not trying to make a masterpiece on day one and keep in mind that when you're struggling with something, that means you are challenging yourself and growing as an artist. Struggle isn't always a bad thing! The harder you work at something, the more likely it is to stick.

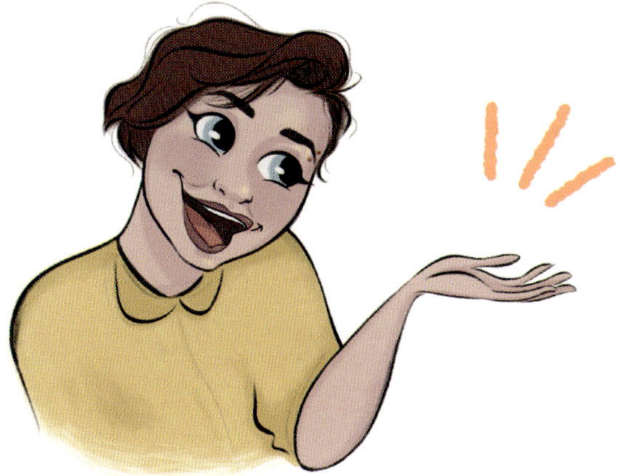

IN SUMMARY...

1. Study the work of a variety of artists.

2. Maintain a semi-regular art practice.

3. Pay attention to the stylistic choices you're drawn to (pun intended!) and enjoy drawing the most.

WORK BY YOURS TRULY

Here's how studying different artists has shaped my own work over the years. I've included both caricature and character design here because of how the two art forms complement each other.

In all honesty, I'm not sure I have one super distinctive style, as I tend to shift between more illustrative, stylized approaches and more realistic ones depending on my mood. But through studying other artists and practicing consistently, I've started to notice certain qualities that feel uniquely mine. The quality of line work and illustrative shading you see in my Dali piece, for example, is something I've been consciously developing and leaning into more. Your style might not be about having one signature look, but about recognizing and nurturing the elements that feel most natural to you.

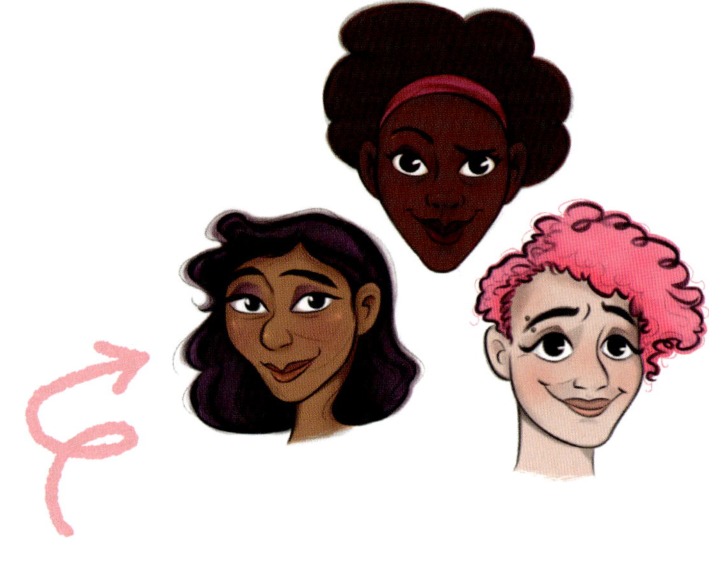

I drew these cartoony caricatures while people watching at a coffee shop!

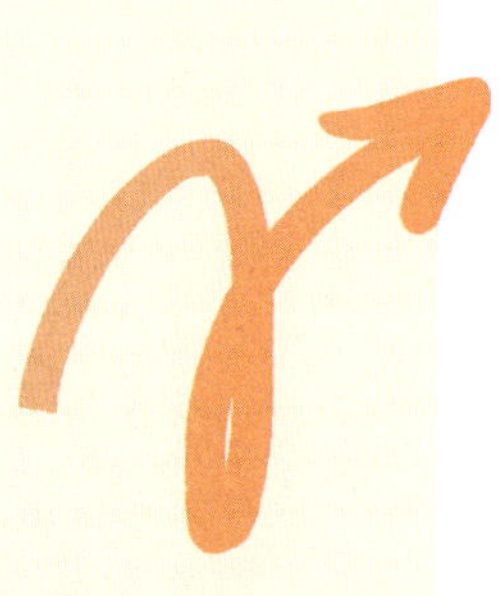

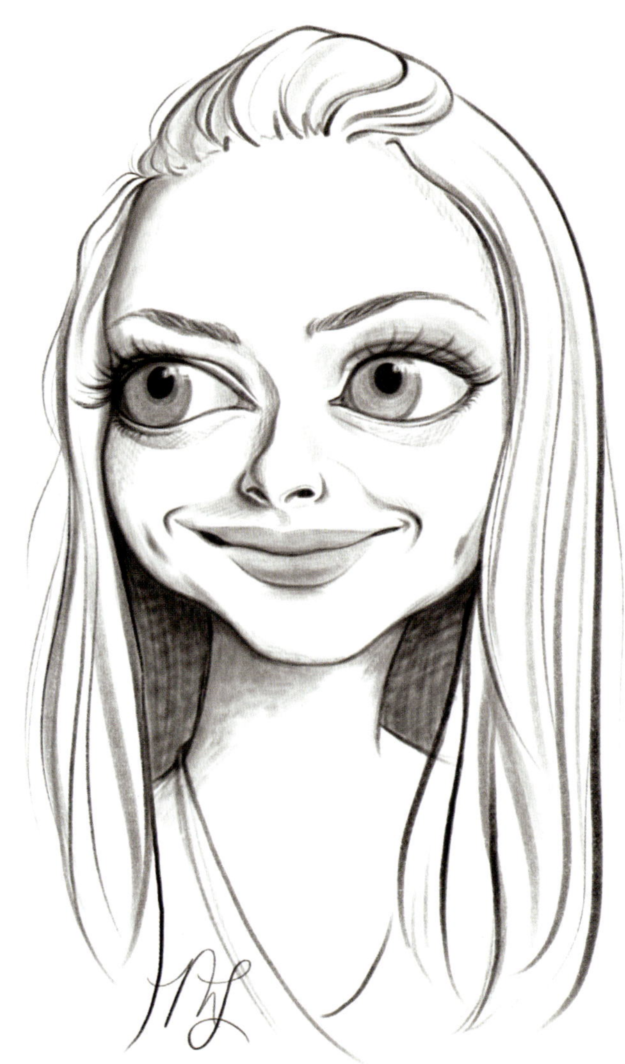

I'm particularly proud of how this Amanda Seyfried piece turned out, so I wanted to give it a featured spot here.

Let me introduce you to Tobias "Toby" Greenwood, a character I designed for a fictional webcomic concept. I drew him back in 2018 for one of my first online courses on Skillshare that focused on character design and caricature. That course was one of the first stepping stones that led me to creating this book, so this piece holds a special place in my heart! Toby remains one of my favorite characters I've designed, but looking at his hands now, I can see how much I've improved since then. They do the job just fine, but I've definitely leveled up my hand-drawing skills!

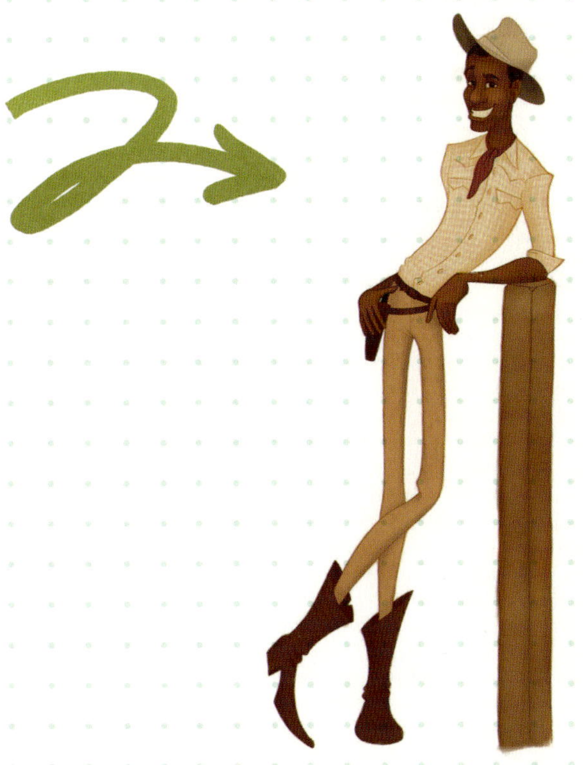

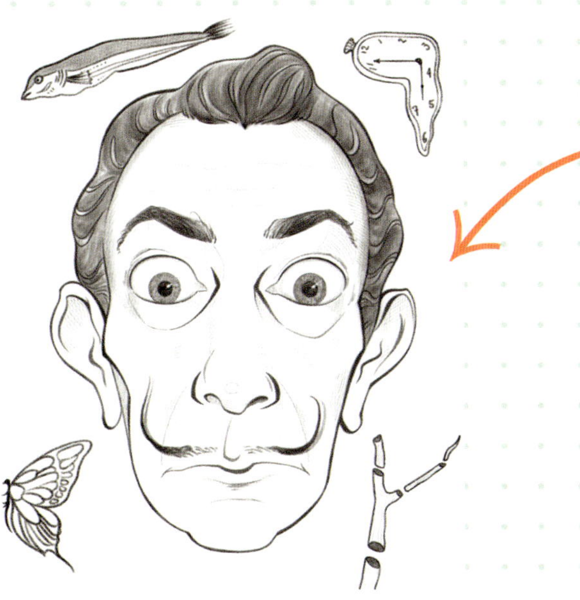

I took my simple sketch of Dali from the Foundations: Spacing & Placement Exercise and pushed the exaggeration just a little further to create this caricature of him.

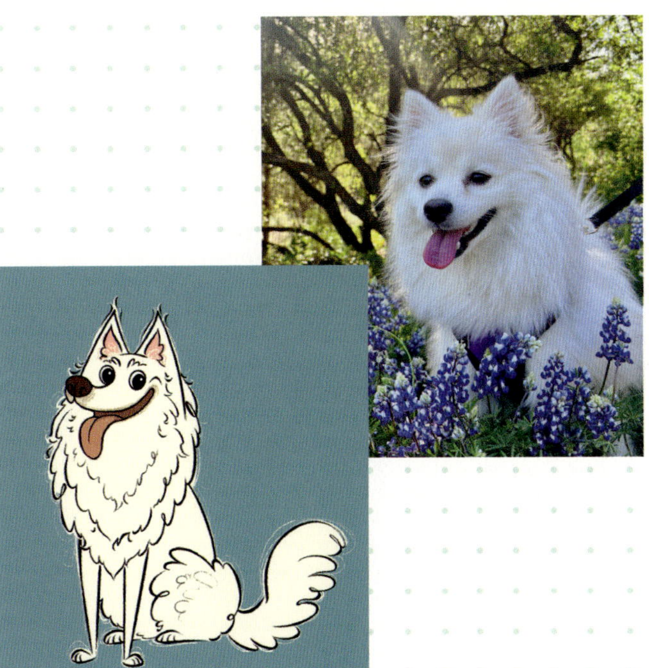

This cutie is my dog, Kaya! I was determined to get her big muppet smile right in this caricature, and I really think I nailed it. See how exaggerating her most distinctive features brings out her character?

THE ART OF CUTE-ICATURE

Cute-icatures (i.e., live caricatures) are typically simpler and a little more flattering than more traditional, highly rendered caricatures. Because this style of caricature is often a souvenir for the person you're caricaturing, the exaggeration is not typically pushed to the extreme—emphasizing a feature that someone may feel self-conscious about can lead to some unhappy customers. I have heard some horror stories about angry or awkward interactions with displeased customers. Of course, it's (usually) not meant as an insult, but unfortunately that is how it can appear to some people. There is a good reason why this style of caricature tends to be a little cuter and more endearing.

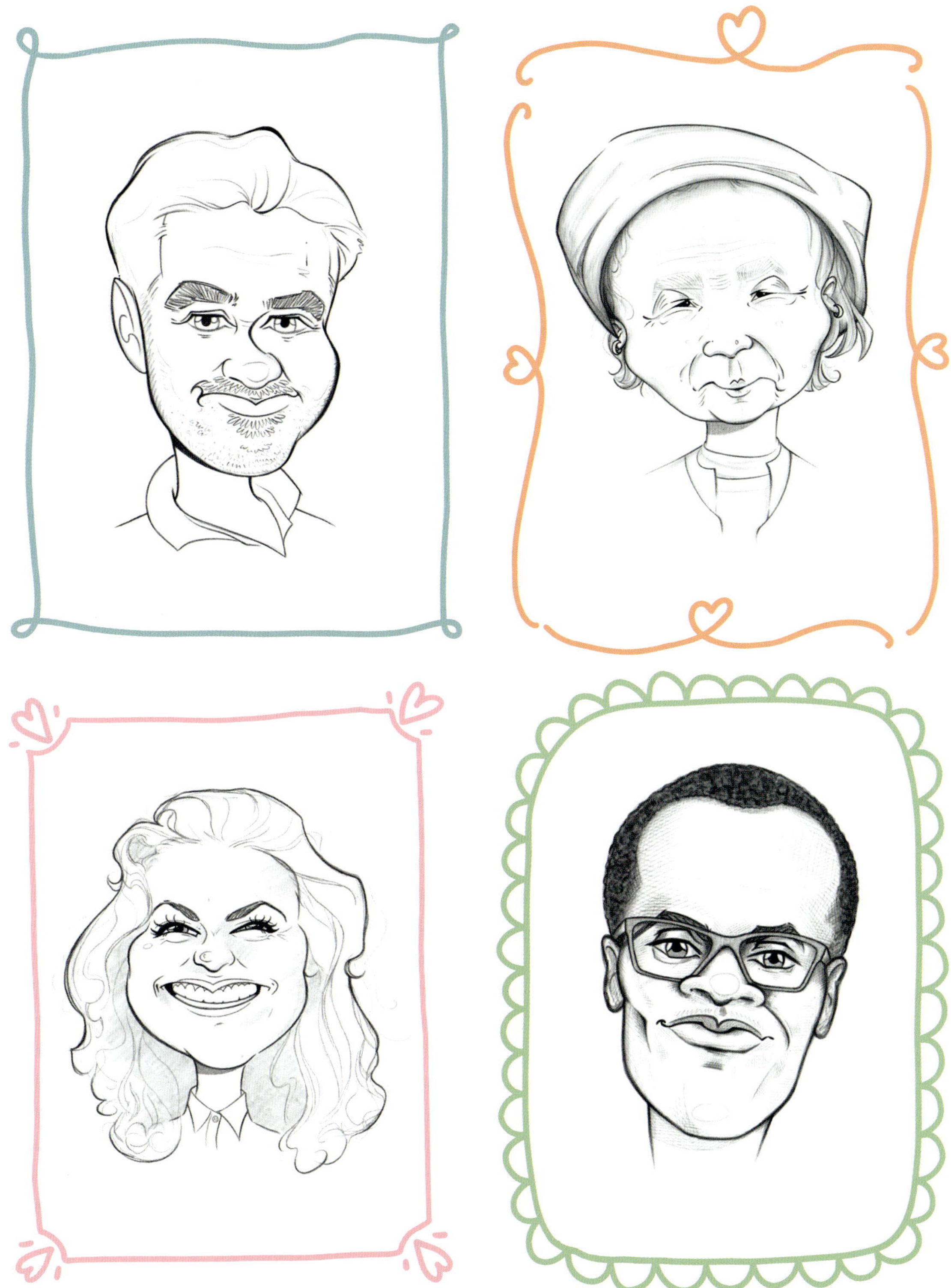

PLOTTING OUT THE FACE

There are several ways you can start a caricature drawing, but I usually start with the basic head shape. If you start with the eyes, for instance, you may find that when you try to fill in the rest of the face and head, things just feel... off. This is because you haven't yet mastered how to build a face, so you don't have the foundational knowledge and muscle memory to pull from.

As you gain experience, you can start to experiment with different starting points—like the eye line or the ears—but the ability to do this effectively relies on having a strong foundational understanding of realistic proportions, and a ton of practice with drawing exaggerated faces. So, for beginners, I always recommend starting with the head first.

Most of the full caricatures in this book are of people looking directly at the camera so, for this section, I wanted to demonstrate how to draw a face at a three-quarter turn.

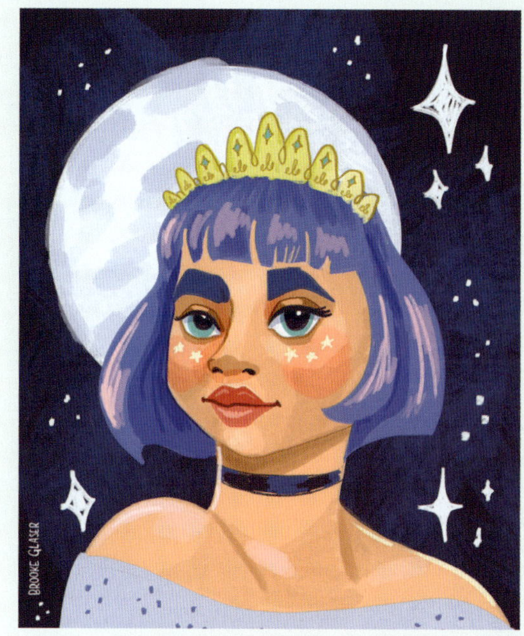

Brooke Glaser (2022, November) Cosmic Girl

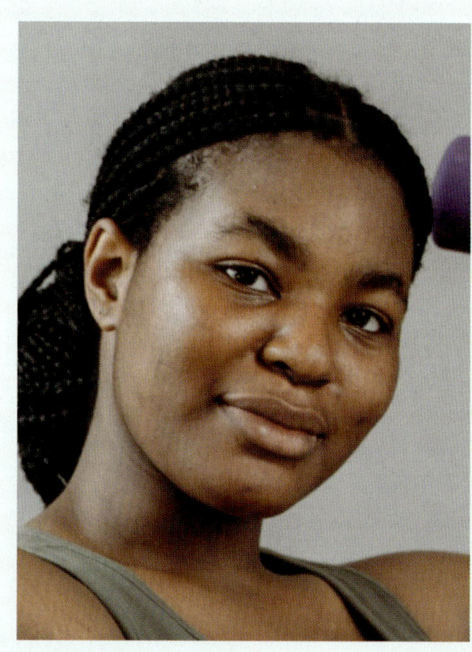

1. Start with a circle (this represents the spherical portion of the skull without the jaw), then draw a vertical line down the center. In this case, it's tilted to match the tilt of the reference photo.

2. Next, draw a horizontal line through the center. The tilt of this line is determined by the tilt of the eyebrow line.

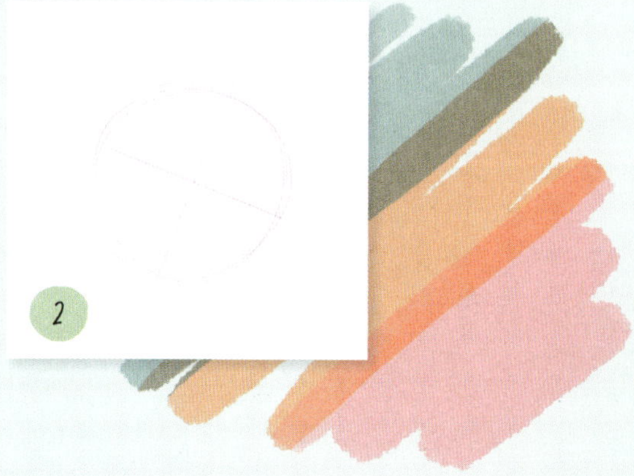

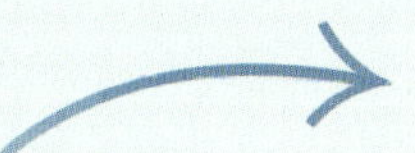

3. Our heads are not perfect spheres, so we need to flatten the sides. Draw an oval on the side of the skull that is facing you and add a cross through that as well. Draw a vertical line on the opposite side of the circle to indicate where the other side is cut off. This is where you can draw in the shape of the eyebrow ridge and cheek. Erase as needed.

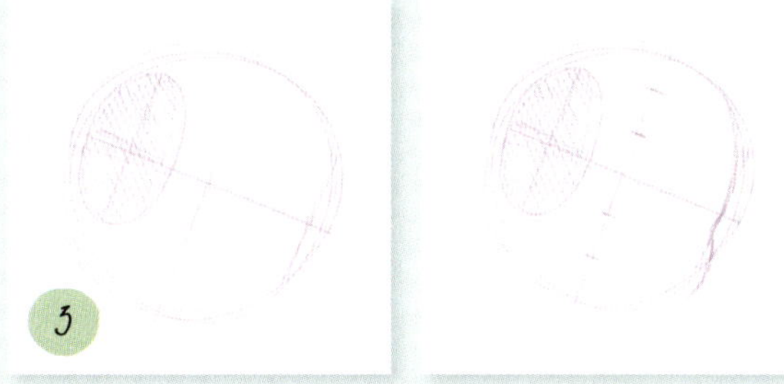

4. Break the top and bottom halves of the circle into thirds so that there are six equal sections. The pink lines represent where the hairline, the top of the eyes, and the bottom of the nose land. Be sure to draw these lines parallel to each other. It can be helpful to use curved lines instead of perfectly straight lines, as the curve better represents the curve of the face.

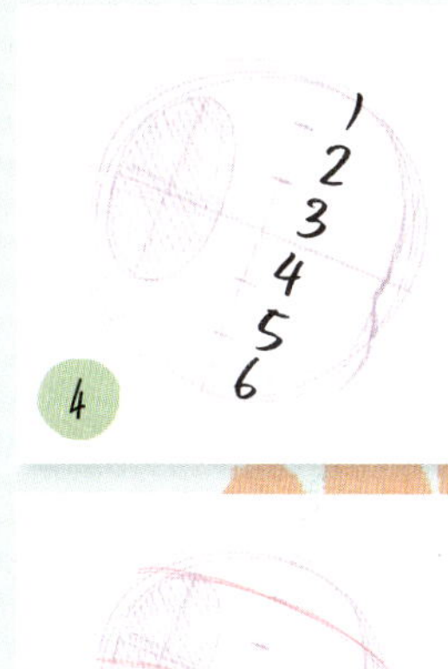

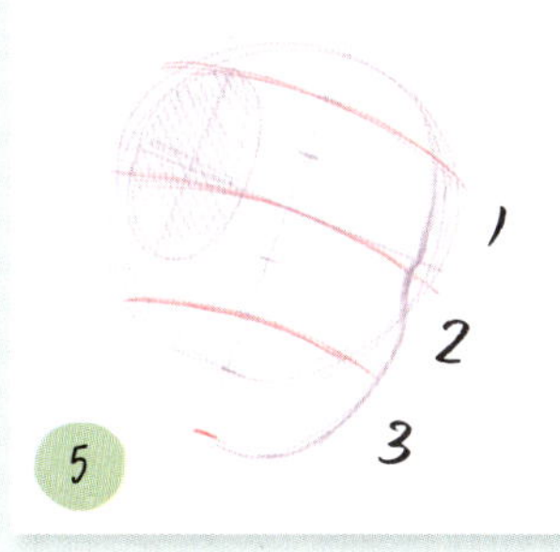

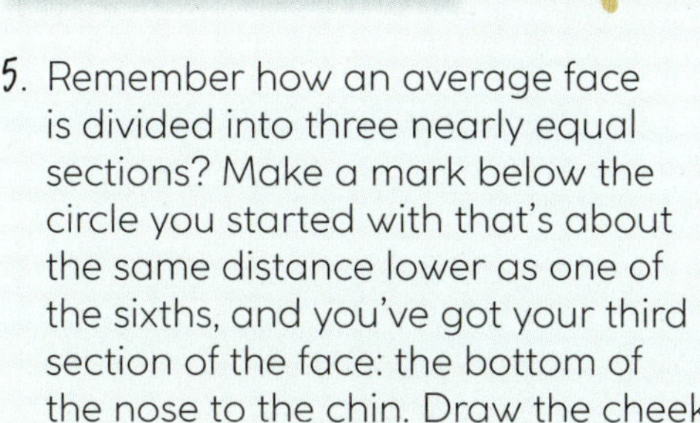

5. Remember how an average face is divided into three nearly equal sections? Make a mark below the circle you started with that's about the same distance lower as one of the sixths, and you've got your third section of the face: the bottom of the nose to the chin. Draw the cheek in a curved line down to the chin.

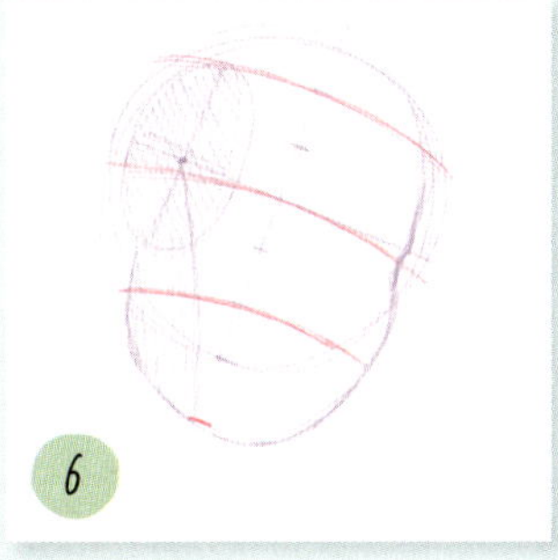

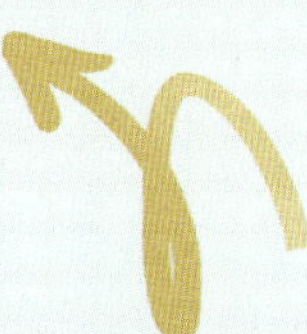

6. The line from the center of the oval down to the jaw helps define where the cheekbone lands. Draw a curved line from the chin to somewhere close to the center line of the oval to create the jawline. No two jawlines are the same. Some are soft and round like this one, and some are more angular and sharp.

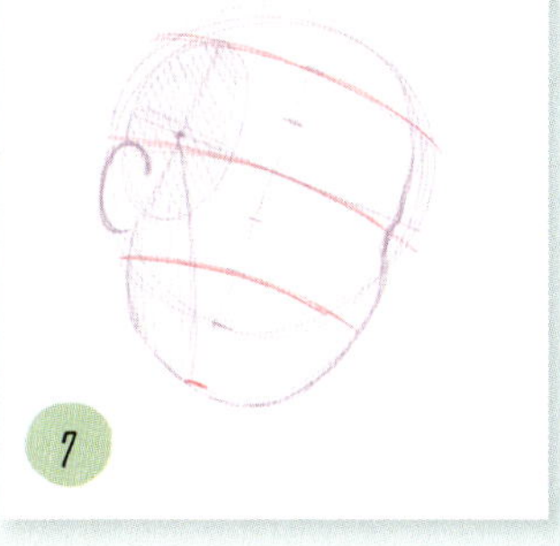

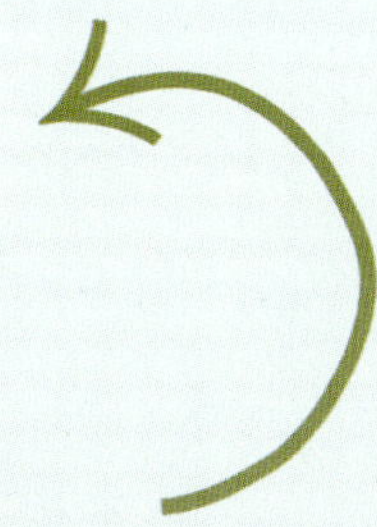

7. The ear sits in or across the lower left quadrant of the oval, in between the brow and nose lines; the second third of the face.

8. To help you place the facial features, draw a line roughly where the center of the face lands. Because this face is turned in perspective, this center line is not in the center of the first circle we drew. More of the side of the face is facing us, so allow for more room for that side.

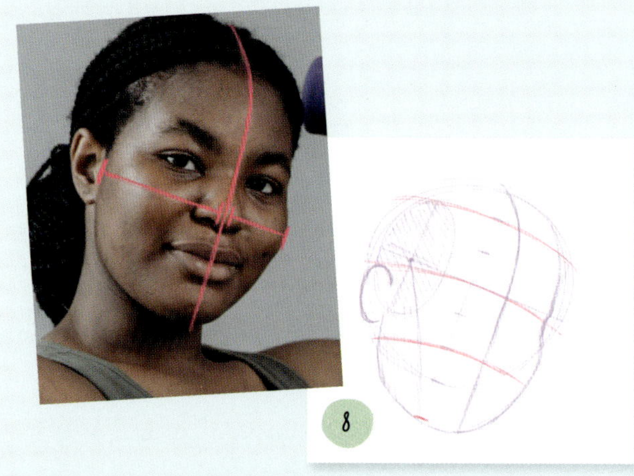

9. It can be helpful to draw a mask shape where the eyebrows and eyes will be. With a three-quarter view, the eye that's closer to you is a little larger than the other, so make the side of the "mask" that's facing you larger. The circles represent the entire eyeball (think spherical), not the iris or pupil, so try your best to draw them as wide as the eyes appear, so in other words, follow the width from corner to corner. Most of these circles will be covered with the eyelids.

10. Next, follow the shape of the eyes, using the circles as your guide. My reference model has almond-shaped eyes and partially obscured eyelids so I've drawn dark eyelid lines following the upper almond shape. You can now add the irises and pupils.

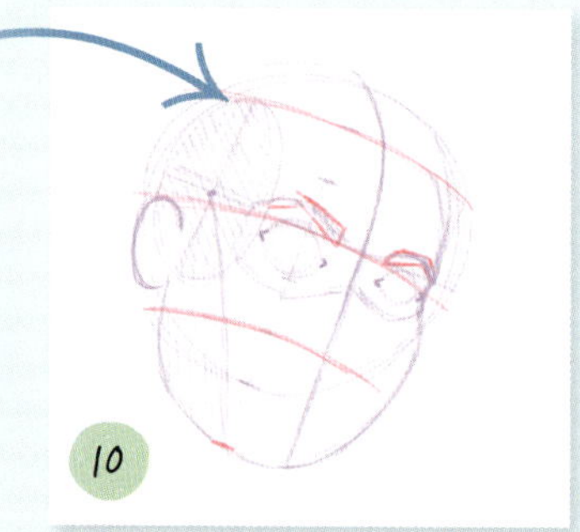

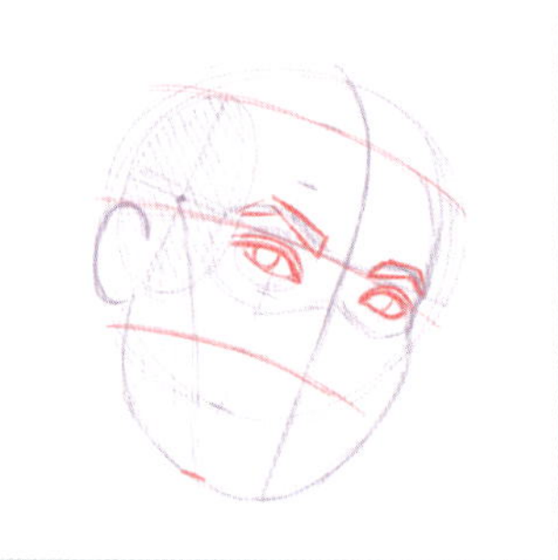

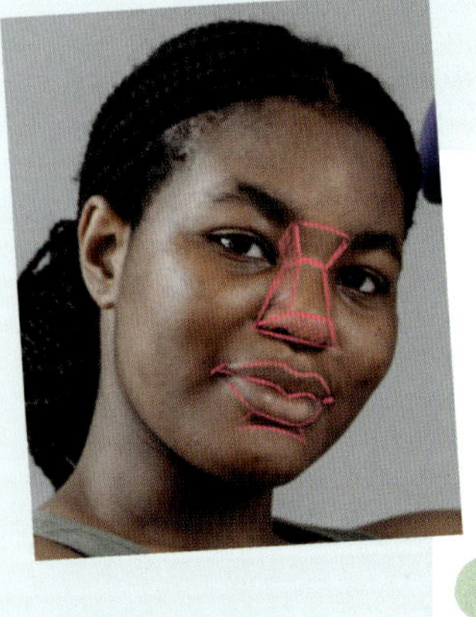

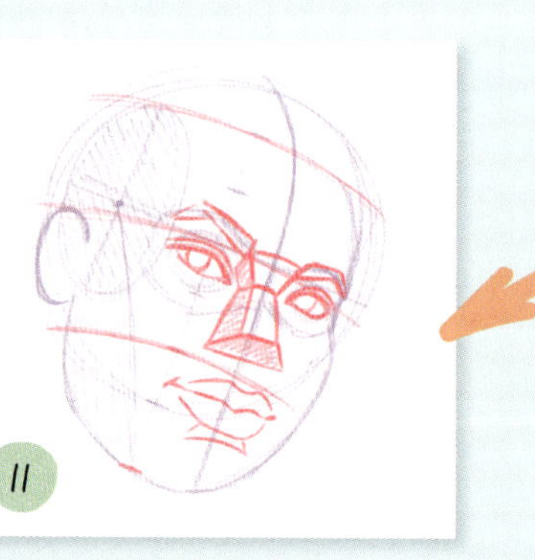

11. Noses are one of the most challenging facial features to draw. Blocking out the nose with simple shapes before adding more natural, curved, and organic lines can help you develop a better understanding of how the feature is built and enable you to make more creative, stylized choices that work.

The center line of the mouth usually lands near to or on the original circle.

To reiterate, the tops of the ears line up with the tops of the eyes, and the bottoms of the ears line up with the bottom of the nose. The inner corners of the eyes line up with the sides of the nostrils. The outer corners of the mouth line up with the centers of the eyes. And the eyes should be about one eye width apart.

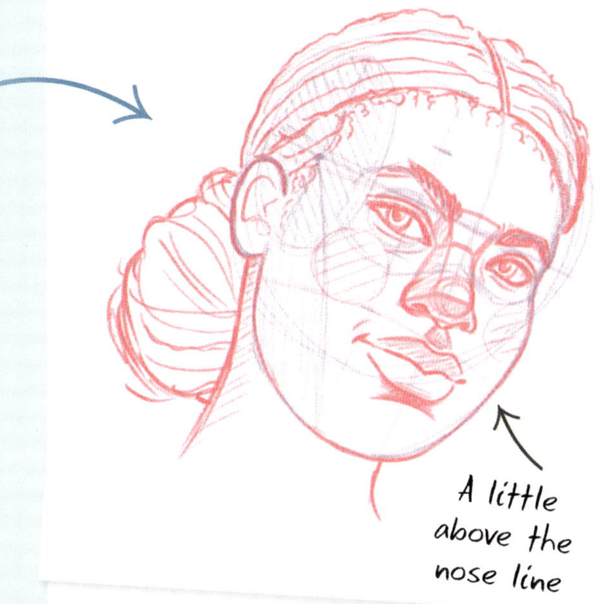

My reference model has a somewhat short nose, so it doesn't line up perfectly with the nose line. She also has a wide nose, so the inner corners of her eyes don't line up with the sides of the nostrils. It's not an exact science! These guidelines can help us make better proportion choices, but don't feel restricted by them.

"But Melissa!" you may be thinking, "You're teaching us how to build a proportionate face again, not a caricature!"

I know. I snuck it in there again! I promise you that this foundational understanding will only benefit you. At the risk of sounding like a broken record, the better you understand construction, the better you'll be able to caricature that construction.

FUN EXERCISE!

Find some reference photos of people's faces (Pexels and Unsplash are great royalty-free websites) and practice breaking down the face into simple shapes. If you want to try exaggerating:

1. *Look for the most interesting shapes and exaggerate them.*
2. *Use complete shapes to help you understand how everything connects, and keep them as simple as possible. You can always erase anything you don't want to keep.*
3. *You're allowed to fake things. Do what's more visually interesting to you.*

HOW TO DRAW EYES

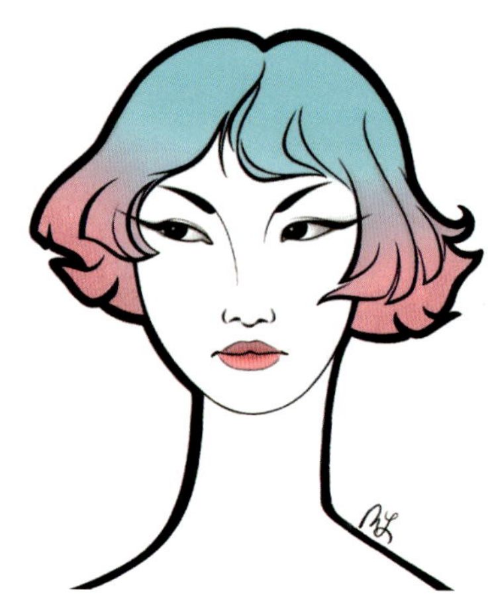

There are a million and one different eye shapes and a million and one different ways to draw them, ranging from extremely simple and abstract to hyperrealistic.

These bunnies and frogs illustrate how small changes in shape, size, and placement of features can alter a drawing, even one drawn in the most simple of styles. You can convey a lot of emotion with very little.

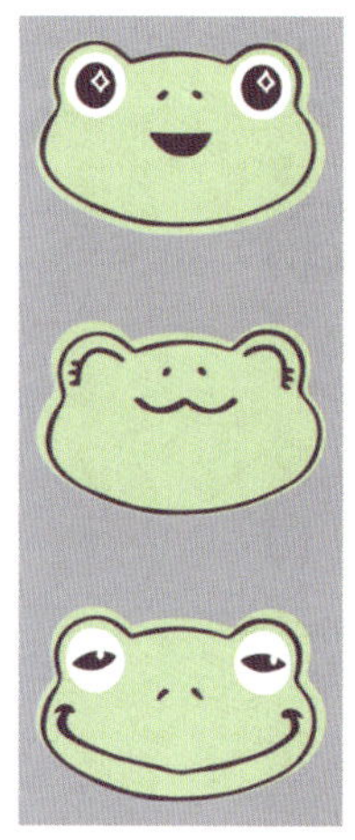

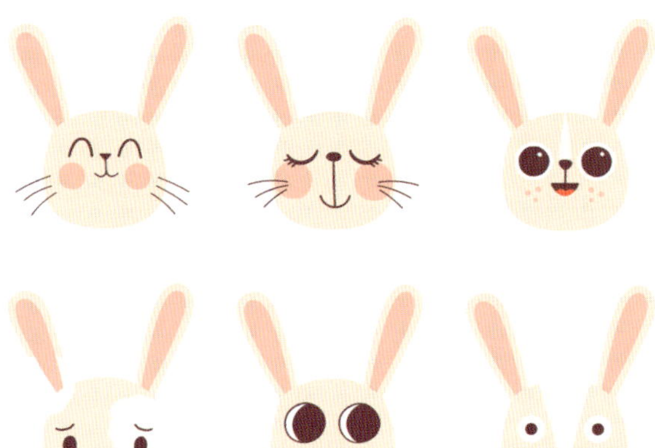

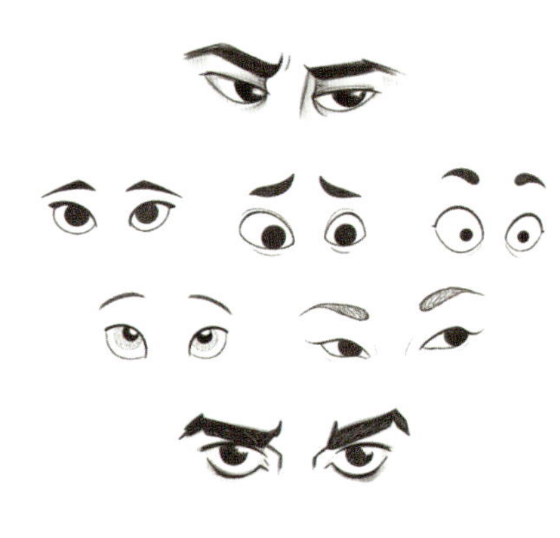

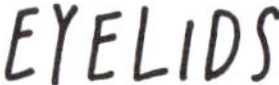

EYELIDS

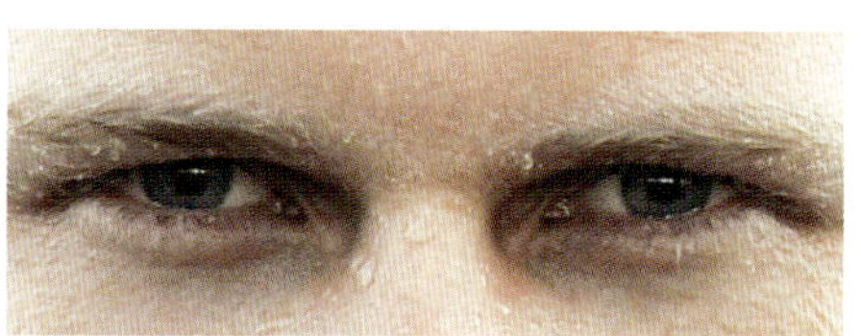

Everyone has varying amounts of visible upper eyelid. Some people have what is called a "monolid," meaning that their eyelids are not visible when their eyes are open, while others may have partially obscured eyelids. The prominence of the brow ridge can also affect the visibility of the eyelids. The lower eyelids tend to be flatter than the upper eyelids. However, many artists, including myself, often overlook this for either stylistic reasons (I love drawing big, expressive eyes!) or to illustrate how the brow ridge can obscure the tops of some people's eyes.

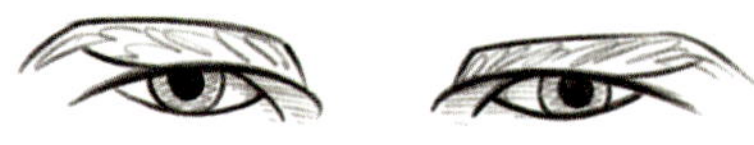

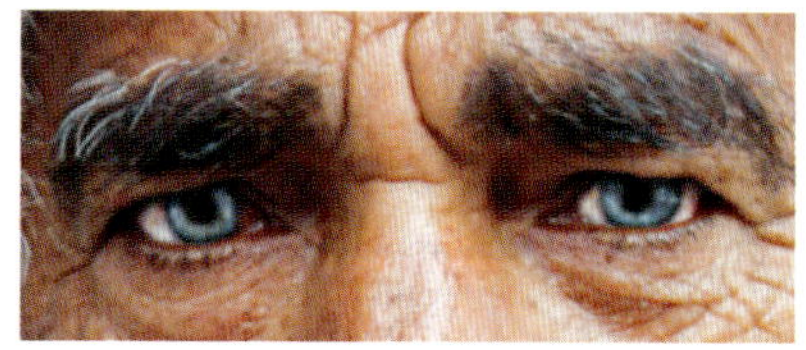

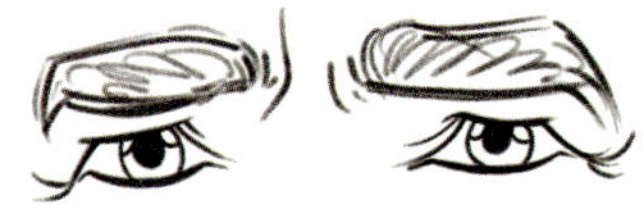

ANGLE OF THE EYE

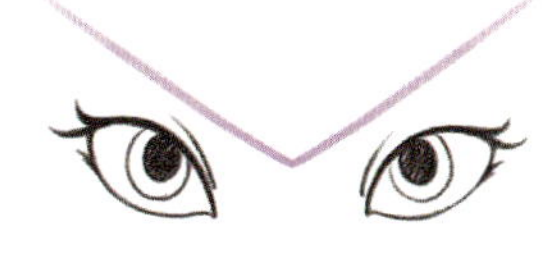
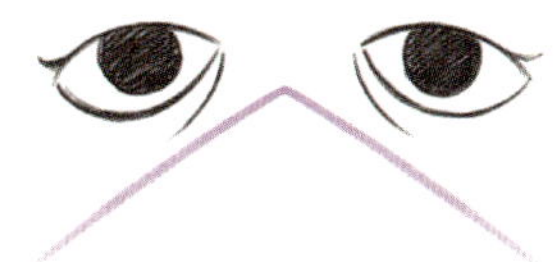

Pay attention to the angle of the eyes. Some outer corners tilt upward while others slant downward. This characteristic affects likeness more than facial expression, whereas the tilt of the eyebrows, on the other hand, can significantly alter expression.

EYELASHES

I love drawing dramatic eyelashes. I usually represent them with a thicker, darker line on the upper lid that tapers into a cat eye of varying lengths. If you want to draw more lashes, a good rule of thumb is to concentrate on adding them to the outer corners of the eyes. You can include lashes in the inner corners as well, but keep them a little more sparse.

Whatever you do, don't draw evenly spaced eyelashes. That's a quick way to make your eyes appear spider-like. Unless, of course, it's an intentional stylistic choice!

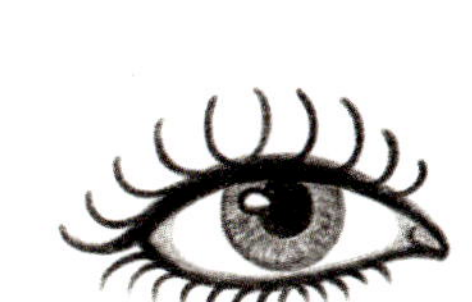
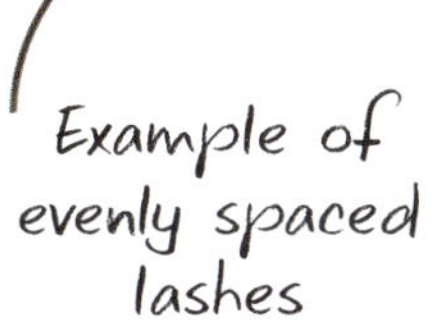

Example of evenly spaced lashes

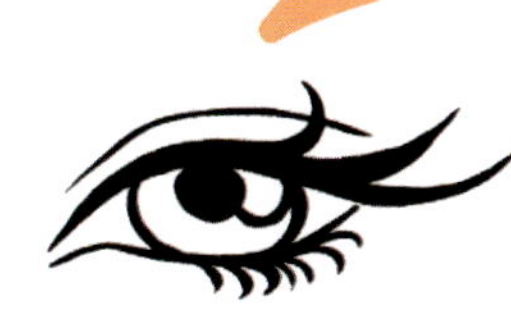

Example of dramatic lashes

EYEBROWS

Eyebrows also come in many shapes and sizes, but a consistent characteristic is that the part of the brow next to the nose is thicker and tapers to a thinner point at the outer end. If you choose to draw the eyebrow hairs, keep in mind that near the center of the face, the hairs tend to grow upward. As you move outward, the hairs become more slanted, and at the top of the arch, they grow almost horizontally.

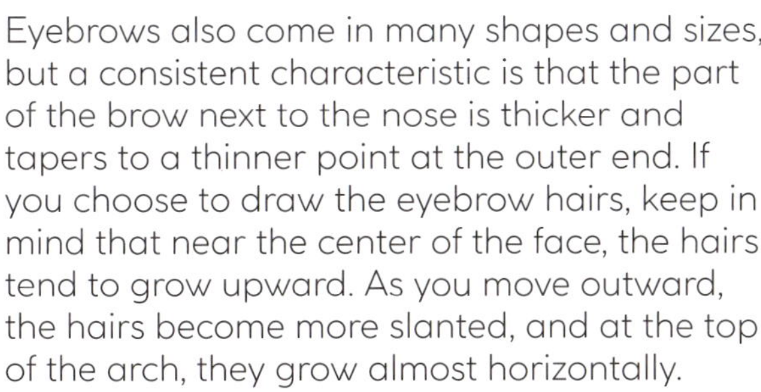
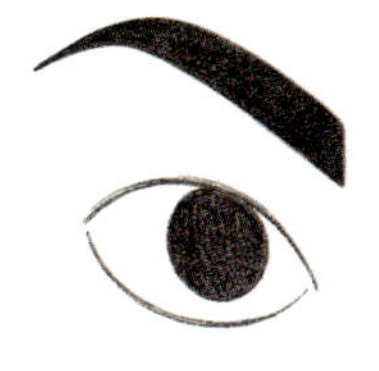
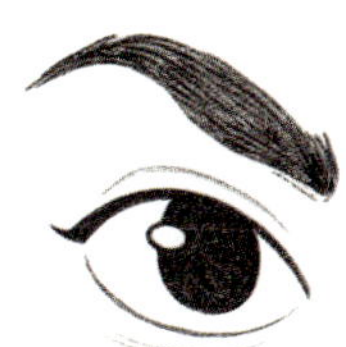
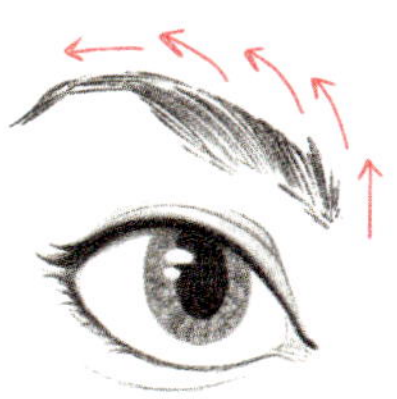

PROFILE

It's important to remember that eyes are spherical (in fact, you can more clearly see how the eyes protrude from the face), so for an eye in profile, you still want to start by drawing a light circle. Then draw a triangular wedge in the circle (think Pac-Man) and add the lids along the circle's edge. Rather than drawing the eyelashes in the inner corner, in profile, you want to draw them sweeping out and upward from the outer upper lid.

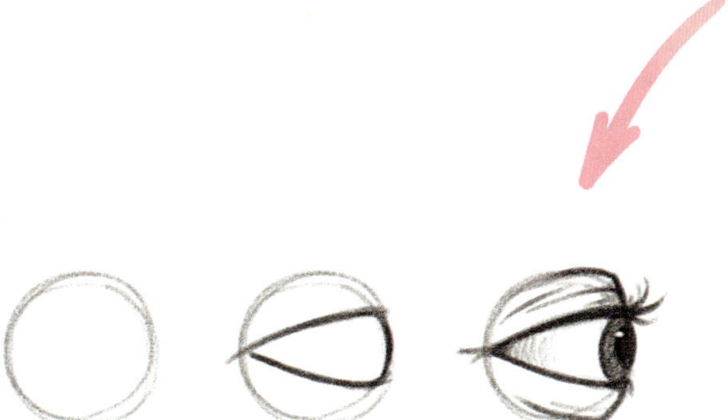

HOW TO DRAW MOUTHS

When drawing a mouth, the center line is the most important thing to pay attention to, and is often the first thing you will draw out.

You don't have to draw the upper or bottom lips, but you'll almost always need to draw the center line. This line can be pointed down in the center or not at all. It depends on both the complexity of style and the shape of the lips that you're drawing.

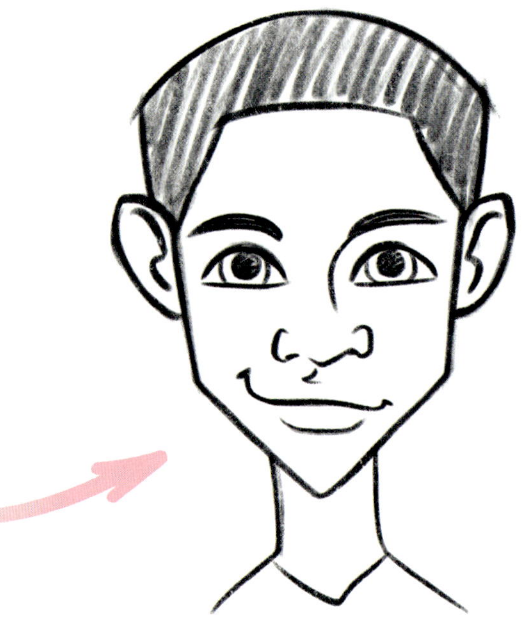

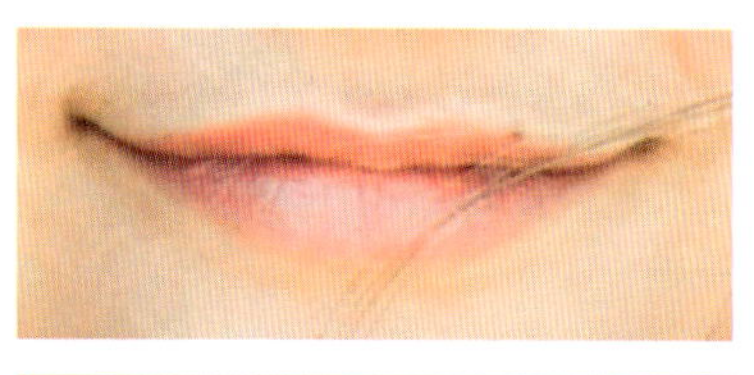

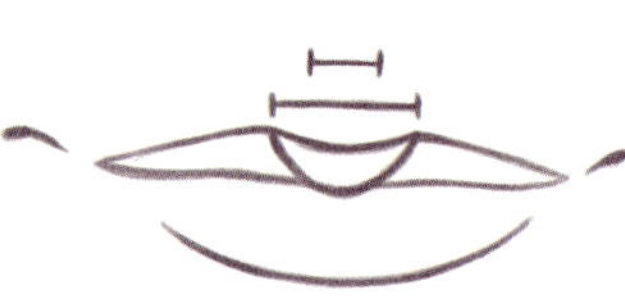

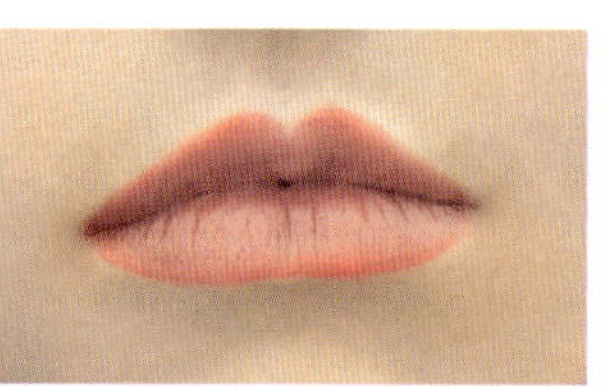

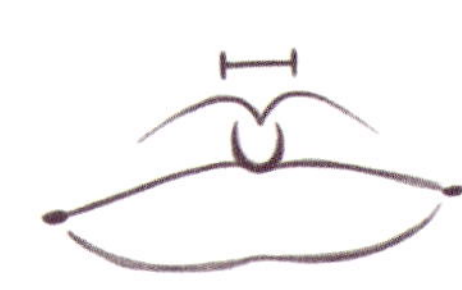

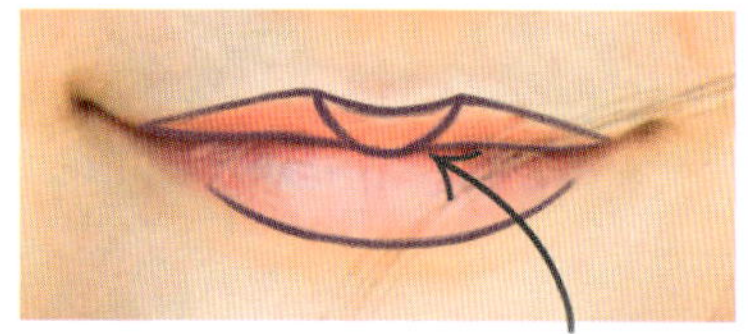

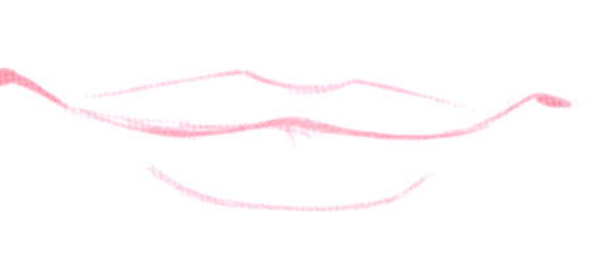

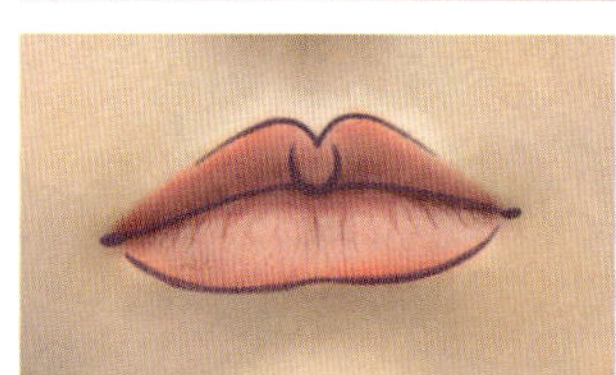

Shallow crescent shape

THE LIPS

The upper lip is made up of three shapes: a heart, shallow crescent, or bean shape in the middle and two rounded triangles at the sides. The bottom lip can be represented as two rounded triangles. The length and width of the philtrum (the divot between nose and upper lip) varies significantly and greatly influences the overall shape of the upper lip. Some philtrums have a pronounced dip, while others are flatter. This also applies to the center bottom of the upper lip. Some bottom lips also curve down a bit in the center (another thing that can affect the shape of the center line), and some don't. Just like every other facial feature, no two mouths are the same.

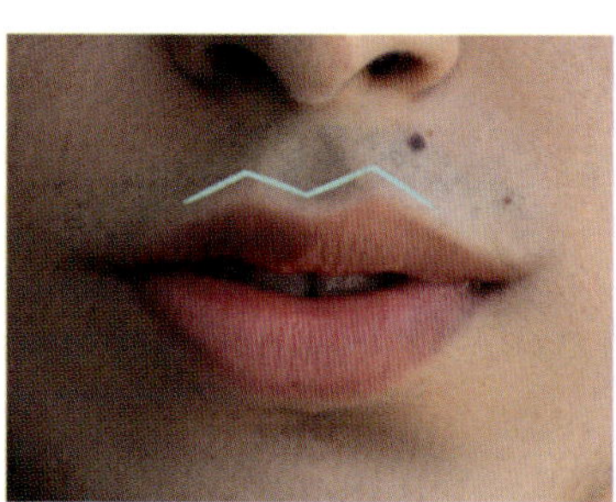

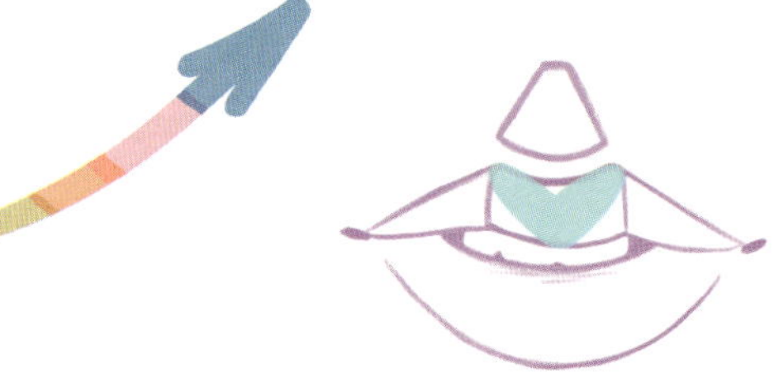

Once the center line is drawn (1), I look at the shape of the philtrum and draw accordingly. From there, I draw a curved line downward toward each corner (2). Finally, I draw the bottom lip (3). I rarely connect the top and bottom lines of the lips to the corners of the mouth. That's a mistake that I see a lot. Typically, lips looks better without those connecting lines. You can indicate where the lip ends with color, but it's not necessary to connect it with lines.

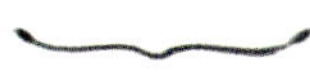

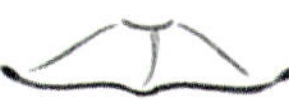

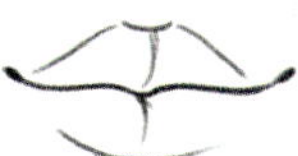

You approach the mouth a little differently when someone is smiling with their teeth. The shape of the lips is pulled and stretched, resulting in triangles and teardrop shapes that are typically longer and less rounded.

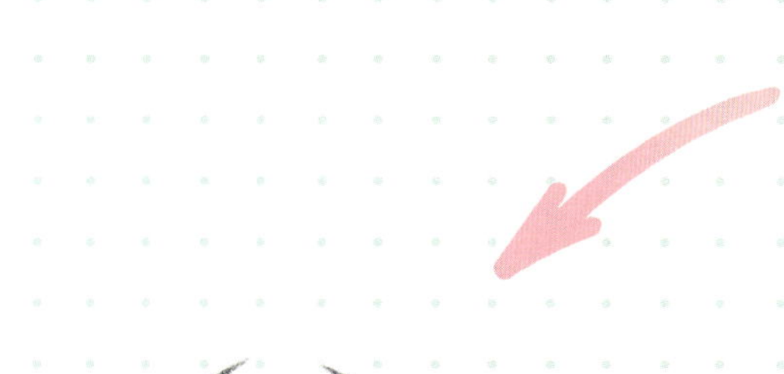

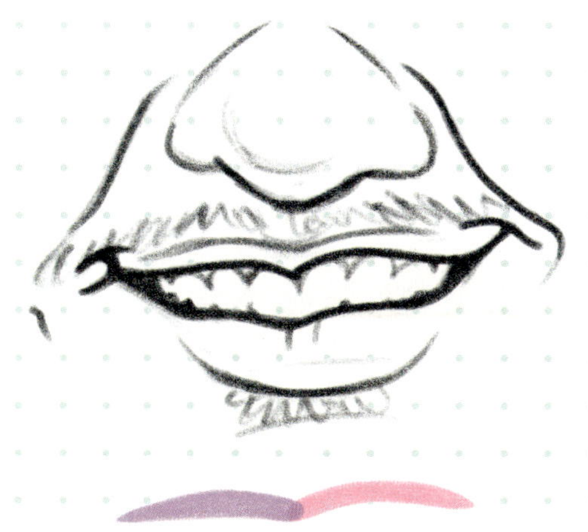

ARTIST INSIGHT

I like to think of the corners of the mouth as anchor points or nodes that you can manipulate to control expression. They pull the lips up into a smile, down into a frown, or sideways into a smirk. Even the slightest movement of these nodes can affect facial expression.

TEETH

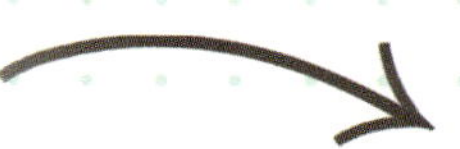

When it comes to drawing teeth, keep it simple. Draw a simplified outline of the teeth; something that suggests the overall shape. Don't make the mistake of drawing the vertical lines that separate each tooth, it's usually not a great look. You can indicate the gum line and the outer edge of the teeth without drawing in the lines separating them. For mouths that are barely open, you can simply fill in the corners.

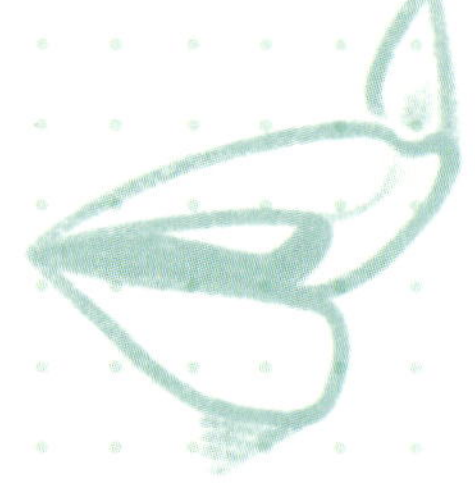

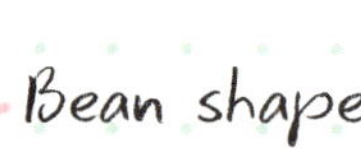

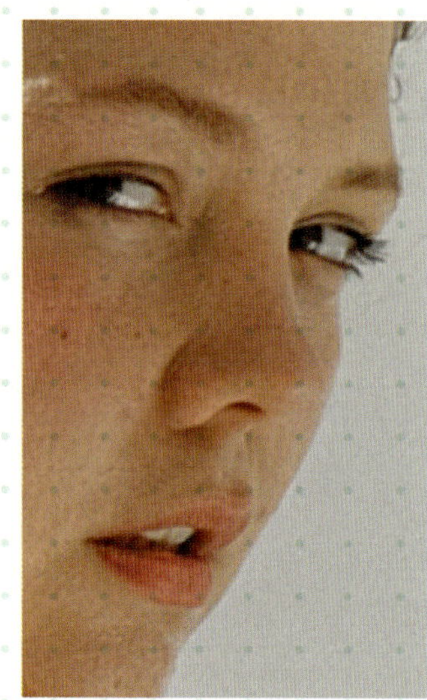

Bean shape

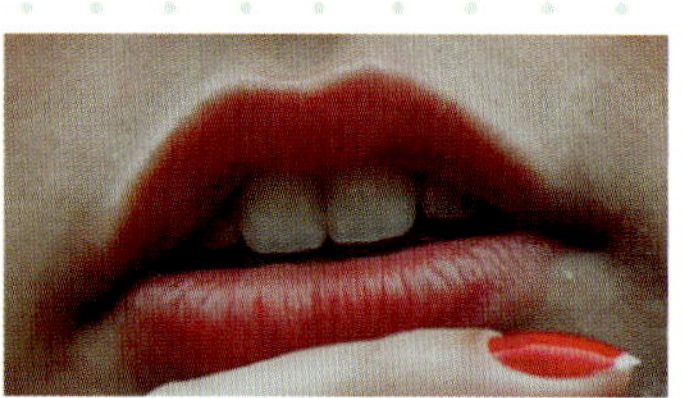

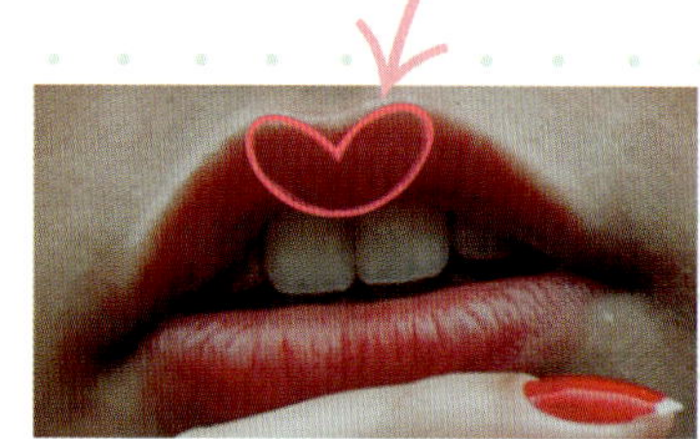

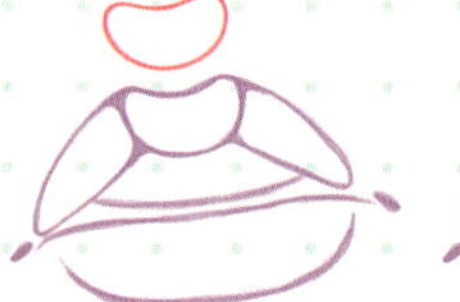

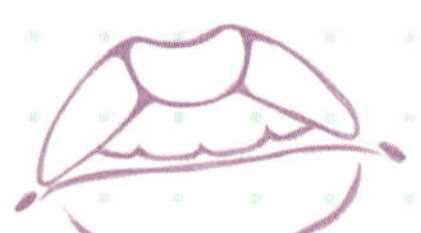

HOW TO DRAW EARS

While ears look quite complicated, they're actually one of the easier features to draw stylized.

For the inside, simply draw an S-shape with a sharp corner and then mirror it on the other side.

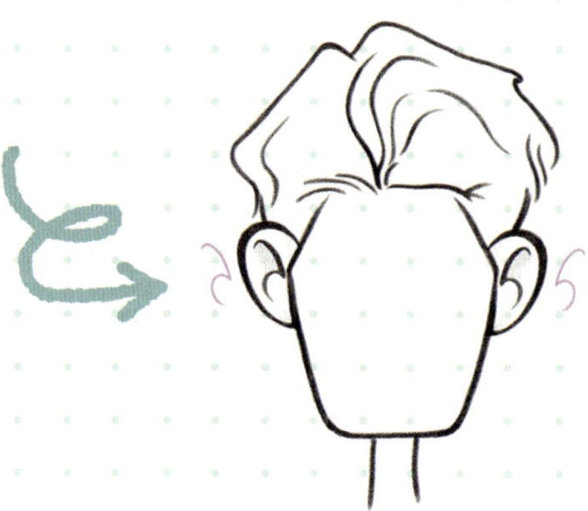

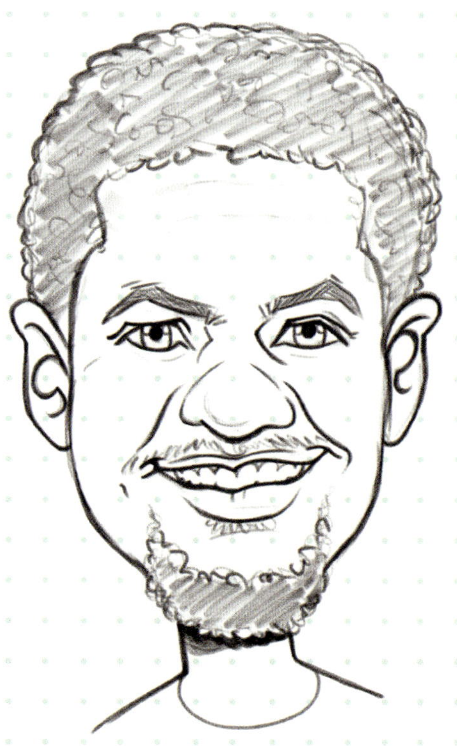

HOW TO DRAW PROFILES

When a face is turned to the side, the side of the upper lip closest to you is about the same length of rounded triangle as before, but the side that is facing away is shorter. How short depends on how far the face is turned.

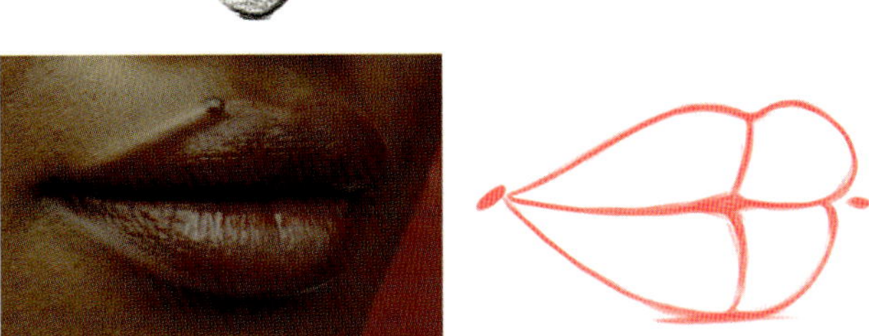

In this profile view, you can see a small portion of the far side of my reference model's lips. The upper lip creates a warped and squished heart shape, or a small vertical teardrop shape stacked next to a larger horizontal teardrop. Think rounded triangles, hearts, beans, and teardrops!

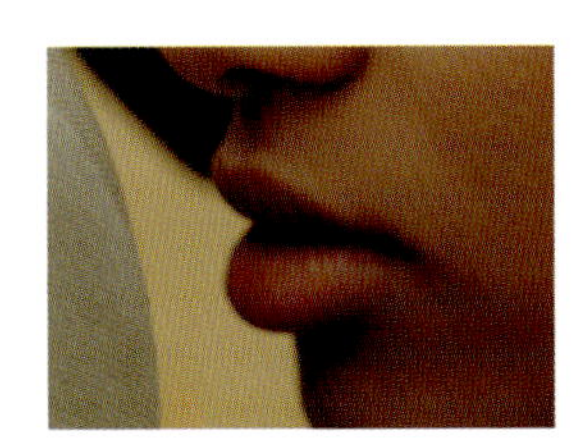

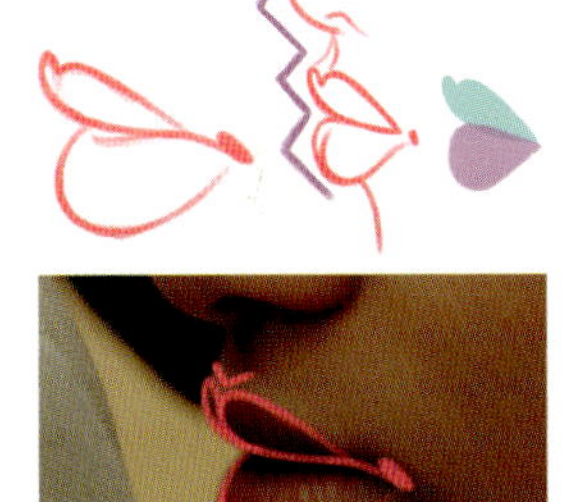

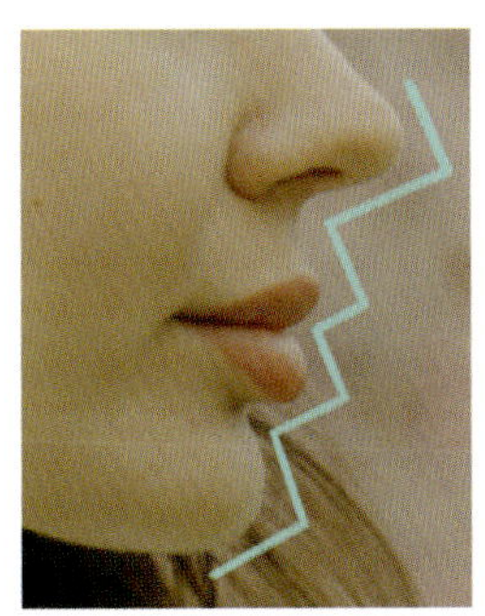

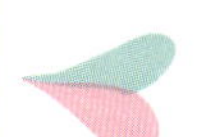

One common mistake I see people make when drawing a profile is drawing the lips extending farther out than the nose, when, in fact, they should be positioned further back. Think of it like a staircase that starts at the nose and descends to the chin. It can be helpful to draw a diagonal line from the nose as a visual reminder not to draw the lips past it.

These heavily stylized mouths barely follow the actual shape of the reference model's lips, but the choices I made here were still informed by my understanding of how mouths are structured.

See that little dip in the center of the drawing on the right? I knew to include that because I understand the shapes that form the lips. In both of these drawings, I cheated the perspective a bit as well. These could work for a face in a three-quarter turn, but I like how they give the impression of a pouty smirk.

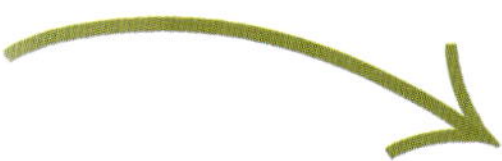

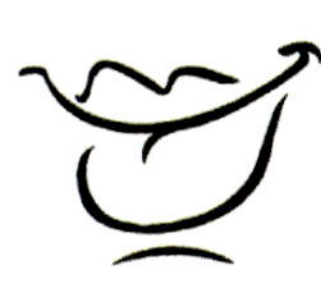

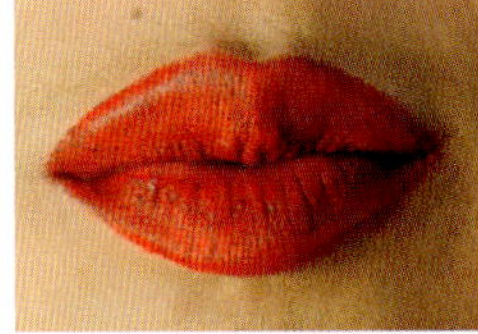

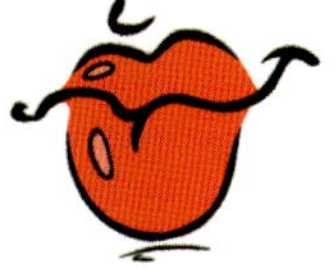

HOW TO DRAW NOSES

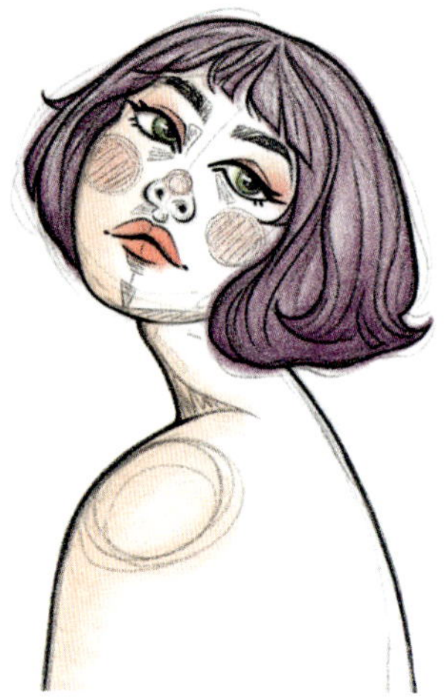

There are a thousand different ways to draw a nose, especially in caricature and cartooning. You can choose to draw all of the nose or just the nostrils, represent it as a simple triangle or oval, or draw every plane, bump, and ridge.

Some artists choose to be consistent with how they draw each individual feature, particularly when it comes to eyes and noses. Personally, I like to shake it up a bit depending on the specific nose size and shape of either, whoever I'm caricaturing or the type of character I'm designing.

Building a nose with rectangular planes can help you understand its three-dimensional shape. Once you establish those planes, it's easier to draw the organic, curved lines of the tip and the wings (nostrils) of the nose.

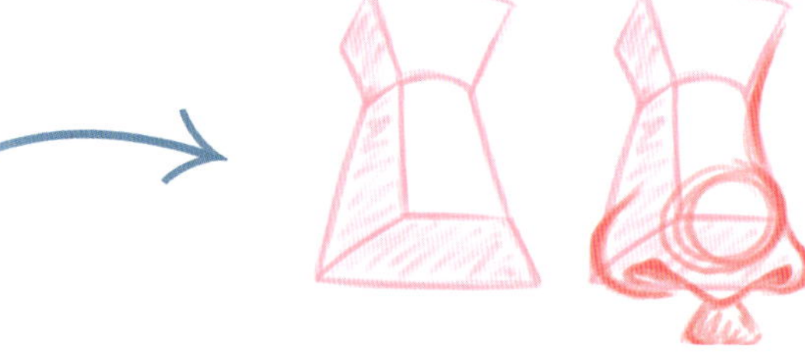

I have so much practice drawing them that I no longer need to rely on this method. I've developed a muscle memory for drawing them. Now, I typically begin by sketching a light circle, oval, or rounded triangle to represent the tip and nostrils, and then once I've established where all of the facial features will sit, I render the organic shape of the nose.

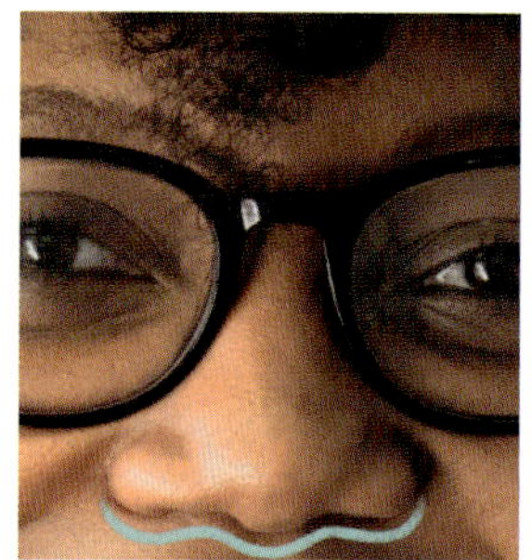

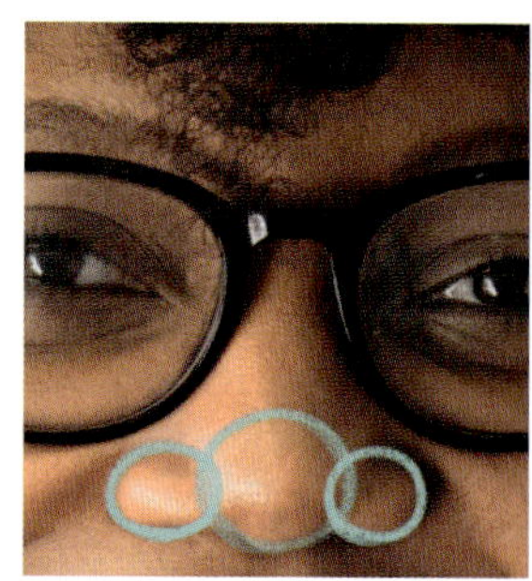

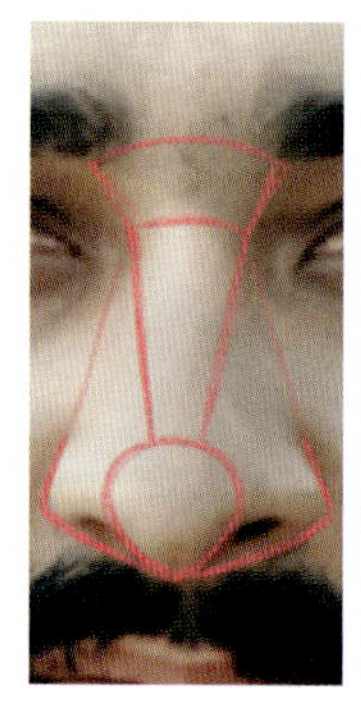

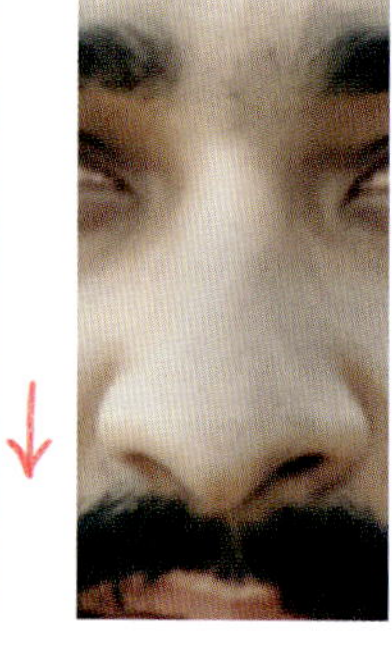

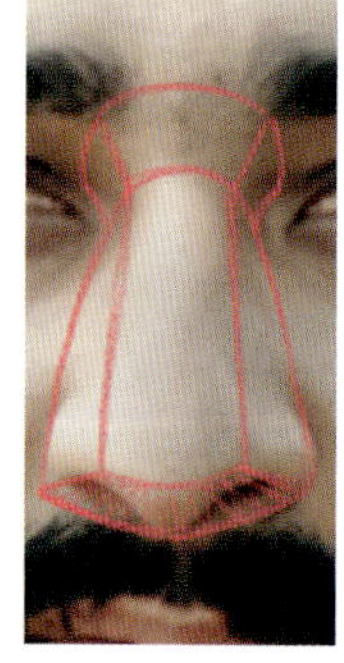

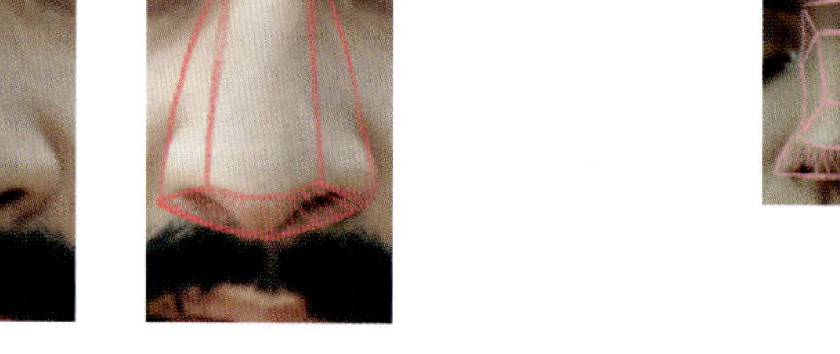

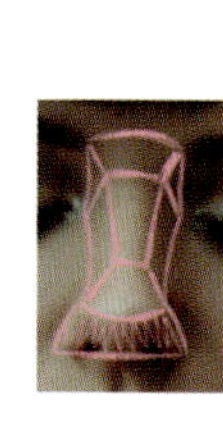

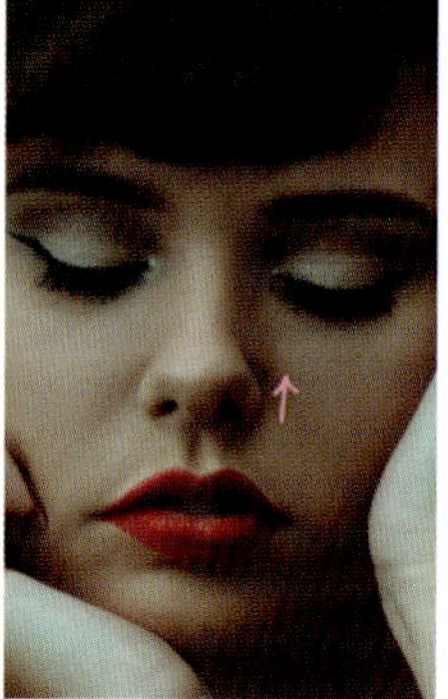

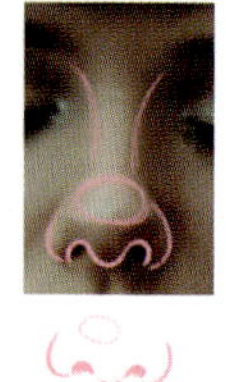

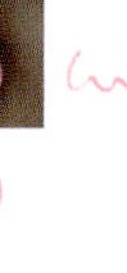

For a more stylized caricature, I follow the shape of the underside of the nose and, if visible, indicate the inside of the nostrils with indentation points of varying sizes. The higher the indentation points, the more visible the nostrils are.

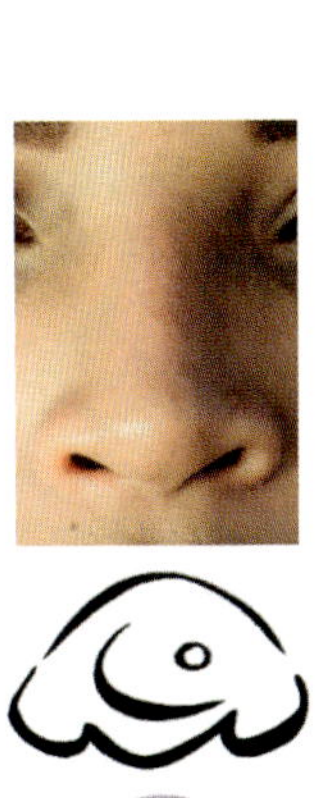

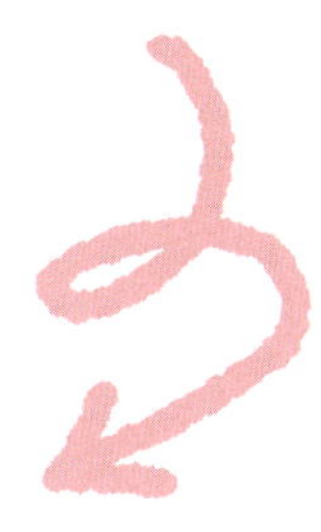

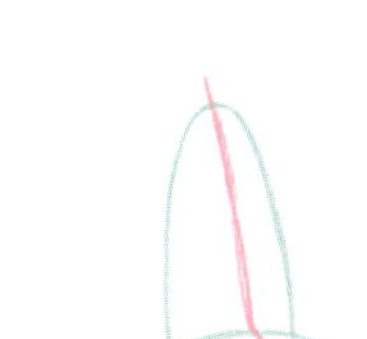

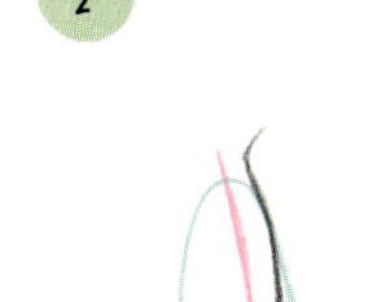

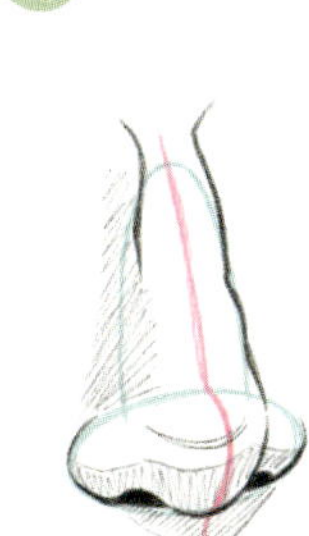

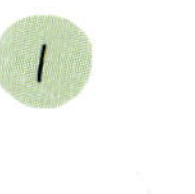

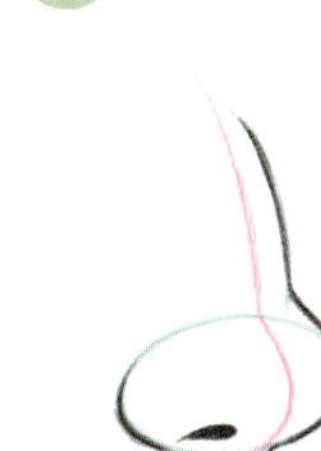

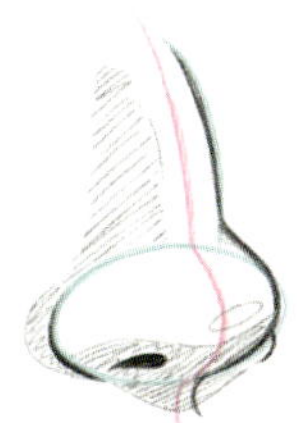

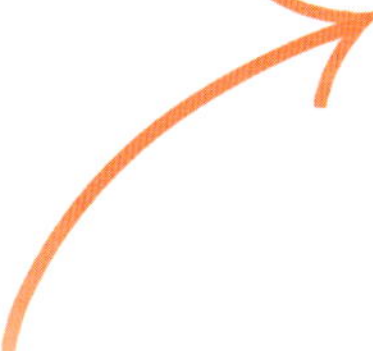

THREE-QUARTER VIEW

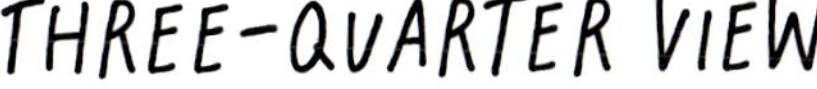

The same methods work for noses in a three-quarter turn. Just be sure to pay attention to perspective or, in other words, how much of the far side of the nose is visible. Sometimes the far nostril is hidden by the tip and bridge of the nose, and sometimes a small portion of the wing is visible.

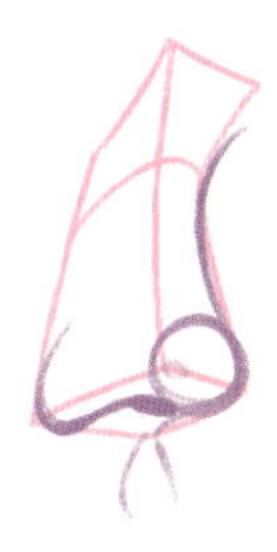

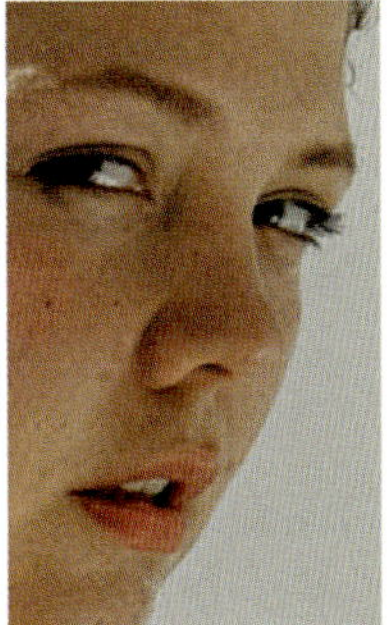

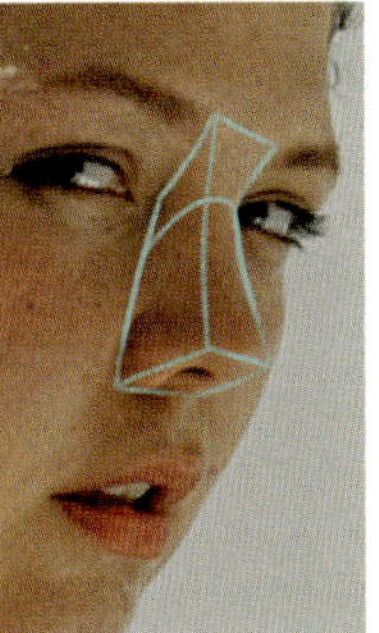

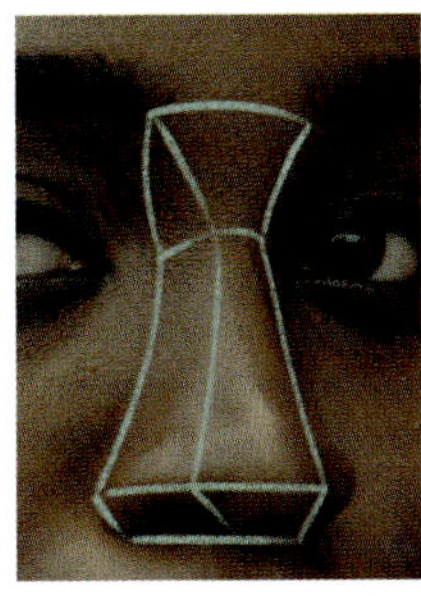

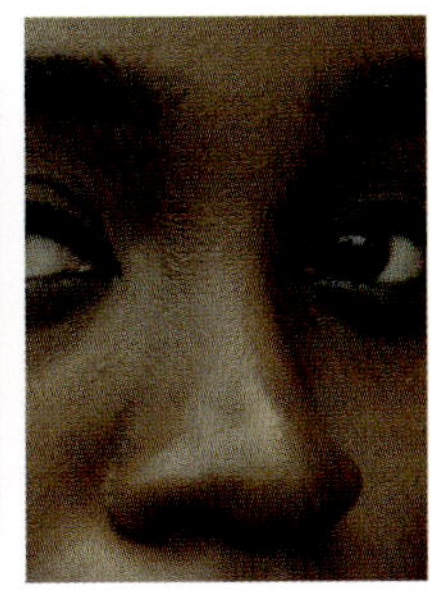

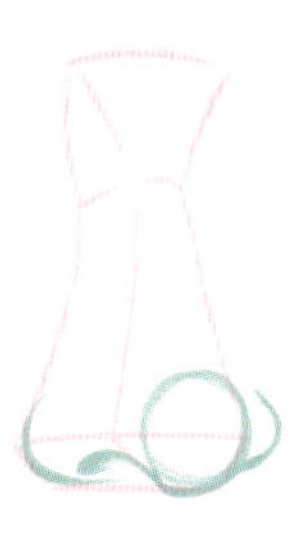

HOW TO DRAW HAIR

Hair sits on top of the skull so you need to account for that when drawing it, as well as taking into account the style, length, and texture of the hair.

In this example, the subject's hair sits relatively flush to her head, but I still drew it slightly offset from the circle I drew for the skull.

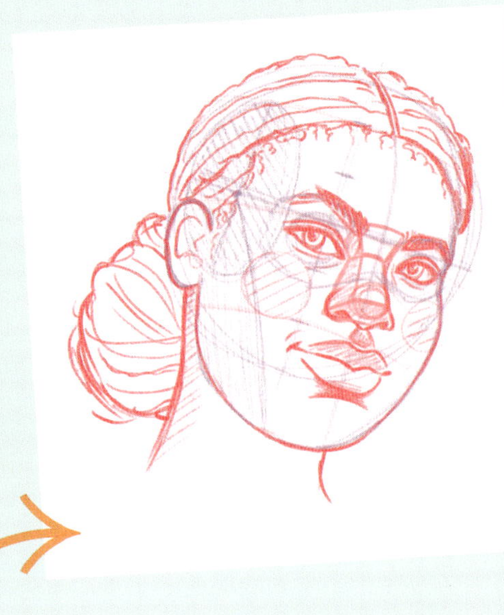

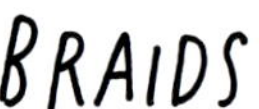

BRAIDS

I drew the model's braids as simple bumpy lines, but if you wanted to add more detail, there are a few ways to go about drawing them. First, with teardrop shapes butted up against each other like hearts. Second, by stacking long scallop shapes. And lastly, if you're going for a sharper style, you can draw two parallel lines and fill the space between them with a series of Y shapes. You could also add rounded edges for a more naturalistic, fishtail-braided look.

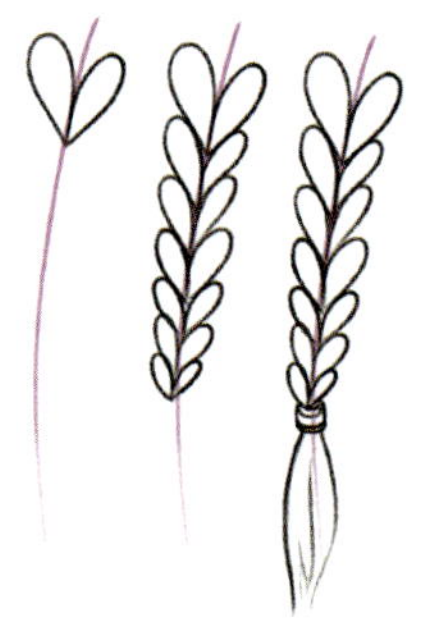

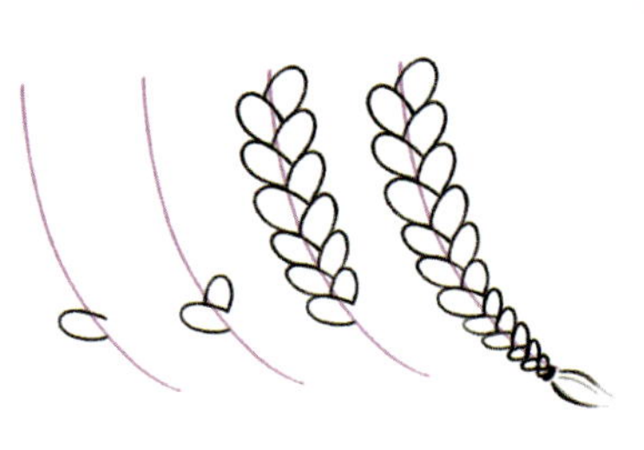

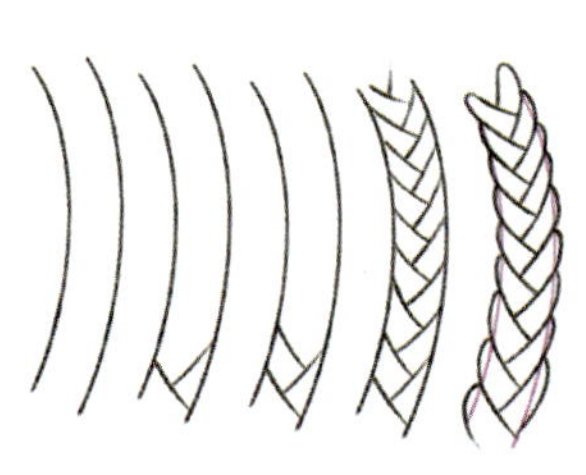

ARTIST INSIGHT

I love adding a few flyaway strands of hair coming off the main shapes. They're fun to draw and contribute a lot to the illusion of hair.

DIVIDE HAIR INTO SECTIONS

It can be helpful to think of hair in sections. Look at it as if it is made of big, solid shapes, rather than thousands of individual strands. Once you've established the sections and blocked out the overall shape, then add lines here and there to represent individual strands.

It can be tempting to add too many detail lines to hair but this doesn't always work well. The level of detail you include should depend, in part, on the level of detail in your drawing of the face. If your drawing is simple and stylized, then the hair should also be simple and stylized.

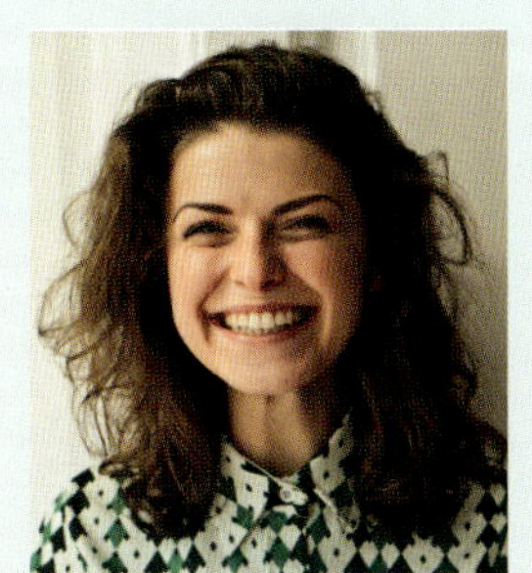
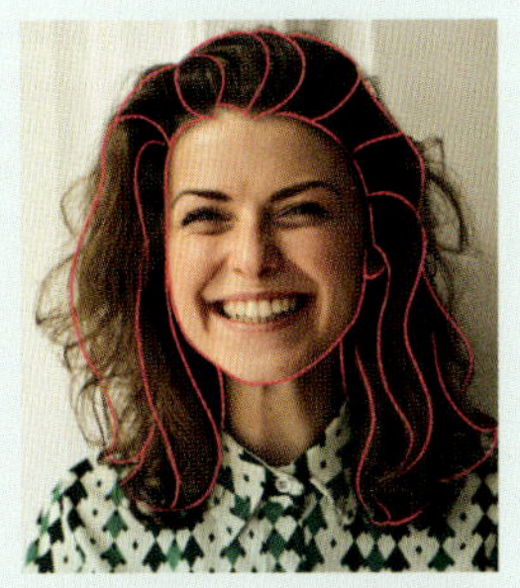
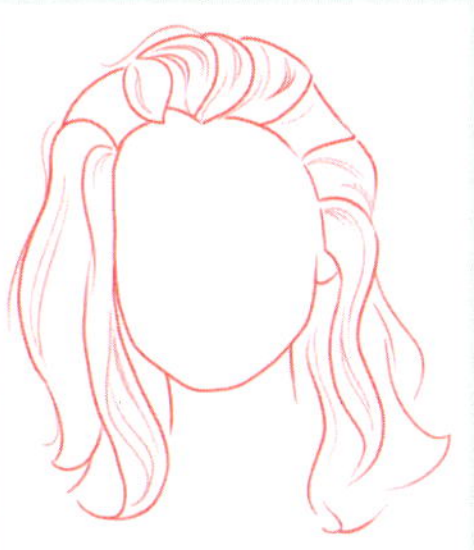
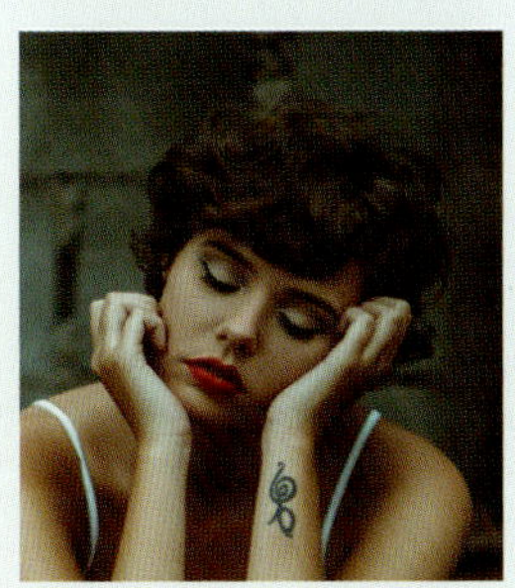
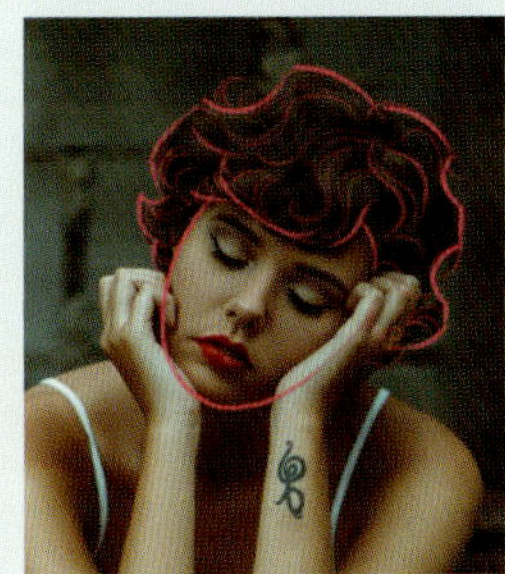
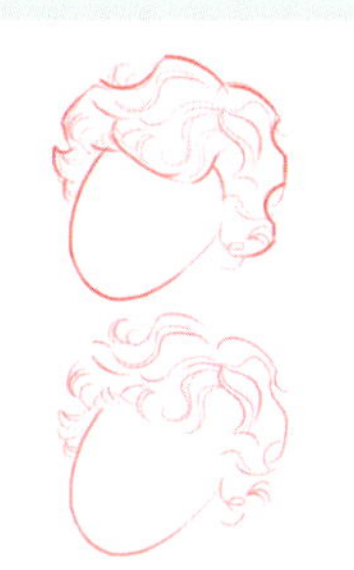

CURLS

In cartooning, putting straight and curved lines next to each other adds visual appeal. Rather than using all curves to represent curly hair, you can do something more like this.

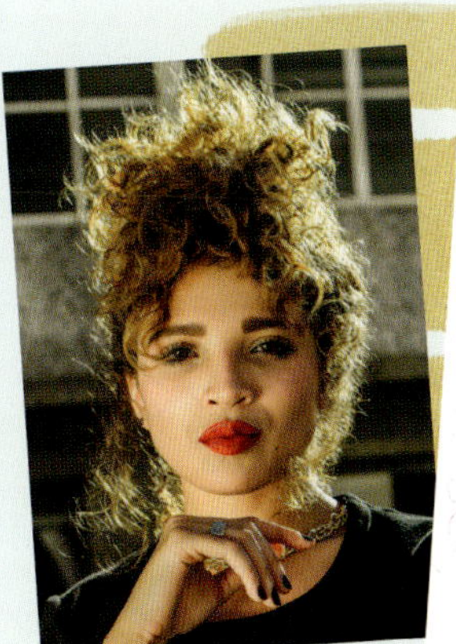
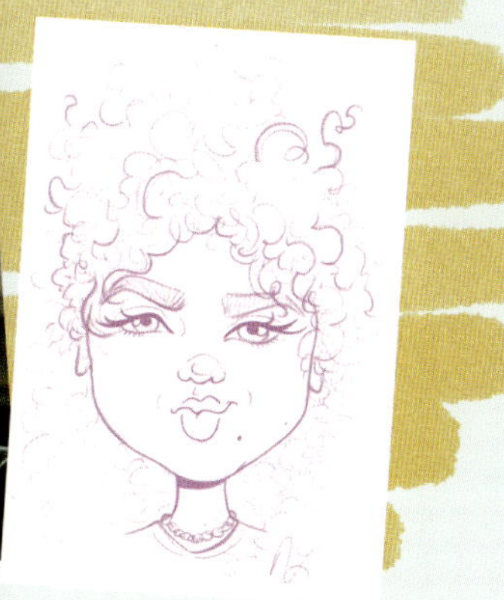

Spirals aren't a bad idea, especially for representing tight curls, but they're not the only option. This alternating pattern of straight and curved lines represents this particular reference model's floofy hair very effectively.

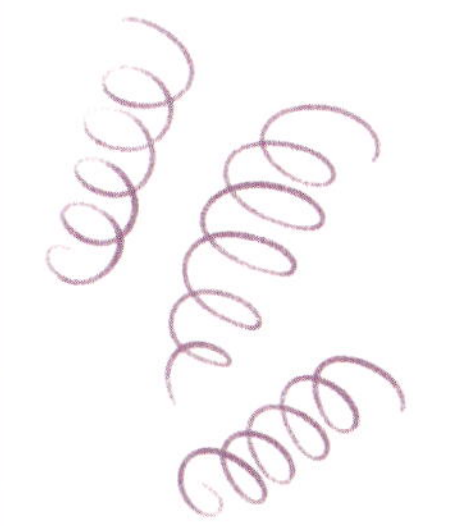
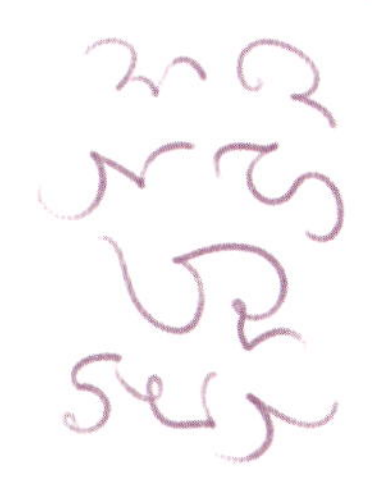

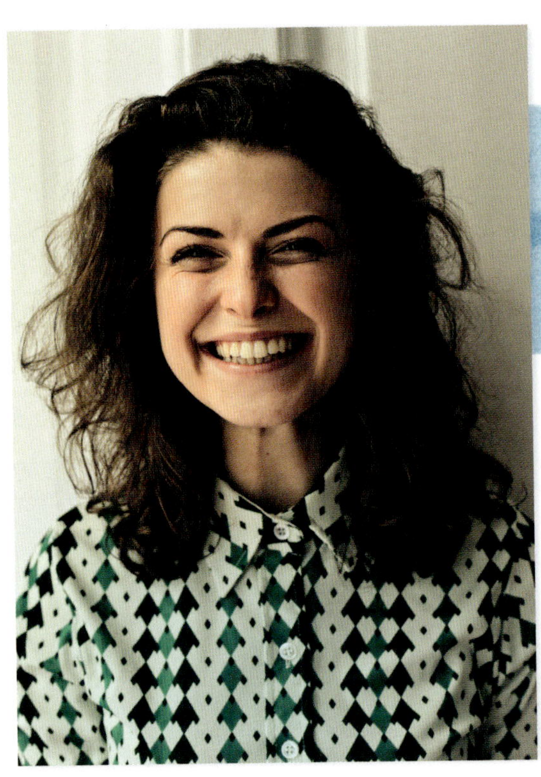

CARICATURE: STEP-BY-STEP #1

Shake out your hands and shoulders, loosen up. You can do this!

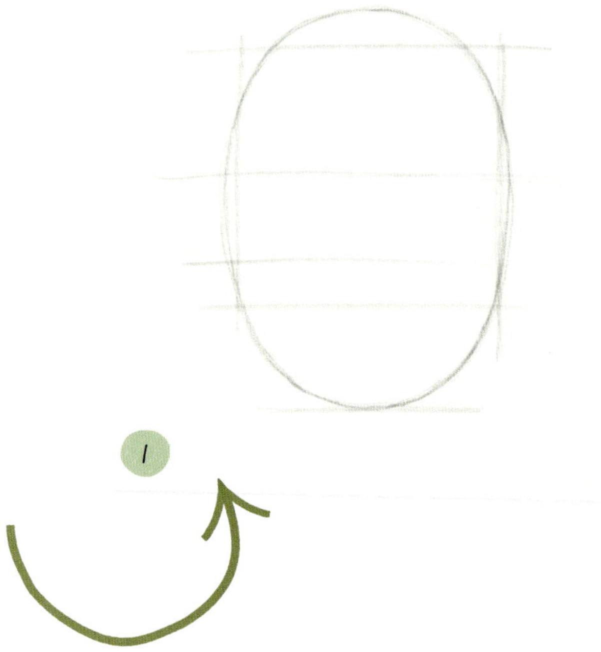

1. Before you put pencil to paper, take a look at the photo you're using for reference and observe the overall face shape of your subject. Once you identify that shape, draw a very light circle, oval, square, or rectangle—whatever shape you think works best for their face. I think a long oval works best for my subject. Next, draw the eye line, nose line, and mouth line about where they appear in reality.

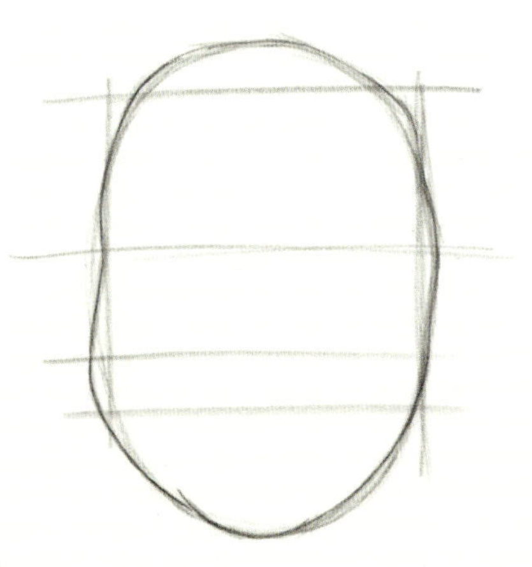

2. Following this, you can draw a more detailed outline of the face; however, in this instance, I have decided to keep the shape simple for now, since my subject's face is a nearly perfect oval. I will look at pushing the exaggeration of the face shape later.

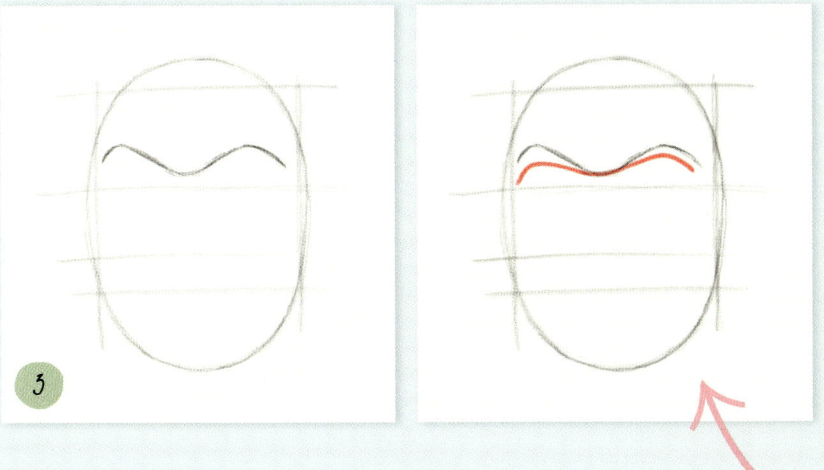

3. When it comes to the facial features, I like to start with the eyebrow line. I've exaggerated the tilt of the eyebrows to give the expression more character. The red line is a tracing of the subject's actual eyebrow line to give a sense of just how much I'm exaggerating it. I love how happy my subject looks, so I'm using the eyebrows to help convey that expression.

4. Next, draw simple shapes for the eyes, nose, and mouth. I drew two light lines to indicate where the corners of the eyes start before actually drawing the almond shapes for the eyes. The person I'm caricaturing has a somewhat short nose, so the spacing from the eyebrows to the bottom of the nose is a bit shorter than the spacing from the bottom of the nose to the bottom of the chin.

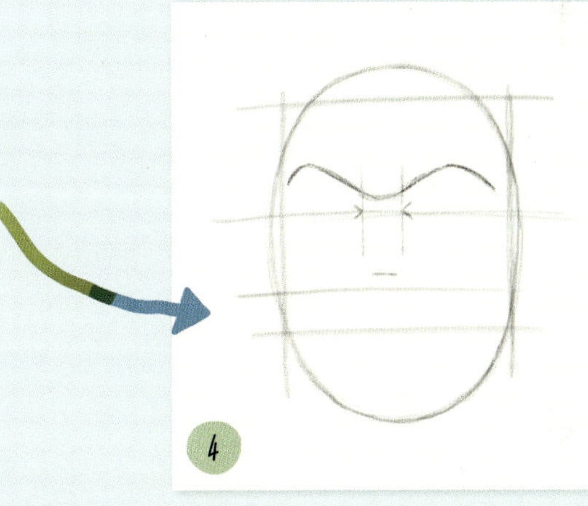

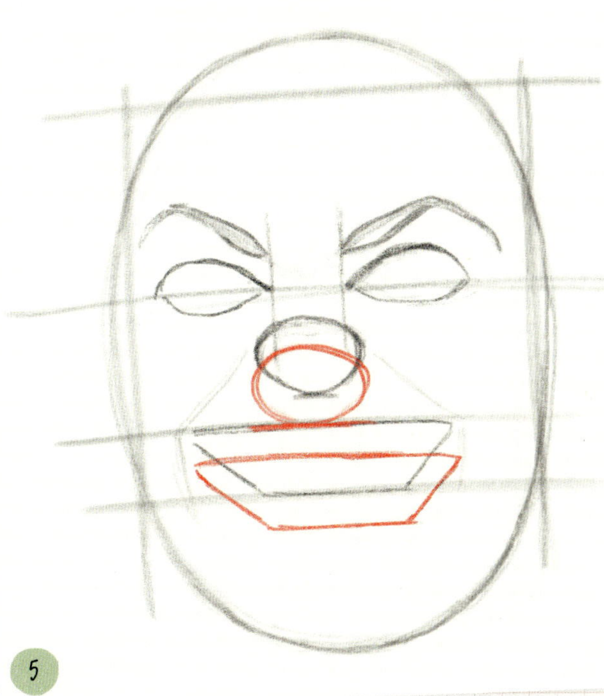

5. With that in mind, the rounded triangle for the subject's nose is drawn a little higher to exaggerate how short it is. I also placed the trapezoid for the mouth a little higher. The subject's philtrum is small, so my instinct was that exaggerating it wouldn't serve her likeness very well. The red shapes indicate where her features are in reality.

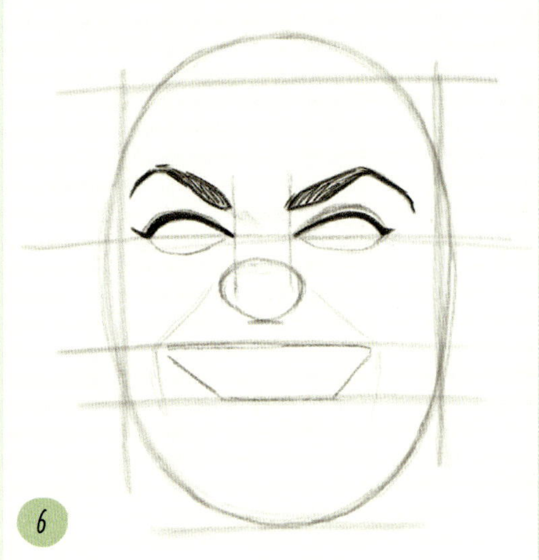

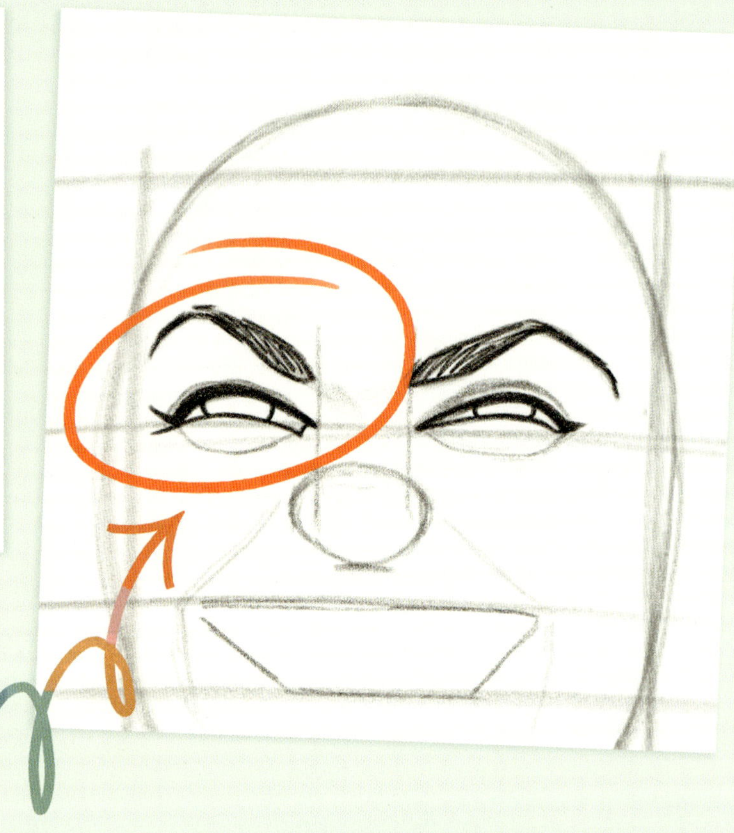

6. I like to work my way down the face, so I start with the eyebrows. I love the curvature of the eyes and how squinted the subject's smile makes them, so I've drawn the top and bottom lines of her eyes very close together. Don't worry about both eyebrows or eyes being perfectly symmetrical. Our faces are naturally asymmetrical and I think that makes us look more interesting. Lean into that asymmetry.

7. Next, I added the irises, pupils, and eyelashes. I love to dramatize eyelashes, so I've thickened and darkened them for emphasis. Don't forget to add highlights to the pupils! Those tiny details make a big difference.

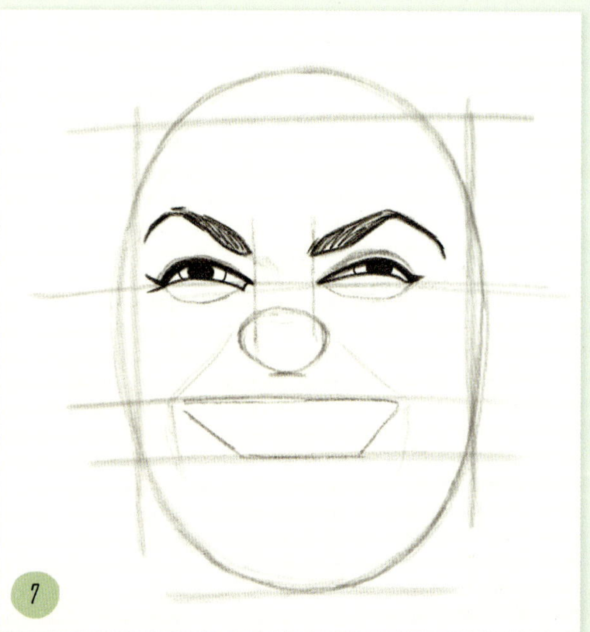

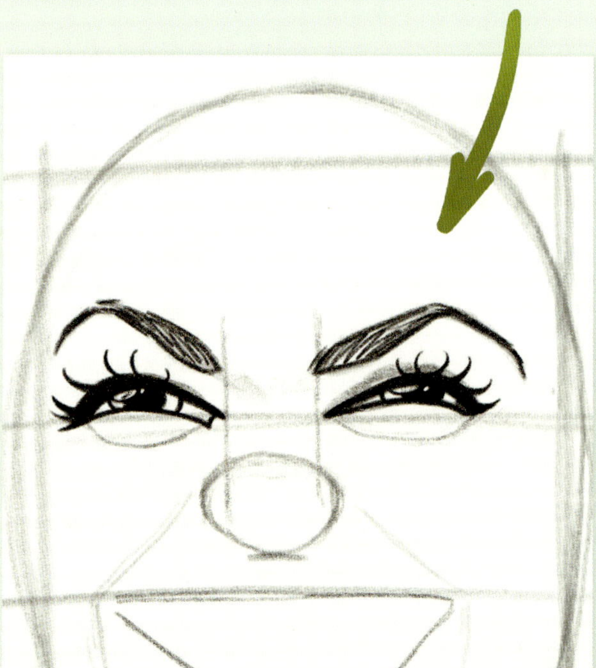

8. The nostrils are not very flared, so I've drawn just the lightest indication of them, following the underside shape of the nose. Pay attention to how the shape of features changes depending on the expression. This person's cheeks are pulling up the corners of her nose, making the nostrils slant up more than they would if she wasn't smiling!

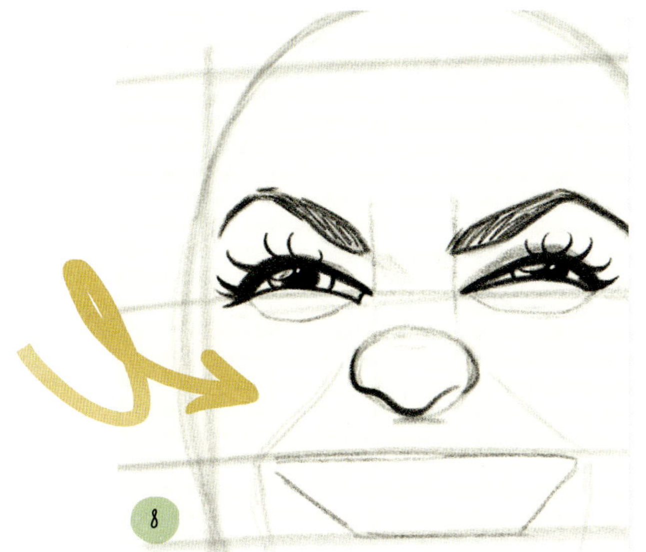

9. My subject has a wide smile, so I've pushed the exaggeration and made her mouth even wider. The red vertical lines from the middle of the eyes represent the width of a typical proportionate face.

Remember, you approach the mouth a little differently when someone is smiling with their teeth versus when their mouth is closed. For open mouths, start with the bottom of the upper lip. The subject's lips curve down in the center just the slightest bit, so for this caricature, I've curved them down much farther.

10. Next, I followed the top of her bottom lip and connected each corner with slanted vertical lines to indicate the teeth.

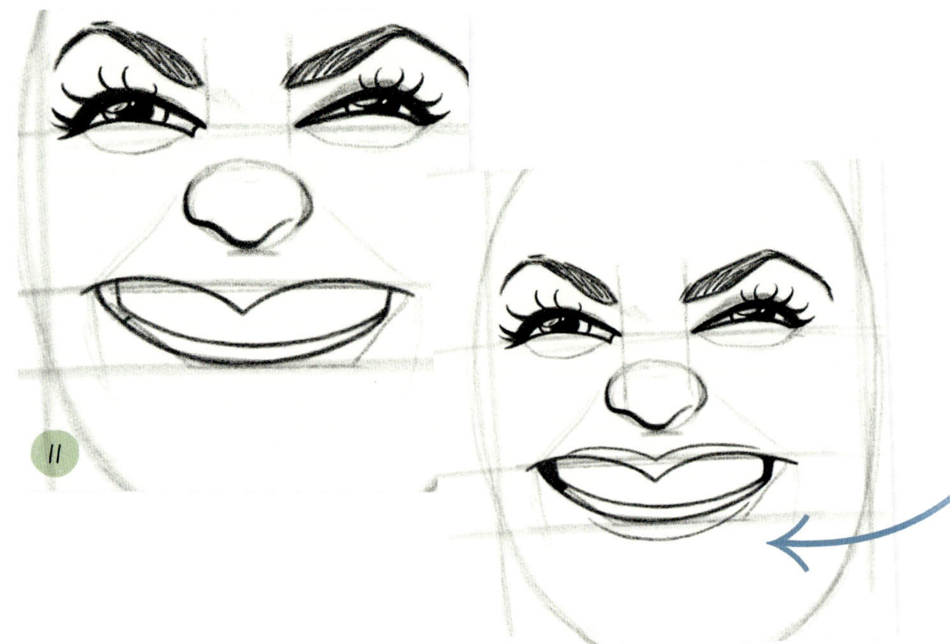

11. To outline the teeth, I've drawn two inwardly slanted lines in the corners of her mouth and a simple curved line, following the same shape as the top of her bottom lip, connecting them.

ARTIST INSIGHT

Instead of erasing your under drawings as you go, you also have the option of using a separate piece of paper and a light board. Simply place the new sheet on top of your under drawing and trace it, exaggerating where it's needed!

12. From there, you can have some fun exaggerating the gum line and the bottom of the teeth. Remember, do not draw in the vertical lines separating each tooth. I didn't fully connect the upper and lower lip lines to the rest of the mouth.

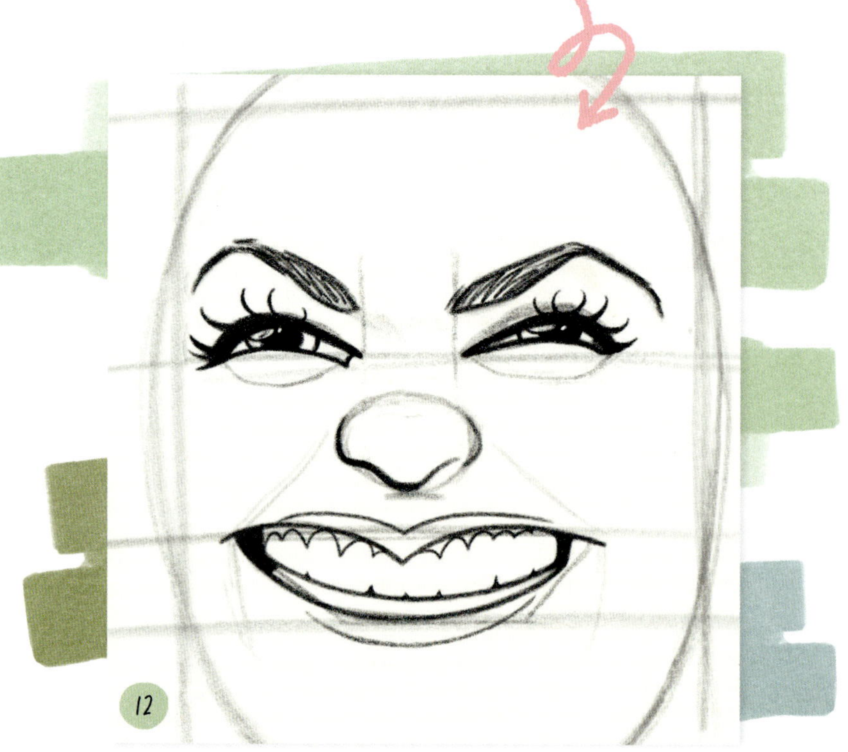

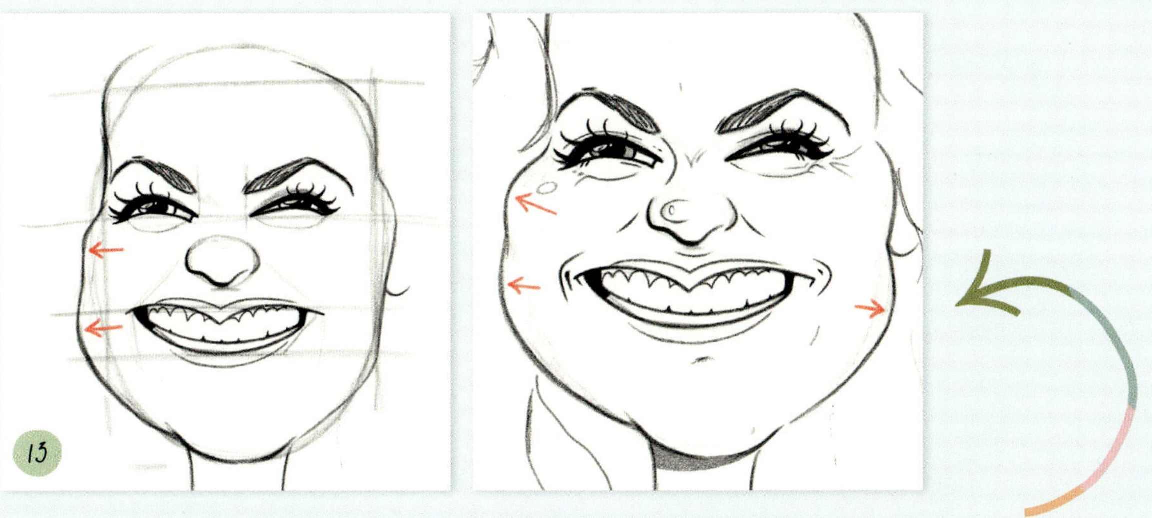

13. I struggled somewhat with how to exaggerate my subject's face shape in a way that made sense. Nothing about her face stands out as a particularly large deviation from the norm. However, her big smile pushes her cheeks out further and big, exaggerated cheeks tend to work well for this style of caricature so that's the direction I took. My first try didn't satisfy me so I erased it and tried again, pushing the exaggeration even further. It's OK to try again and keep pushing the exaggeration!

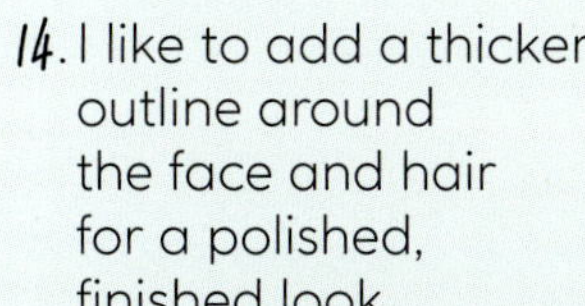

14. I like to add a thicker outline around the face and hair for a polished, finished look.

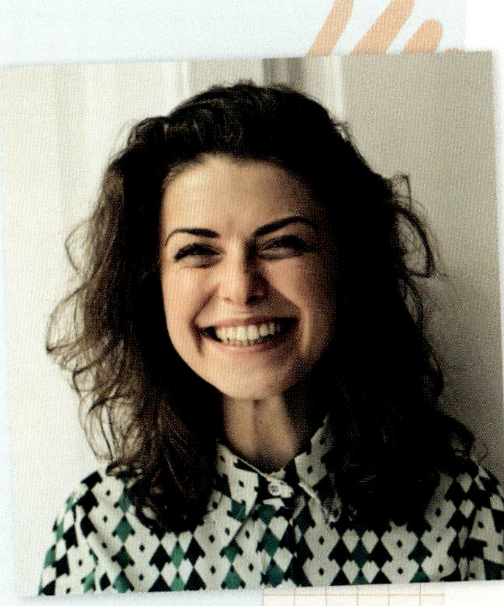

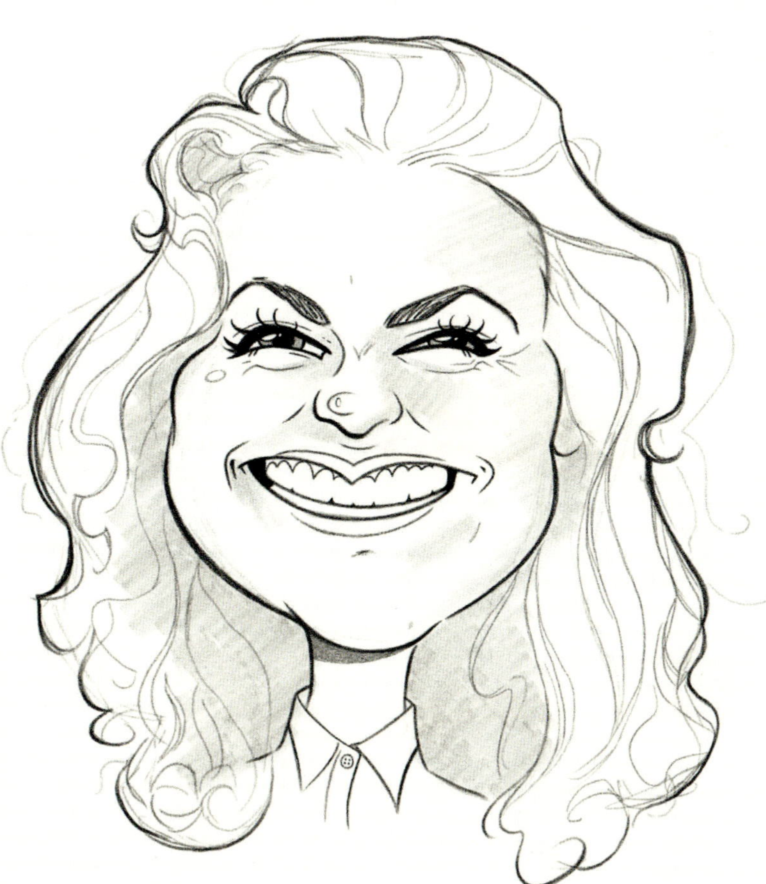

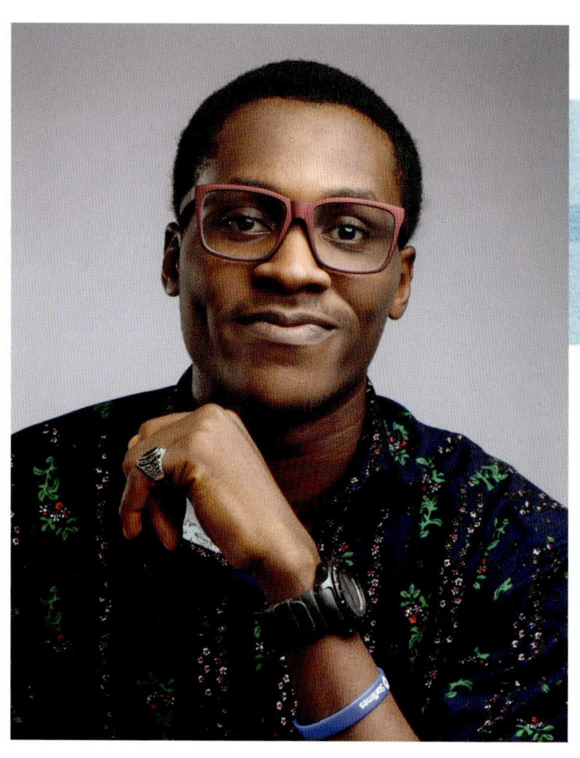

CARICATURE: STEP-BY-STEP #2

In this case, instead of starting with the head shape and then drawing the eyes, nose, and mouth lines, I started with just the eye line and built the forehead and jaw shapes around it. It's helpful to try out different techniques to discover what may work best for you.

1. Draw the eye line. Because the reference model's face is tilted slightly, the eye line is tilted also.

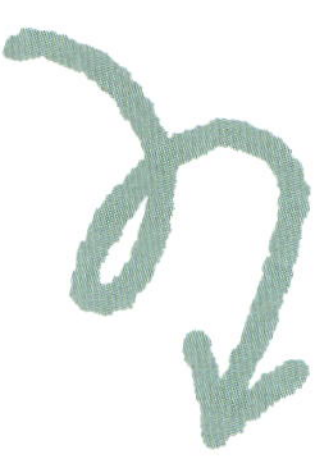

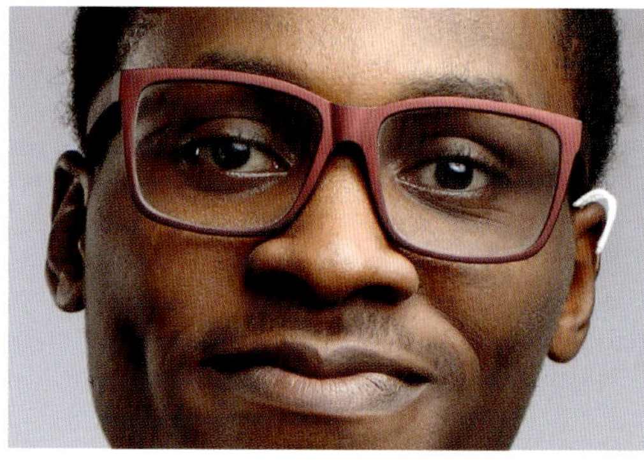

1

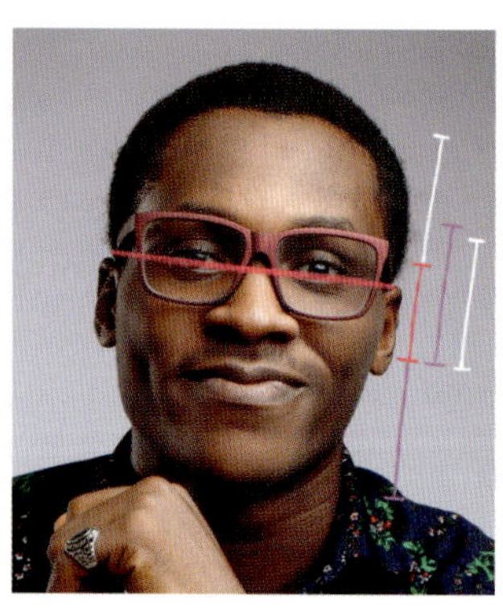

2

2. The reference model has a long face. Both the upper and lower thirds of his face are longer than the middle third—from the top of the eyes to the bottom of the nose. This tells me that I can likely maintain his likeness by exaggerating his forehead and chin.

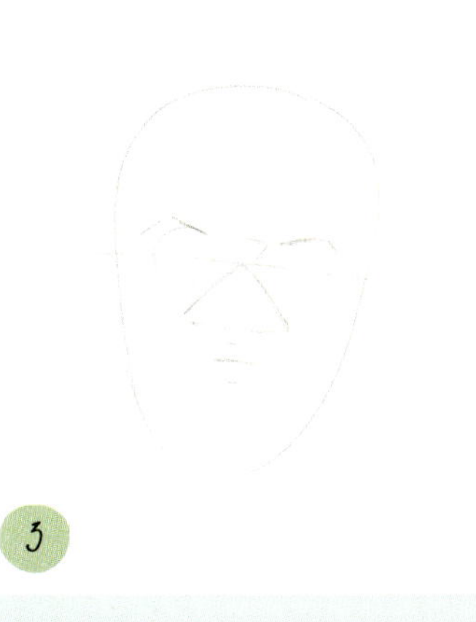

3. Next, I blocked in the eyes and nose with basic shapes and used faint lines to indicate the eyebrows and where I want the mouth to sit. I also realized that my initial oval face shape was too close to reality, so I exaggerated it further.

4. I've chosen to make the middle third of the model's face smaller than it actually is to really emphasize the exaggeration of his forehead and chin. As a result, I've also drawn the glasses a bit smaller than they are in reality. Another approach to caricaturing this subject could have involved making the glasses much larger. There's no one right way to caricature anyone!

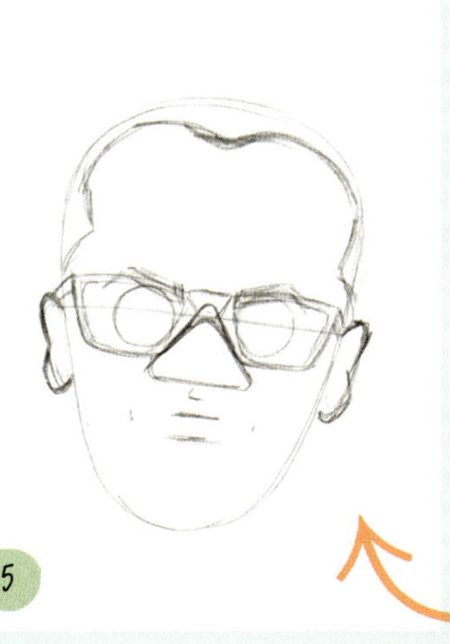

5. I like how the reference model's ears jut outward a bit at the top, so instead of drawing a simple curved line for the outline of the ears, I pushed that feature a little. I also filled in the hairline.

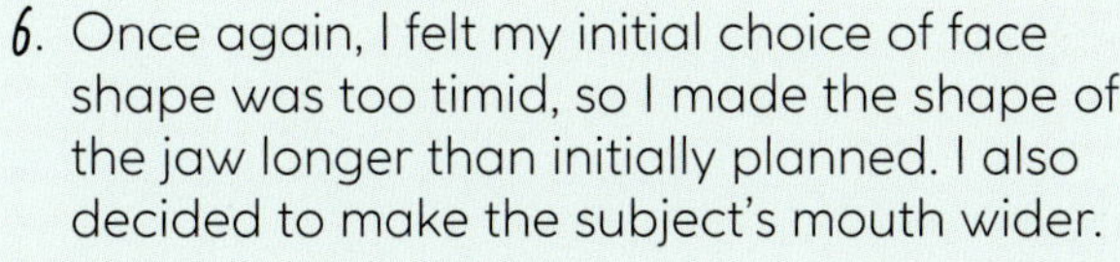

6. Once again, I felt my initial choice of face shape was too timid, so I made the shape of the jaw longer than initially planned. I also decided to make the subject's mouth wider.

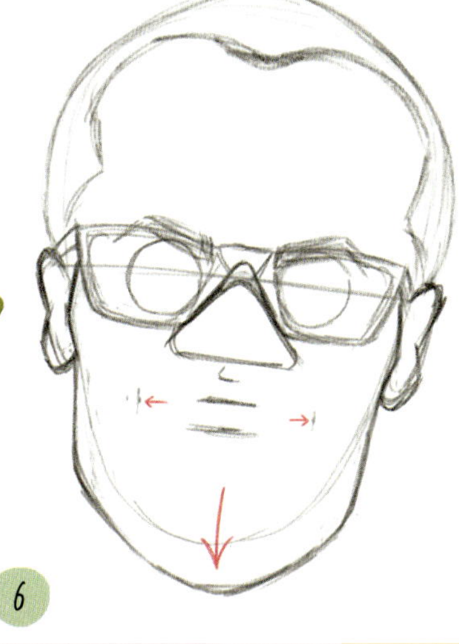

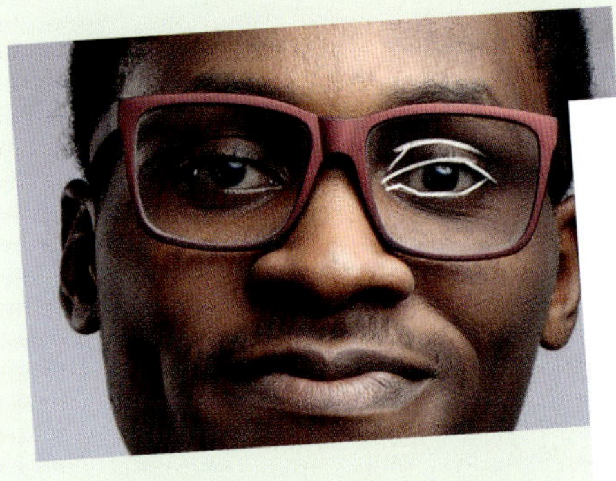

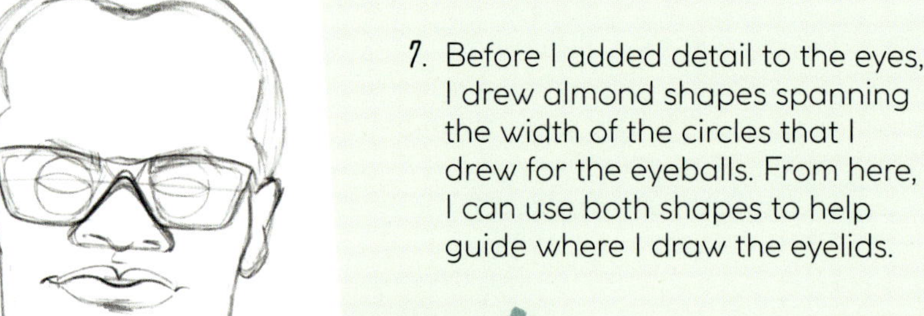

7. Before I added detail to the eyes, I drew almond shapes spanning the width of the circles that I drew for the eyeballs. From here, I can use both shapes to help guide where I draw the eyelids.

8. Here, I've started to define the features. My reference model's upper lip has a pronounced heart shape in the center so I used that to give his mouth character. He also has pretty prominent dimples so I made sure to include those as well. Take advantage of details like this when you see them.

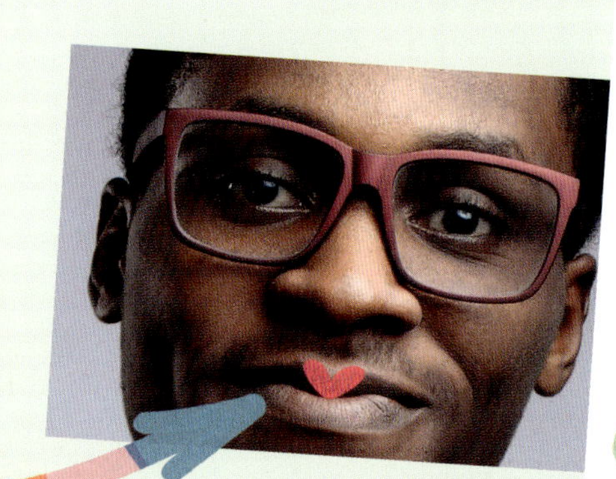

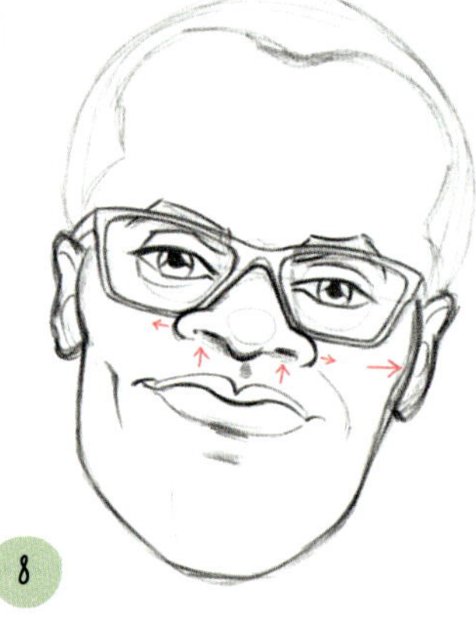

9. When I defined his nose, I made it a little shorter and wider because why not? He was starting to look a little too gaunt, so I also widened and rounded his cheekbones further.

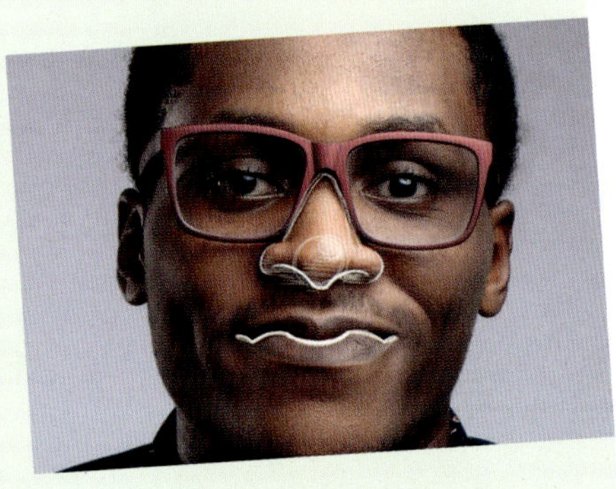

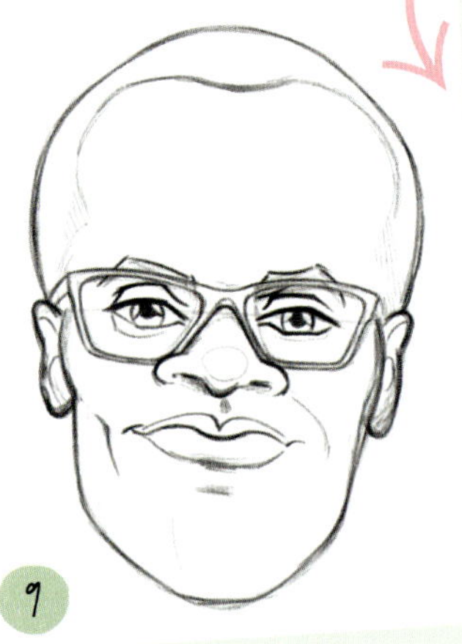

10. Yet again, I felt the subject was looking too proportionate (ha-ha!), so I made the top of the head taller and slightly wider. The red lines represent where his head and hairline sat before.

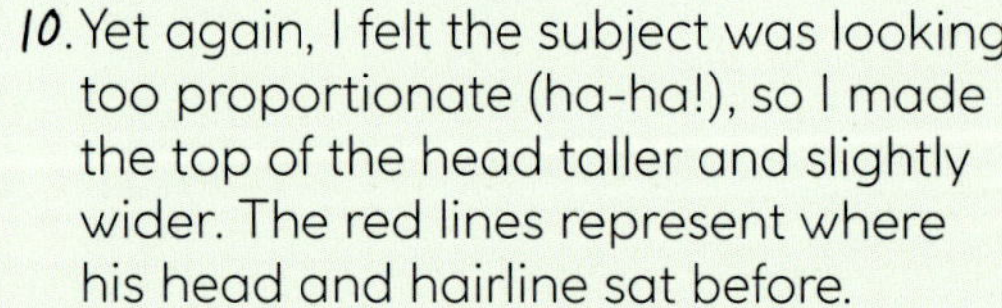

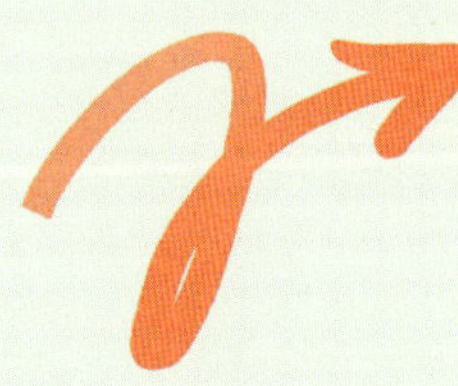

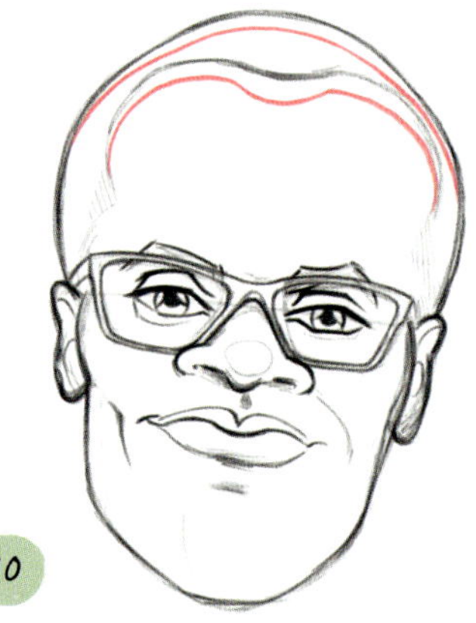

11. The model's brow ridge isn't very pronounced, but it is prominent enough to make his eyes somewhat deep set. As a result, the creases of his eyes are very visible, so I drew them as thick, dark lines.

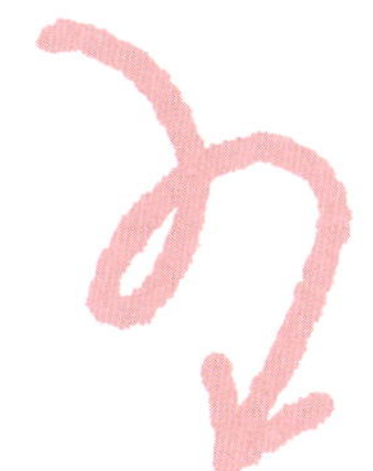

11

ARTIST INSIGHT

I often have to erase and push my designs further and further because my initial choices are timid. It takes me 30 to 40 minutes to draw a caricature like this. Don't be discouraged if both your progress and the time it takes you to draw caricatures feels slow, you are improving with each and every piece you draw, even when it's difficult to see that improvement.

12. I have added shading with cross-hatching, but don't feel like you need to follow in my footsteps if you'd prefer a simpler, cleaner look!

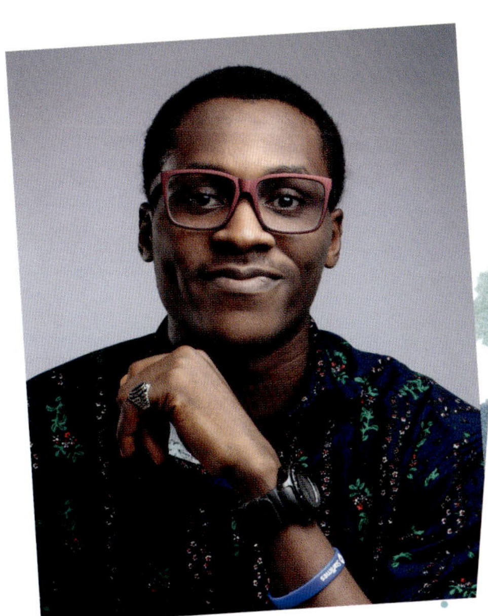

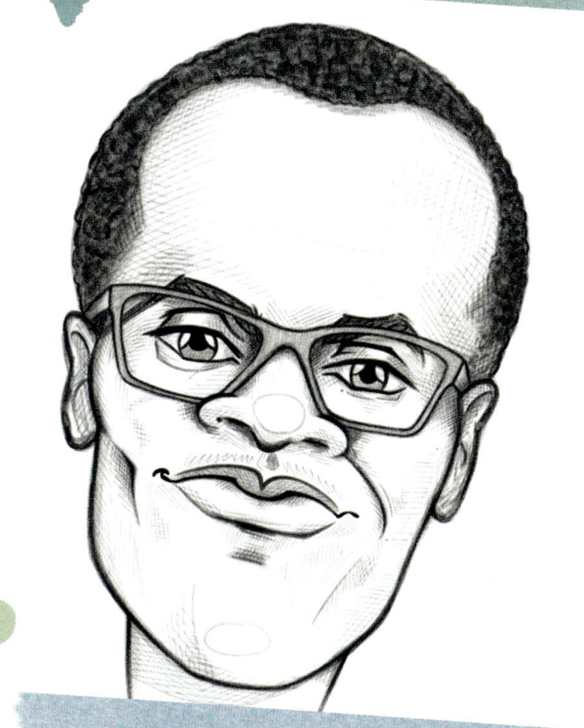

12

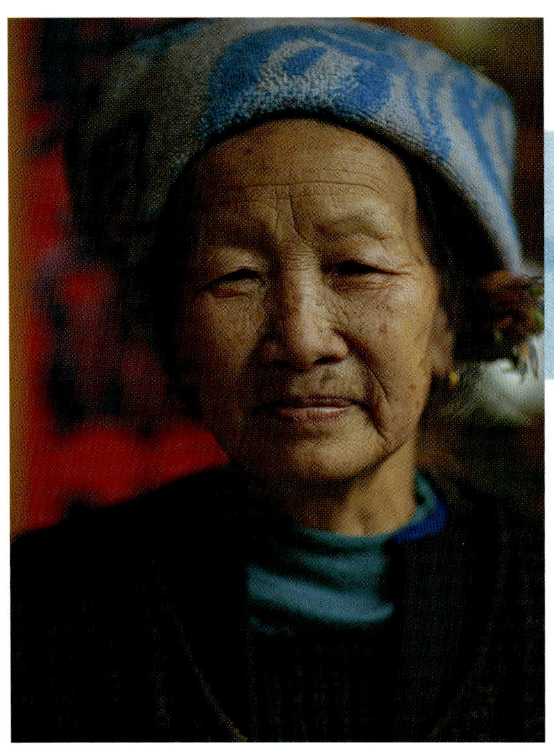

CARICATURE: STEP-BY-STEP #3

I wanted this caricature to feel distinctly cartoony and stylized, so I deliberately set out to start with a much bolder, more unrealistic shape.

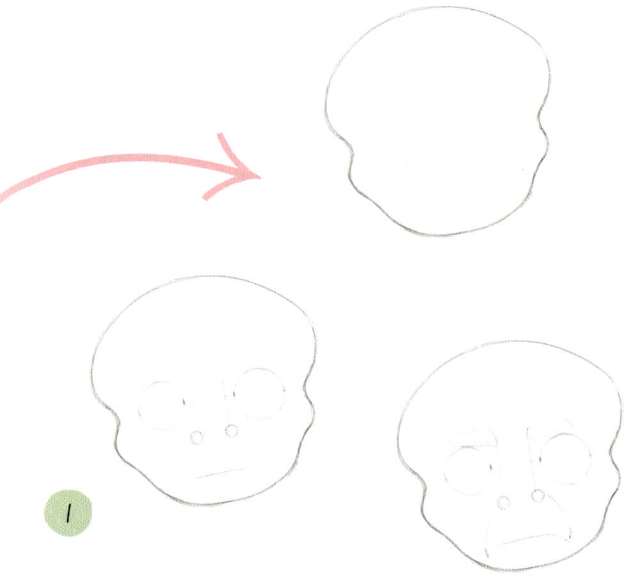

1. I began this caricature by considering the overall shape of the head. I was determined to think outside the box and start with a more interesting shape than a simple oval. My reference model does not have a particularly round or short face, so the initial shape I put down may seem like an odd choice at first glance. However, after closely studying the model's face, I was confident that how I drew the features and their planned placement would do most of the heavy lifting in maintaining her likeness. Her cheekbones shape her face, which is why I went with this odd, bumpy shape. I drew the basic shapes to establish feature placement.

2. Using the basic shapes as guidelines, I drew in her eyes and mouth. Her mouth is smaller than average, but I like how much character the wrinkles around it add. Instead of making the wrinkles and the center line of the mouth smaller, I opted to make the lips tiny instead. This approach creates the impression of a small mouth without sacrificing those prominent smile lines. Remember, the circles represent the whole eyeball or socket, which is why they're butting up against the eyebrows.

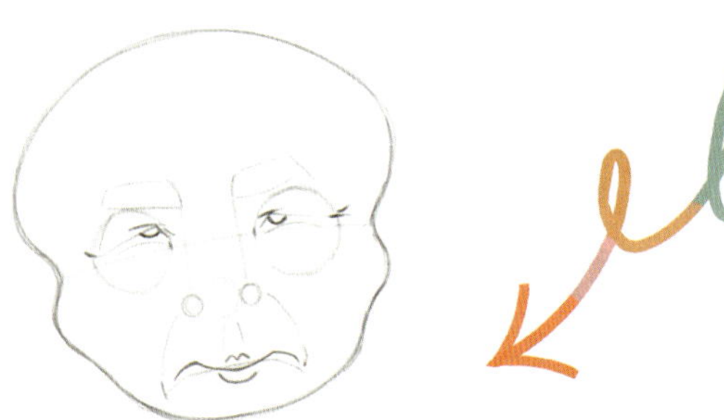

2

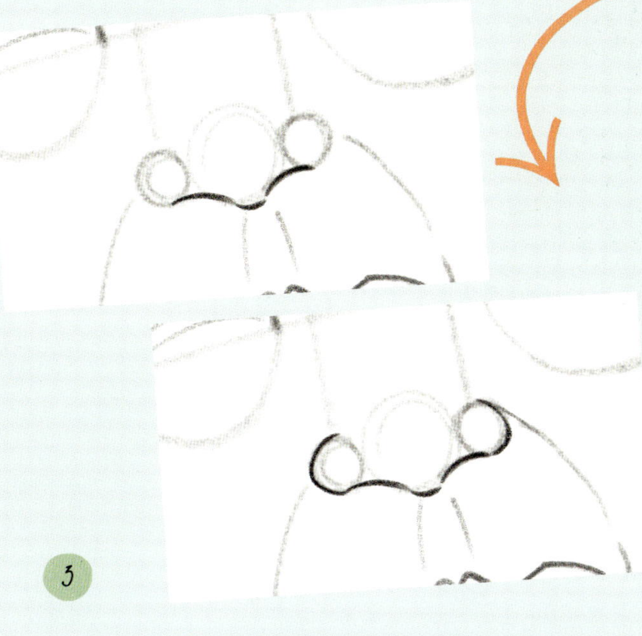

3. Next, I drew the nose by following the shape of its underside, starting with the nostrils and then connecting them with the septum. Since the bridge of the nose is so small, I chose not to draw it at all. Though I did indicate it later with some shading.

3

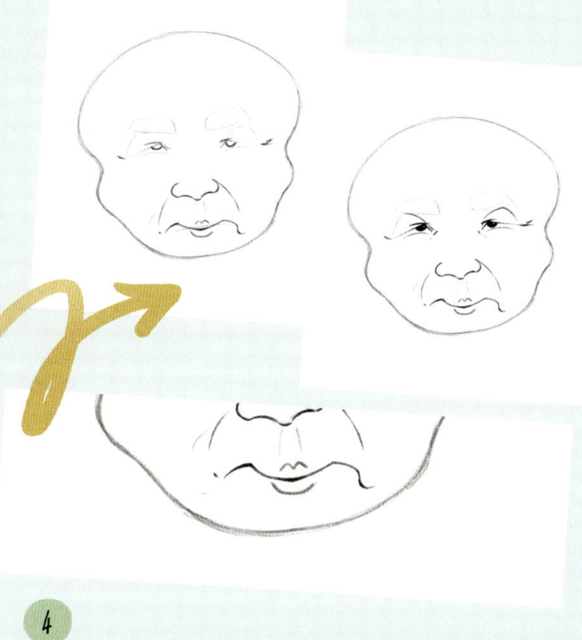

4. I like how the reference model is subtly smiling and I thought my drawing was looking a little too grumpy. Capturing such a subtle smile in a simplified style can be challenging, especially when the reference has such strong smile lines that curve down from the corners of their mouth. To counter this frowning appearance, I cheated a bit and tilted one corner of the mouth upward, then erased it and tilted it even more. I also erased the under drawing and defined the eyes a bit more.

4

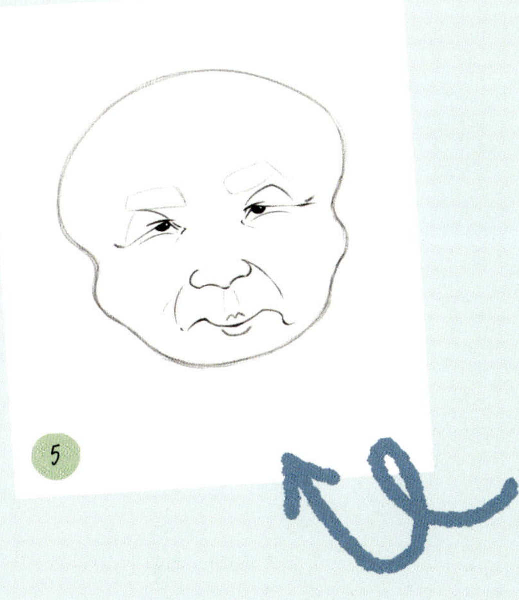

5

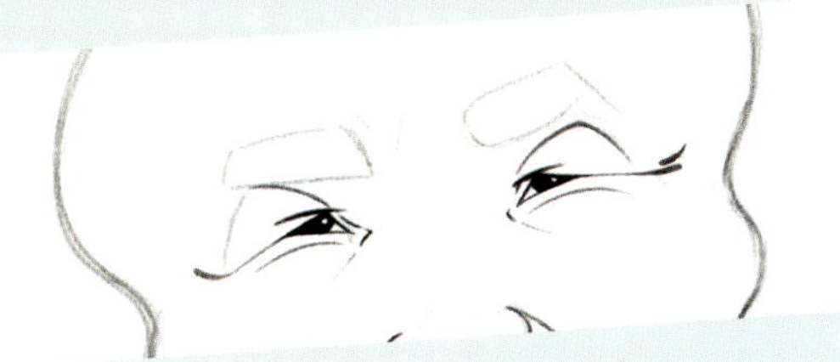

5. The visible sections of the reference model's eyes, under her eyelids, form a tiny triangle shape, so I decided to close the triangles and erase the parts of the pupils that overlapped them.

6. I was satisfied with the shape of the face (for once, ha!), so I cleaned up the lines a little and started adding more of the fun details, including wrinkle lines on the forehead.

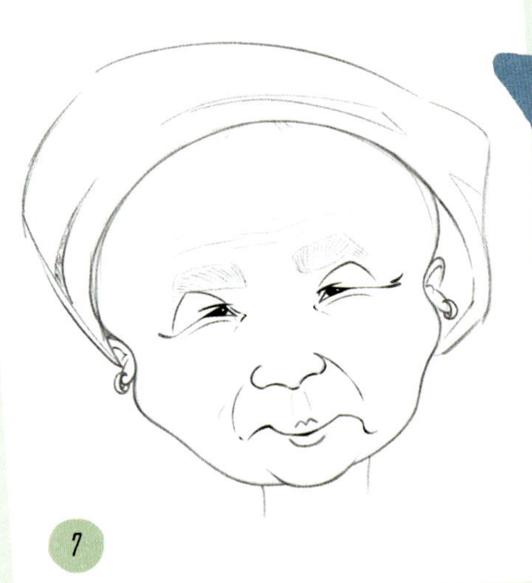

7. Next, I drew in the shape of her headwear, using scalene triangles (triangles with all three sides different lengths) to indicate the wrinkles in the fabric.

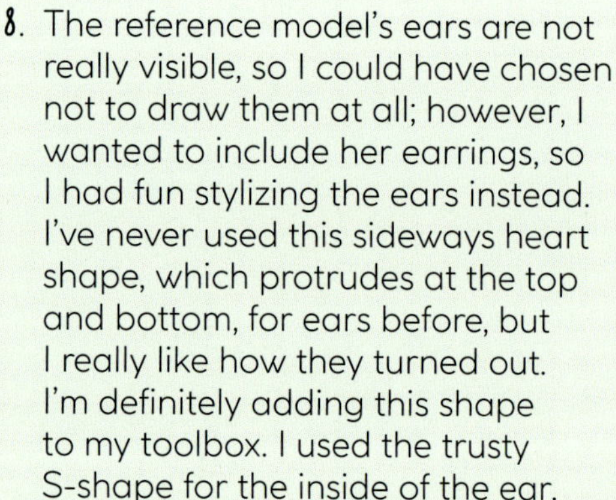

8. The reference model's ears are not really visible, so I could have chosen not to draw them at all; however, I wanted to include her earrings, so I had fun stylizing the ears instead. I've never used this sideways heart shape, which protrudes at the top and bottom, for ears before, but I really like how they turned out. I'm definitely adding this shape to my toolbox. I used the trusty S-shape for the inside of the ear.

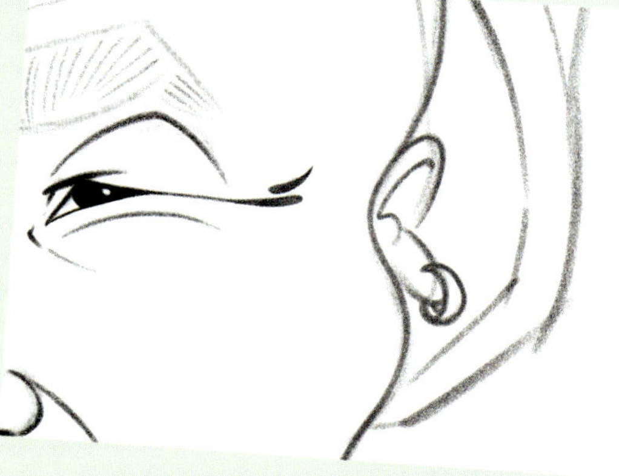

9. Next, I added some simple, flowing lines for the hair and added more details to the face.

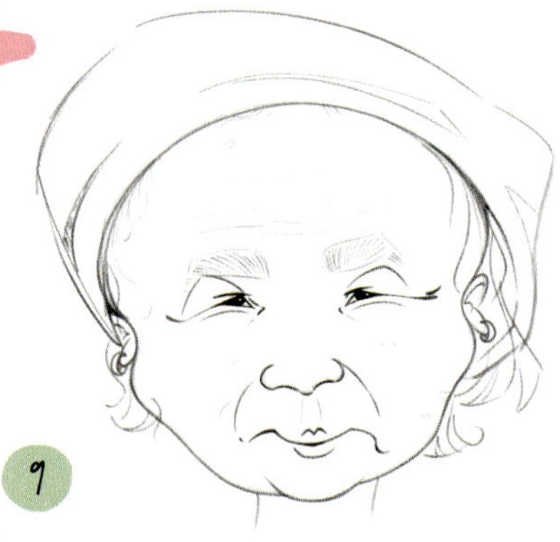

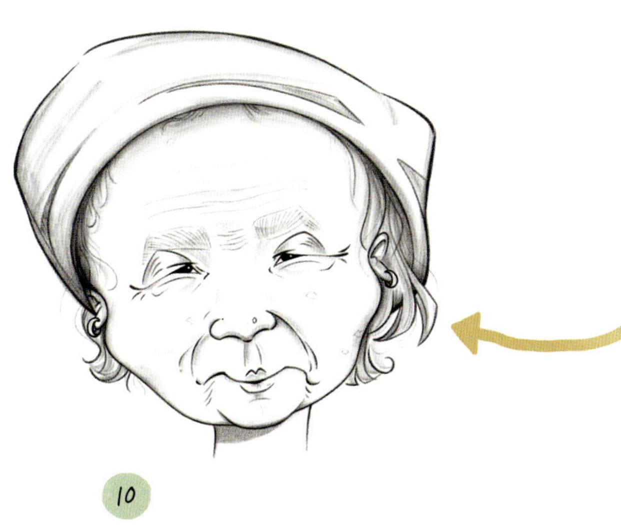

10

10. This is my favorite stage of the process: detail, detail, detail. I added shading using the side of my pencil (this technique works for both traditional and digital mediums), some flyaway hairs, more wrinkle lines, and I defined and darkened my lines.

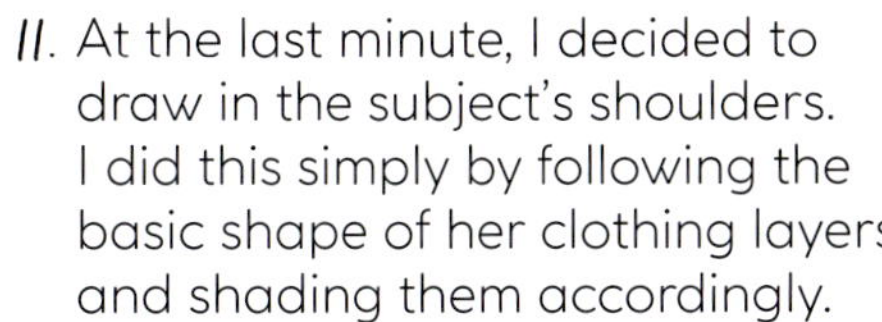

11. At the last minute, I decided to draw in the subject's shoulders. I did this simply by following the basic shape of her clothing layers and shading them accordingly.

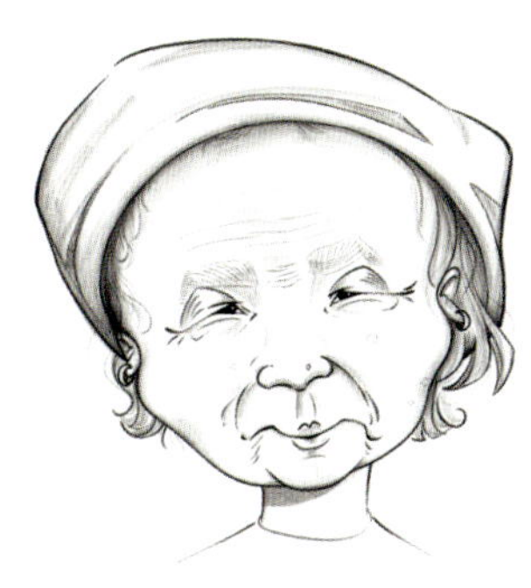

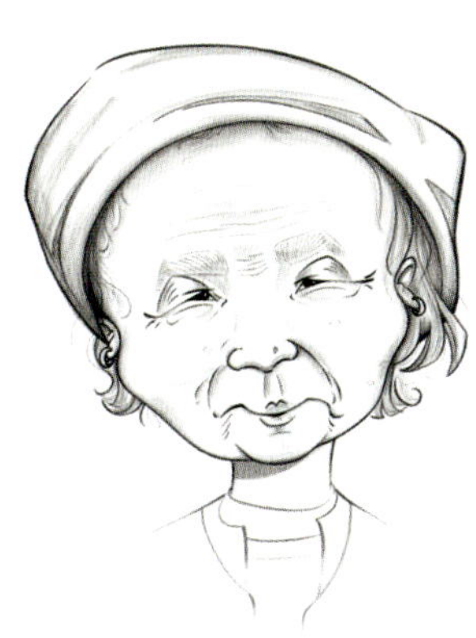

11

12. Ta-da! Finished.

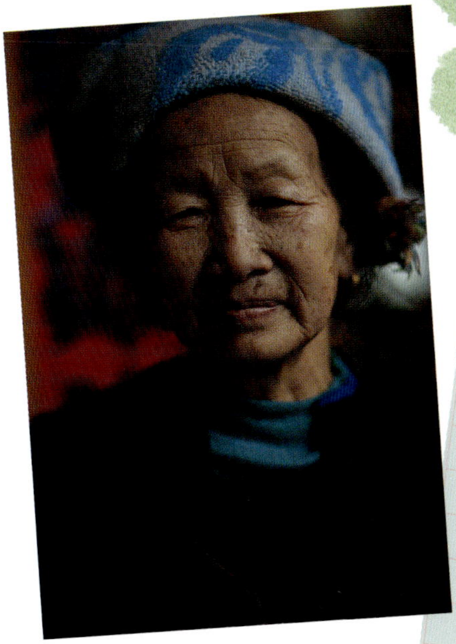

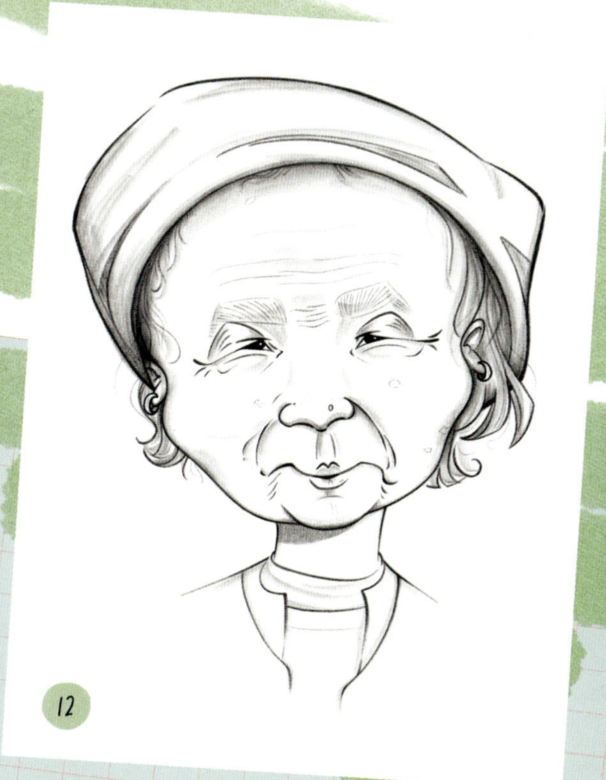

12

RENDERED CARICATURE

Drawing a highly detailed caricature, from sketch to final render, is a little more complex than drawing its amusement park counterpart. While both styles share the fundamental principles of exaggeration and likeness, the comprehensive approach elevates these concepts through multiple layers of refinement. The core tenets remain consistent across both styles: identifying and amplifying distinctive features while maintaining recognizability. However, the detailed rendering process allows us to explore how patience and technique can transform these shared foundations into finished artwork with much more depth and dimension.

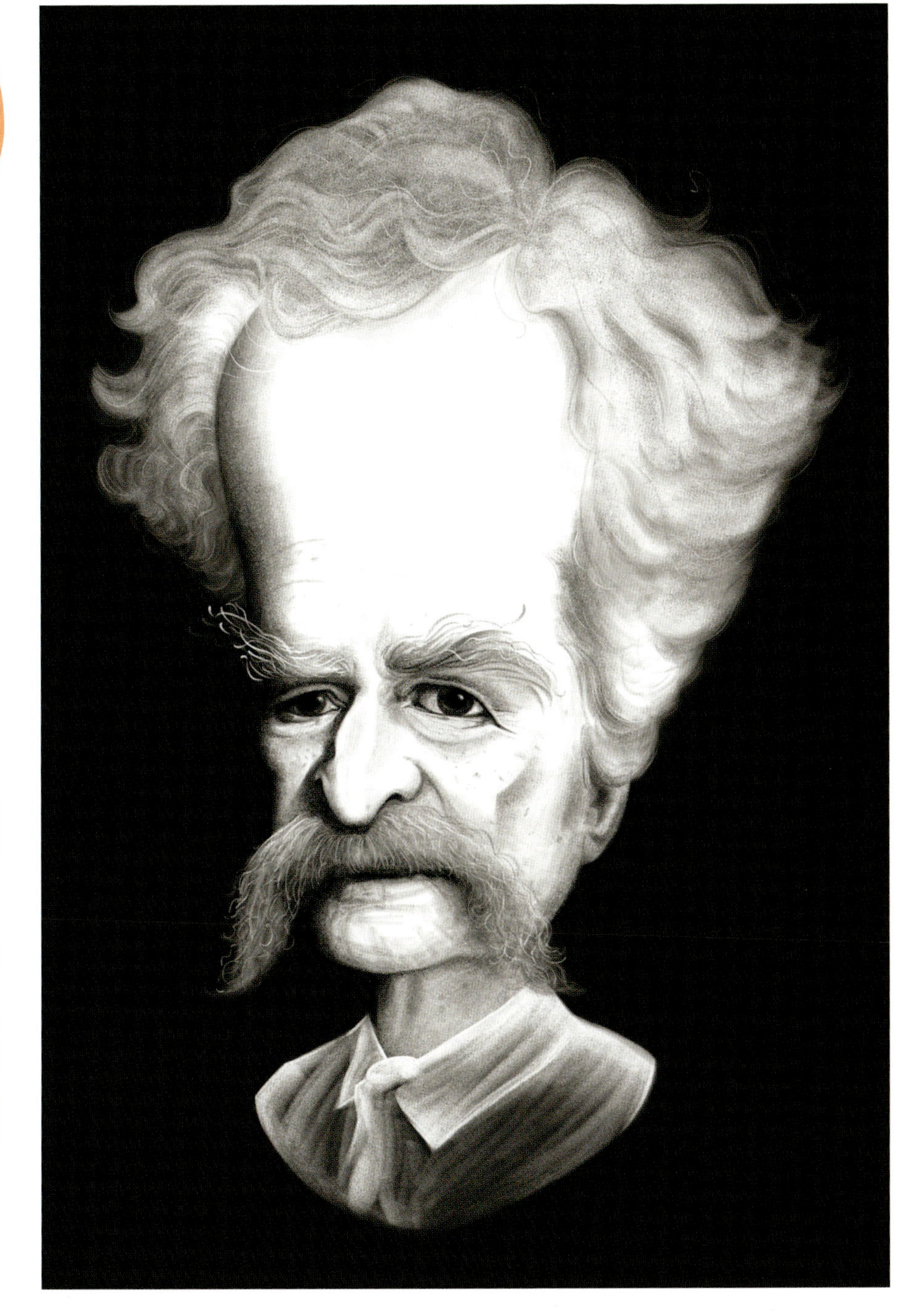

STEP 1: THUMBNAILS

When it comes to more highly-rendered and complex caricatures, it's important to start by creating thumbnail sketches. I realize this obsession with under drawings and thumbnail sketches can feel exhausting, but trust me, they are necessary. In the same way you can reduce your reliance on references for certain subjects, the more you practice drawing something, the less time you'll need to spend on thumbnails and under drawings before creating the final design; experienced artists wouldn't harp on about it so much if it weren't important.

Actually wait, scratch that, the first thing you need to do is warm up! See Shape & Proportion Exercises in the Foundations chapter for my warm-up drawing tips. Now you can start on the thumbnails.

When creating a caricature, it is helpful to have more than one reference photo to work from. You'll be able to observe more details about your subject's likeness that way. Even if you plan to draw them from a specific photograph or angle, having multiple reference images from different viewpoints can provide you with information that will help strengthen your design.

Remember when I talked about how I always start a new drawing with a little bit of fear and how important it is to learn to appreciate the value of your "bad art"? That same principle applies here; deciding that your first few pages of sketches are going to be "bad" will help you push past that initial hesitation and get started.

Sometimes your first sketch does end up being the best one, but that is very rare (particularly for beginners), so try your best to embrace the process of making mistakes and refining your work. This approach frees you up to explore and ultimately reach stronger final designs.

ARTIST INSIGHT

Embrace the process! Take the idea of "I have to work so hard" and flip it around to "I get to play!" You get to try all the media that interest you, every drawing technique that interests you, different styles and subjects, and so on. And that is so much fun! It's easy to feel like you're not being productive because progress can be difficult to see, but it is productive to play and experiment because all that practice is leading you to your goals, and you get to have fun while doing it.

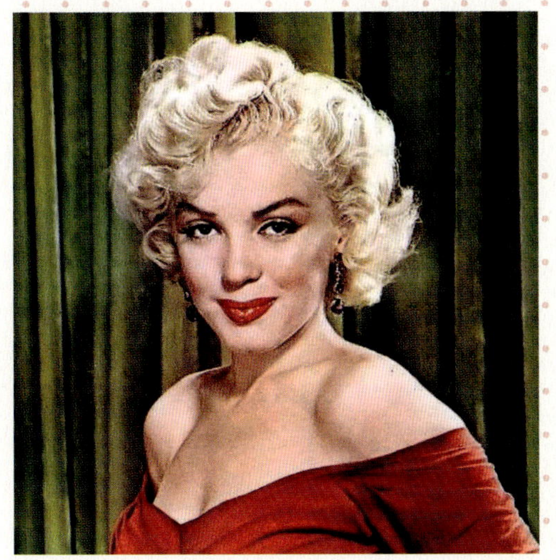

EXAMPLE 1: MARILYN MONROE

Accept that your initial sketches may not be great, and that that's OK. Caricature is the result of manipulating shape, spacing, placement, and proportion; however, for this first step, it's helpful to focus on just one element to avoid overwhelm. Don't worry about anything else but trying out different forms of exaggeration. I always start by exploring different head shape options, as this will be the foundation for everything else.

For now, put aside worrying too much about likeness and let yourself explore all the fun, wacky shapes that are secretly trapped in your brain, yelling to be let out. Thinking too literally stops you from taking risks, and often those risks can pay off (especially in caricature).

My exaggeration choices are still informed by my reference images (in this case, Marilyn Monroe), but I am also intentionally experimenting with shapes that I, instinctively, would not normally associate with her likeness.

If you feel that you need more direction, start by drawing a few simple shapes that do very closely mirror the head shape of whoever you're drawing. In this case, I drew a square, a heart, and a triangle that are, more or less, proportionally accurate to Marilyn. Then build upon the simple shapes you've drawn, making them more pronounced and exaggerated.

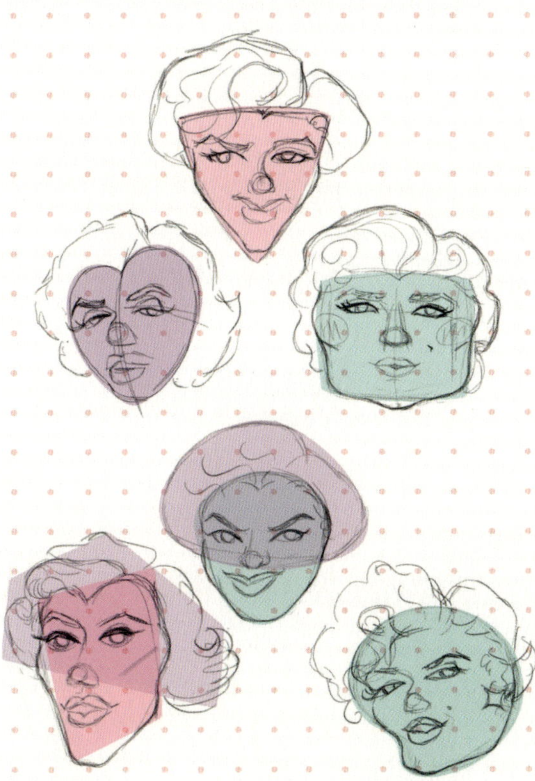

Think simple shapes and minimal detail! This is SO HARD if you're like me and you love detail and precision and you tend to overwork things, so believe me when I say that I understand. But you have to be loose at this stage.

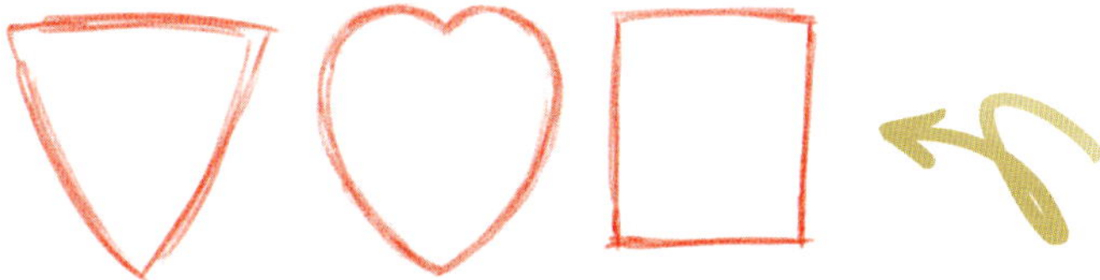

STEP 2: REFINE YOUR THUMBNAILS

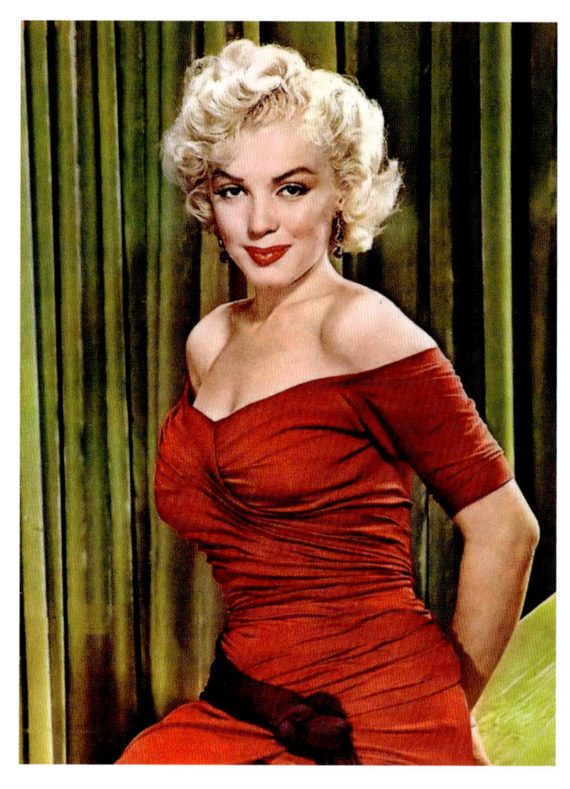

Once I have my quick thumbnails down, I add a little more detail to each of them. This time, I'm considering the subject's likeness more, as individual features are just as important as the overall picture.

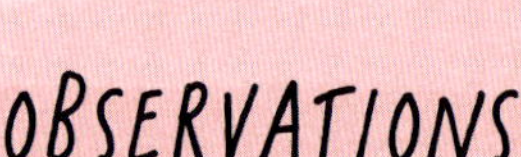

OBSERVATIONS

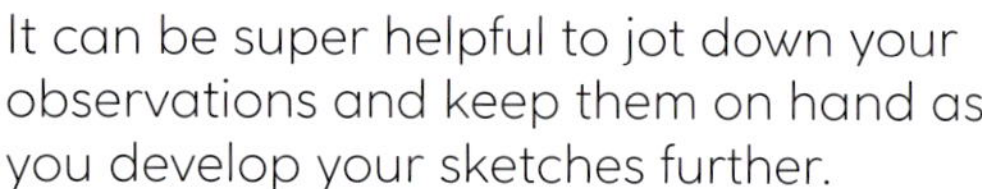

It can be super helpful to jot down your observations and keep them on hand as you develop your sketches further.

Here are some of my observations about Marilyn's face:

- Heart-shaped face
- Small nose and mouth
- Bridge of nose isn't much narrower than the end
- Three main sections of the face are pretty equal
- Eyes tilt downward on the outsides
- Sculpted and pointed eyebrows
- High cheekbones

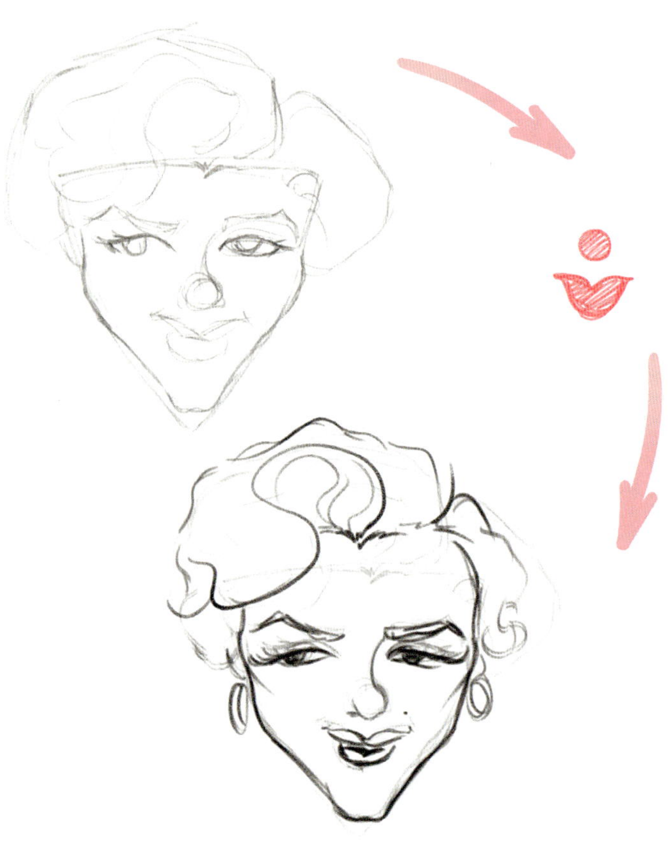

From there, take note of which qualities in each thumbnail you like and dislike. What's working and what isn't.

While this is a pretty illustration, it feels too safe. The proportions are too true to life. However, I do like how I drew her mouth.

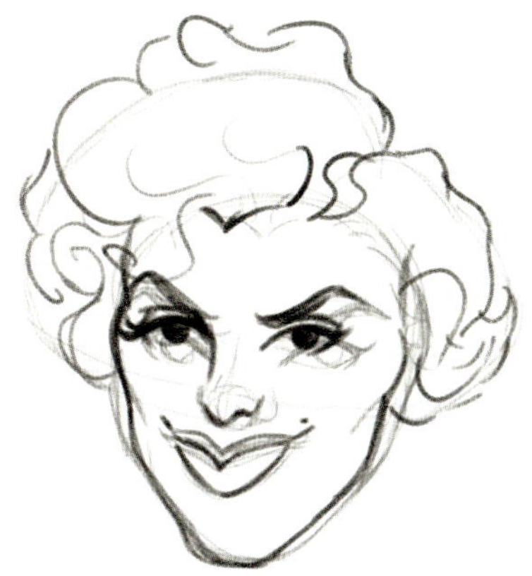

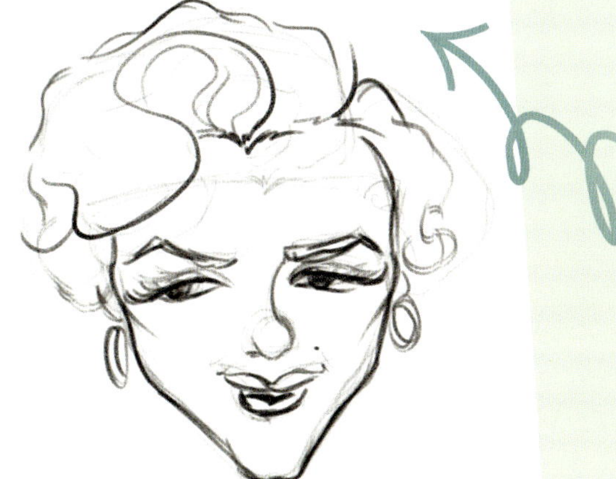

Here, I like how her mouth is smaller and the outside ends of her eyes slant down.

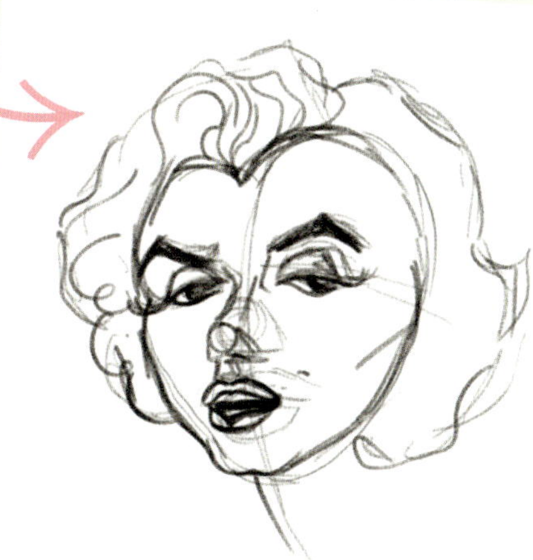

I like the eyes in this one, but overall, it feels a little stiff and awkward. I could potentially develop this more and improve it, but I was feeling more excited about some of my other options.

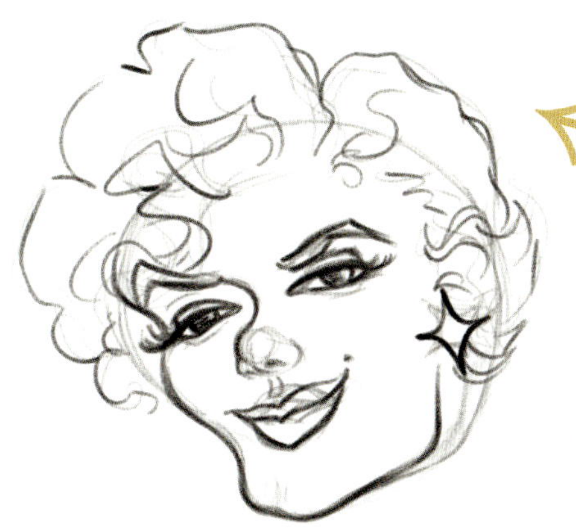

I love how I drew her chin, cheekbone, and jaw here, and like the idea of developing this further. I feel this sketch has the most potential of all of them.

STEP 3: DRAW OVER THE TOP

The next step is to pick your favorite thumbnail and draw over the top of it, continuing to refine it as you work.

I'm sure it's no surprise that this is the thumbnail I chose to develop. As previously mentioned, I love the shape of her cheekbone, chin, and jaw, and knew I could push that oddity further while still maintaining her likeness.

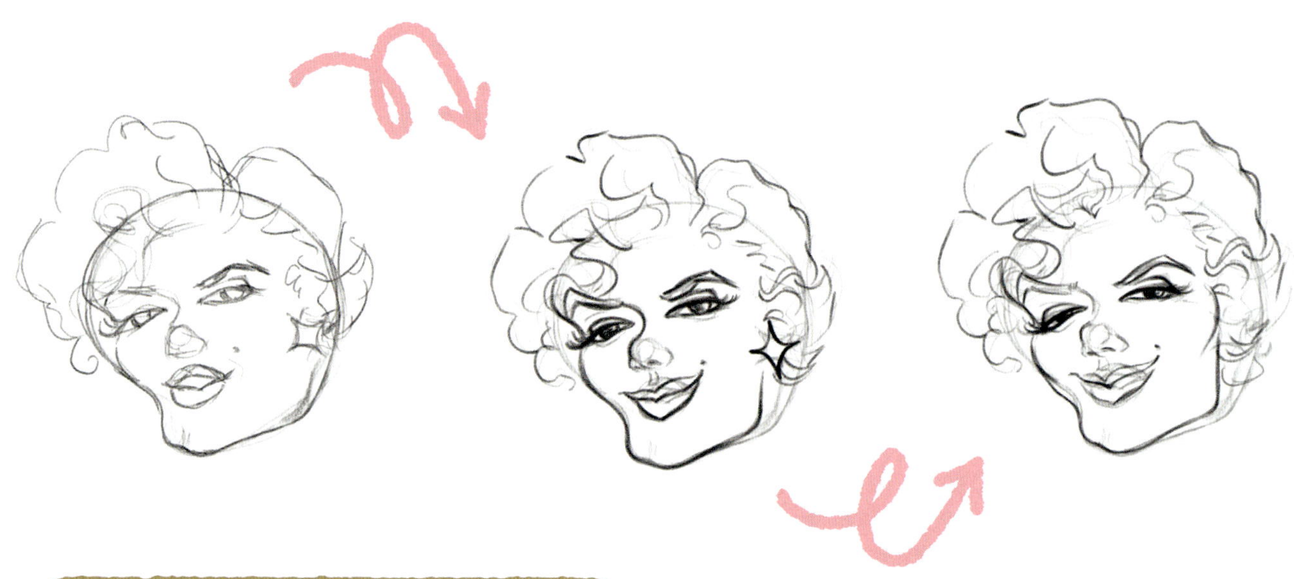

ARTIST INSIGHT

If you're working digitally, you can simply add a new layer and lower the opacity of the first layer at this point—as I've done here. If you're working traditionally, either use tracing paper or, ideally, a light box and a fresh sheet of paper for each new overdrawing.

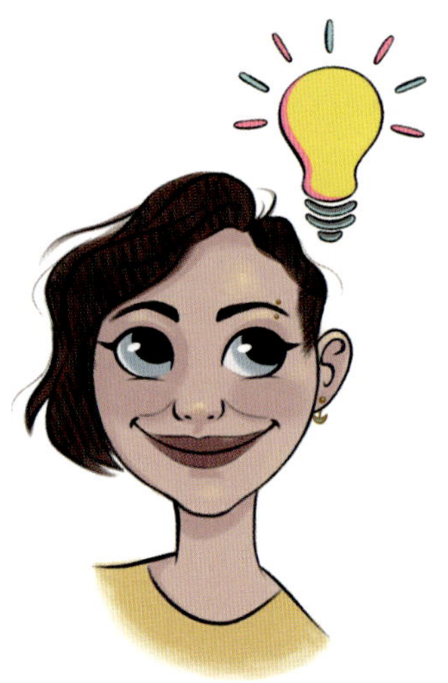

I referred to the smaller thumbnail when redrawing her mouth, so that I could emulate how I drew it originally. That said, you still don't want to spend too much time rendering at this stage. We'll work on the details in Step 4.

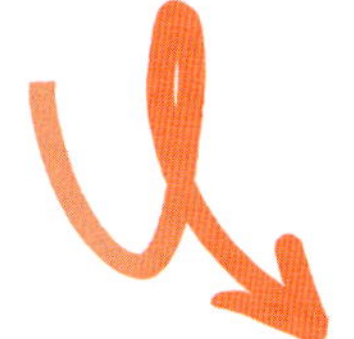

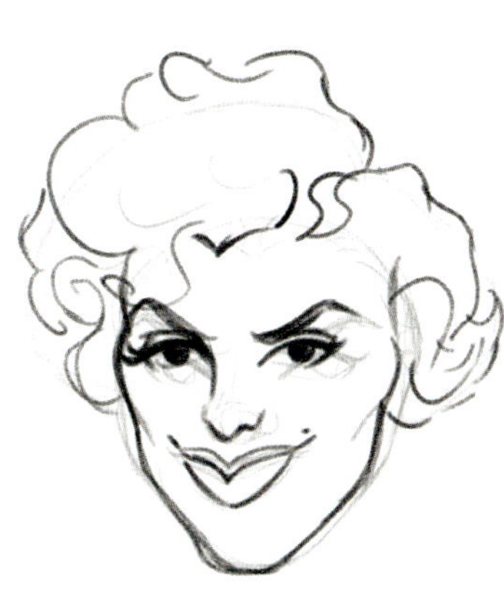

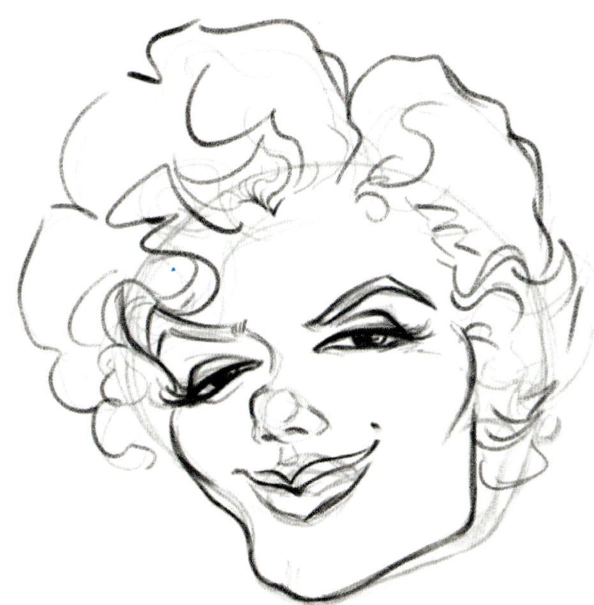

PUSHING THE EXAGGERATION

The practice of redrawing and pushing the exaggeration is beneficial for all artists, regardless of experience, but I especially recommend it for beginners. In my experience, it's easier to make bold exaggeration choices when building on top of the exaggeration choices you've already made. In the same way it's easier to exaggerate from a solid foundational knowledge of proper proportion. The more layers you add, the more you can push your design to the extreme. This goes for character design as well!

ARTIST INSIGHT

If you're still feeling unhappy with your sketch, guess what? Your sketch is not the end result! You do not have to have an amazing sketch in order to make a great piece of art. I have found that sometimes when I'm drawing this sort of rendered caricature, it really only starts to come together when I've begun defining the details. The details are where the likeness can really start to take form.

RINSE AND REPEAT

Once you've got to the point you're happy with your piece, draw it one more time over the top. Basically, push yourself to repeat this process as many times as you can tolerate, continually tweaking to make it better. As difficult as it can feel to let go of your earlier sketches, I've found that the new sketch is always stronger.

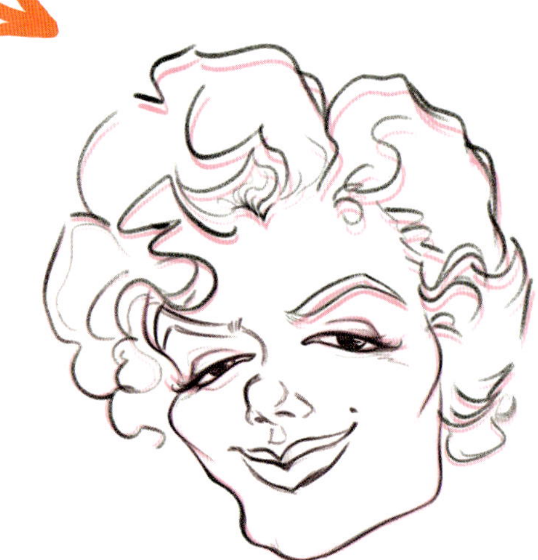

AMANDA SEYFRIED

This is a caricature I drew a few years ago of actress Amanda Seyfried. I refined my thumbnail sketch and then redrew her two more times. I felt that my initial refined thumbnail sketch (first on the left) didn't capture her likeness well enough, so I really pushed myself to make new (but informed!) choices with each redraw.

Sometimes, a person's head shape isn't actually the most important characteristic to exaggerate, and that is usually because it doesn't deviate much from the average. Even though Amanda Seyfried's head is actually more oval-shaped than the round shape that I chose to explore, it didn't detract from creating a good likeness of her.

I decided to emphasize her big, striking eyes, as I think they are a defining characteristic. I also pushed her expressive mouth and dimples. These features go a long way toward creating her likeness, even with a head shape that may seem antithetical to maintaining it.

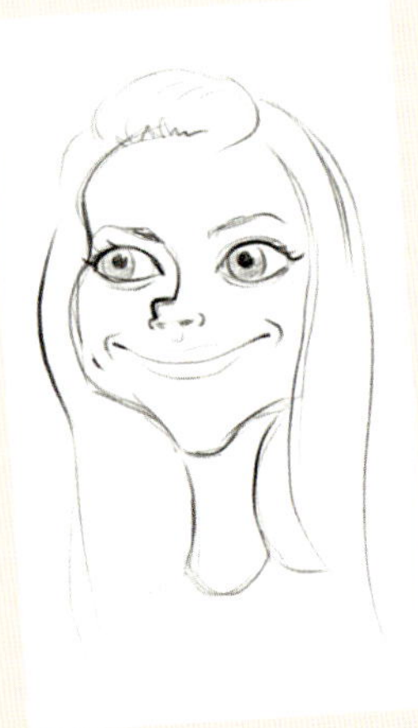

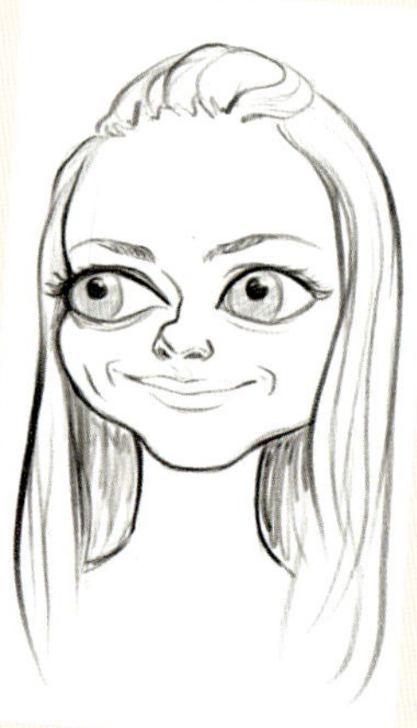

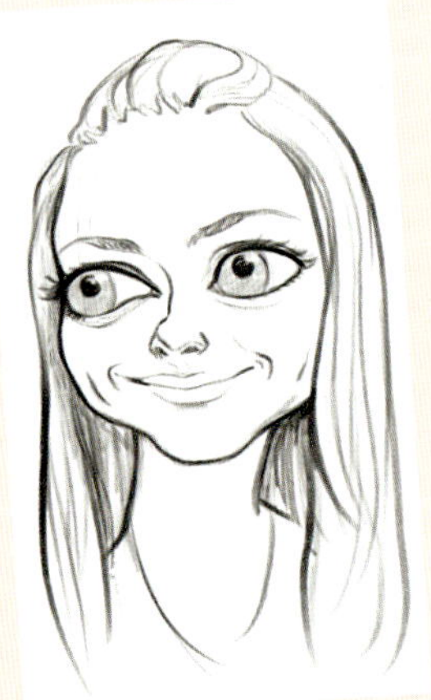

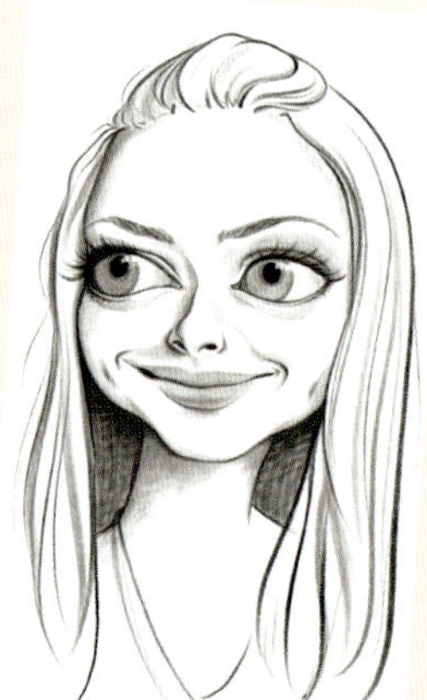

Now, back to Marilyn. As previously mentioned, I purposefully chose Marilyn to caricature for this book because she has a fairly symmetrical, handsome face. There are no features that obviously deviate from the norm. I find both beautiful and more average symmetrical faces more challenging to caricature for this reason. Symmetry can make it harder to see what you should exaggerate (think of the ladder and how you want to avoid it). Instead of simply enlarging or stretching features, I really focused on exaggerating her expression and iconic characteristics, such as her hair and signature makeup. I had a lot of fun drawing her hair!

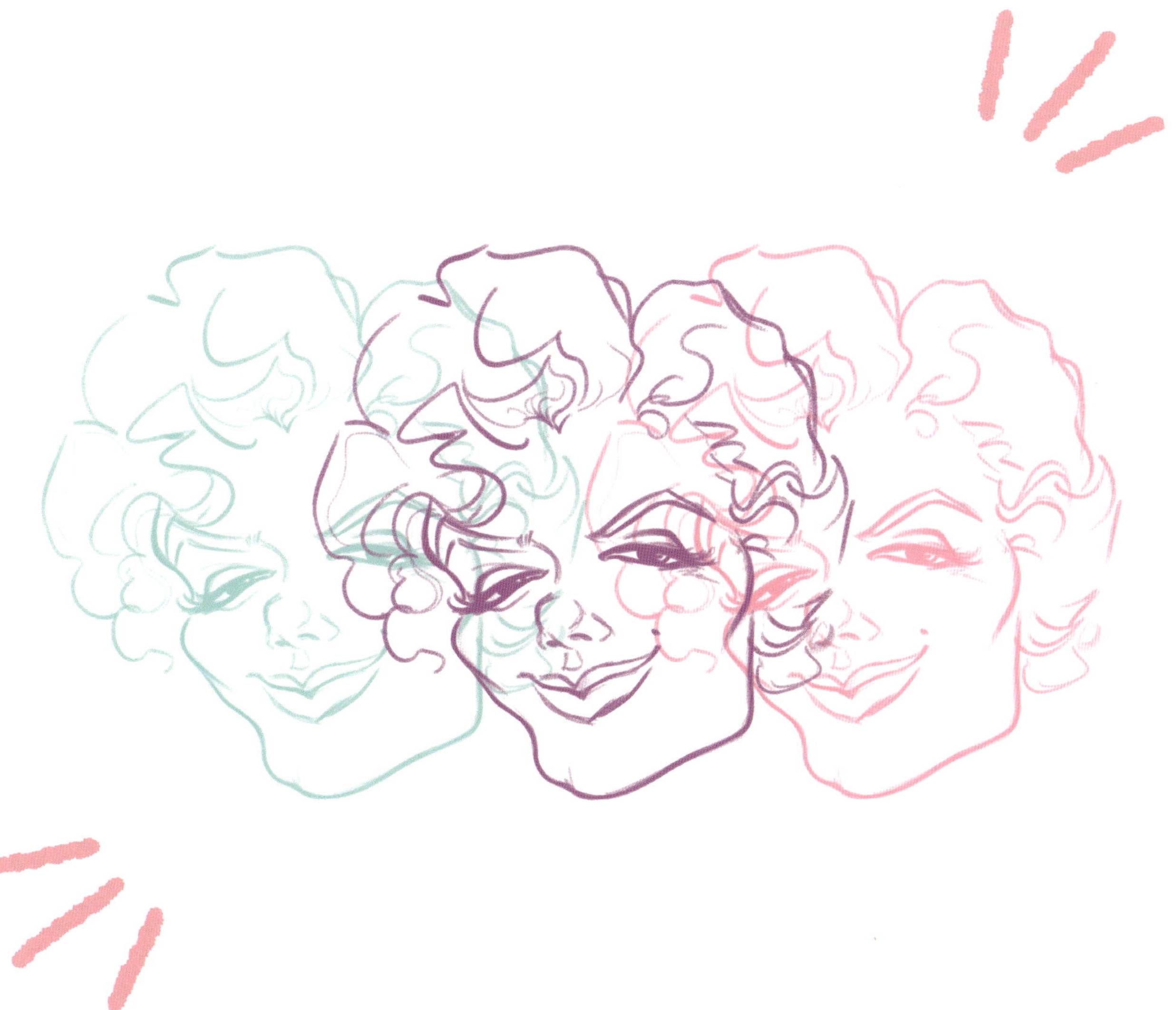

STEP 4: RENDER & REFINE

At last, you've reached the point of the process where you don't have to design anymore! Phew! You should feel so proud of yourself for getting here. It's been quite the journey, but know that you'll have a stronger piece at the end of it. And remember that if you struggle, it means that you've started to change the fabric of your brain. Literally. As you work harder and focus more on what you're doing, that struggle creates stronger, more long-lasting neural pathways in your brain.

I believe it was Court Jones who said that he doesn't always go through every single one of these steps for each of his caricatures, but that it's good to have a process to fall back on when he has a difficult subject. I think it's really important to put this much work into caricaturing when you're a beginner, or even if you're an intermediate caricature artist. I still work through all the thumbnails and rough sketches the majority of the time when I draw a caricature in this style.

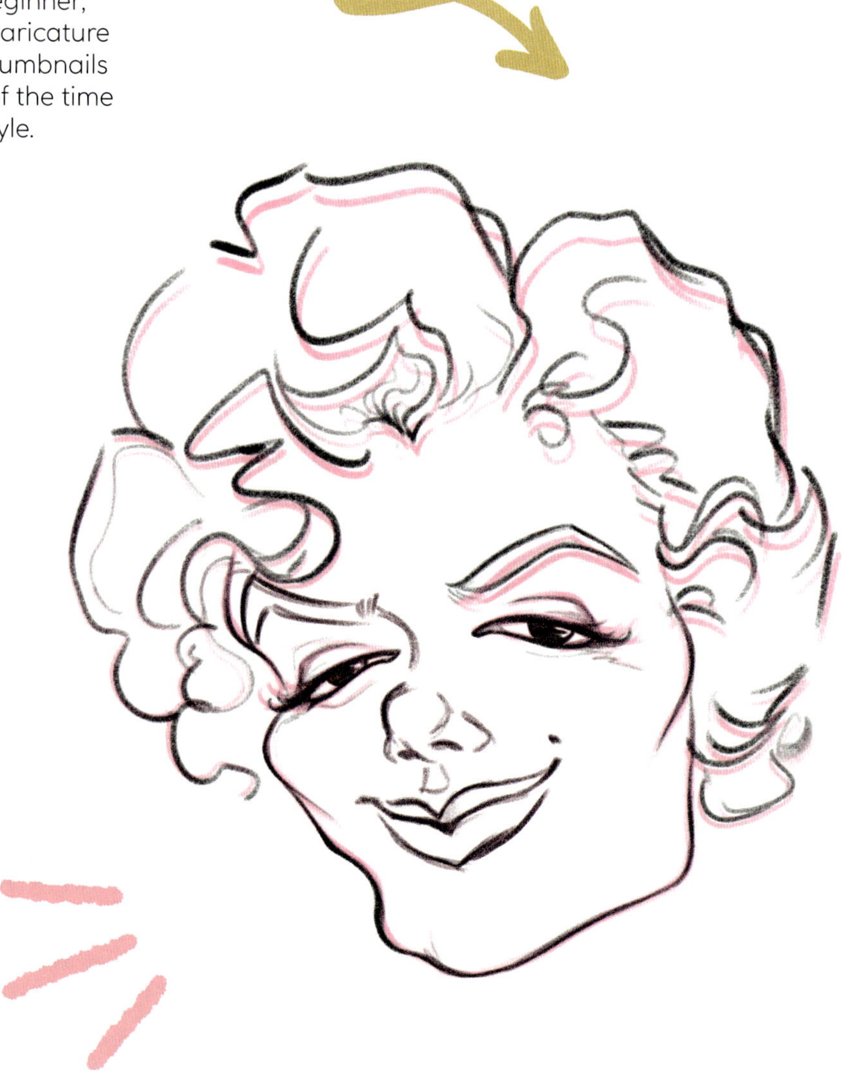

I ended up redrawing Marilyn's face four times. Well, I actually redrew it twice and then traced most of it the final two times, with some minor tweaks here and there.

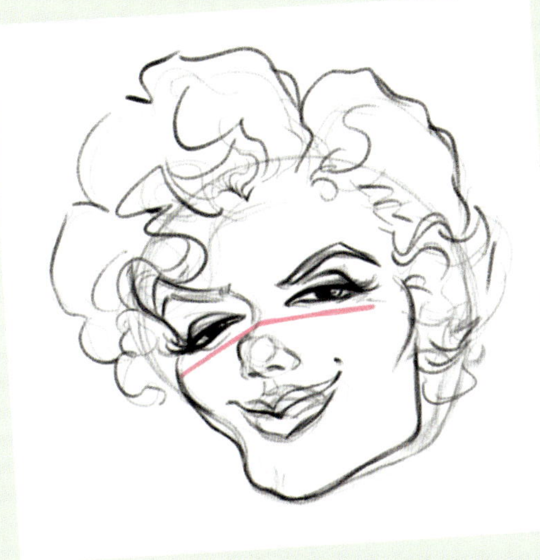

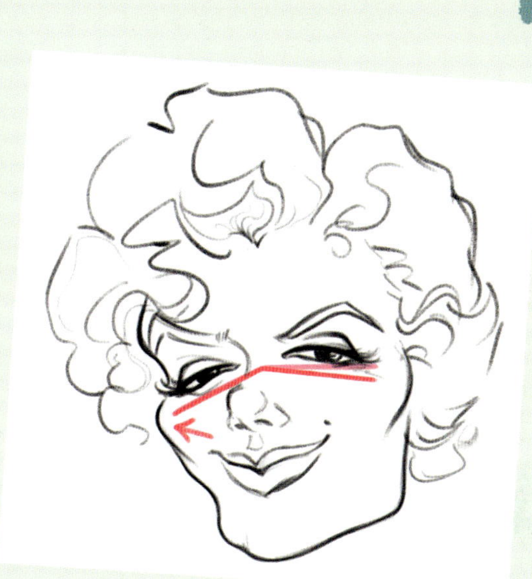

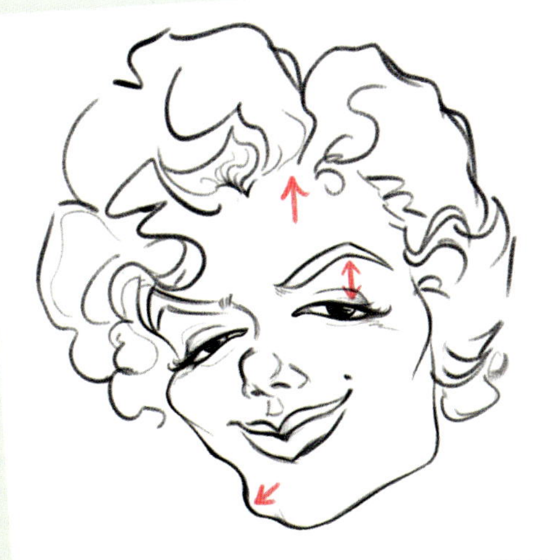

Specifically, I was finally able to slant her eyes to my satisfaction, and pushed her chin and cheeks just a little more.

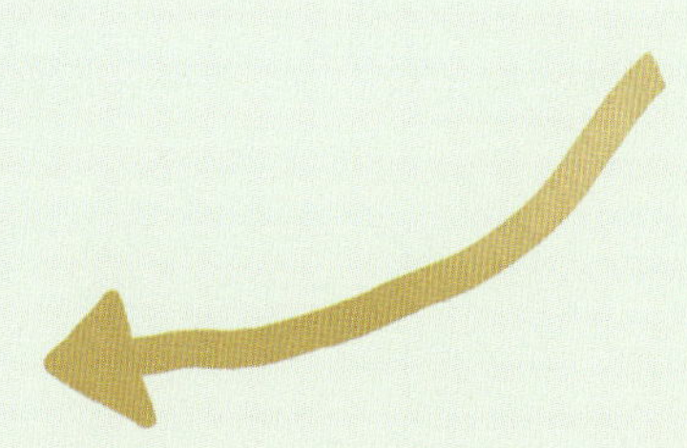

THE MESSY MIDDLE

Up to this point in the process, I often find myself doubting my ability to capture someone's likeness, but time and time again, the further along in the details I get, the more and more the likeness starts to shine. I refer to this phase of doubt as the "messy middle." Thoughts like, "this is too hard!", "who am I to think I can even do this?", and "I'll never be as good as [insert name of skilled artist that you admire here]" often cross my mind. Almost every single creative project I do has a messy middle, and I think that's true for all creatives.

I've learned that it's important to trust the process. So much of building skills or habits lies in your mindset. It's crucial to train yourself to shut down that doubtful voice in your head. If you can push through and persevere to the finish line, I think you'll surprise yourself with what you can create.

Comparison is the thief of joy and the killer of progress. Don't unfairly compare yourself to an artist who almost definitely has had hundreds or thousands of hours more practice than you.

ARTIST INSIGHT

Our initial reactions to our own work are not always accurate. If you're not happy with your piece, set it aside for a day before going back to it. Giving yourself distance can help you see it and appreciate it with fresh eyes.

THE FINAL RENDER

Here, I've paid close attention to all of the anatomical traits present in Marilyn's face, including the interplay of light and shadow, bone structure, and musculature. Basically, the only aspect that doesn't reflect reality are the proportions of her features.

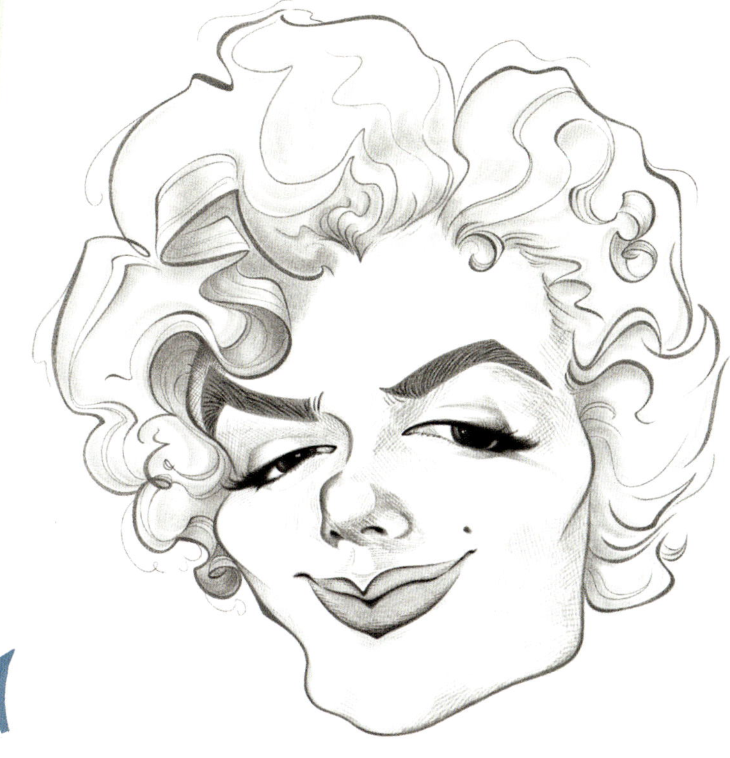

Don't forget to look for any beauty marks, smile lines, laugh lines, dimples, etc. I almost forgot her beauty mark!

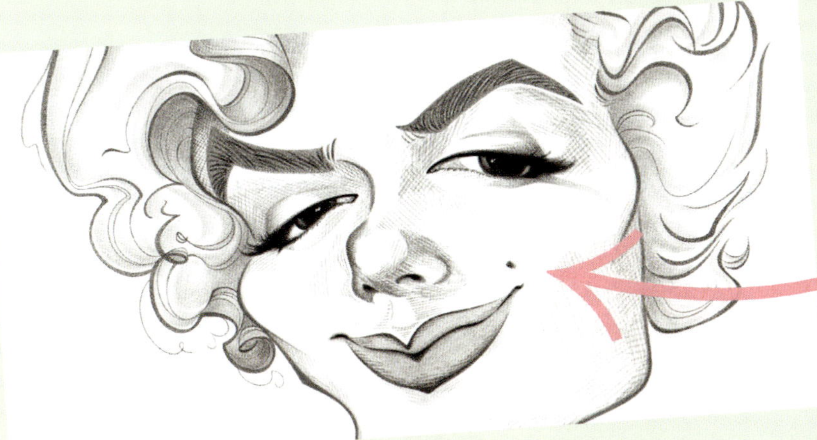

STEP 1: THUMBNAILS

The second person I'm demonstrating is the author, Mark Twain. He has such a unique face that naturally lends itself to caricature, and provides plenty of options to play around with. I mean, just look at his mustache and eyebrows!

The subject's hair definitely influenced the shape choices I made, so for the fifth sketch I tried to focus solely on his face and put his hair shape aside. If you find yourself getting too caught up in a specific feature, it can lead to a stagnation of ideas. When I find myself feeling stuck like this, I try to focus on another characteristic, such as the forehead shape, jaw size, or chin width and push that instead.

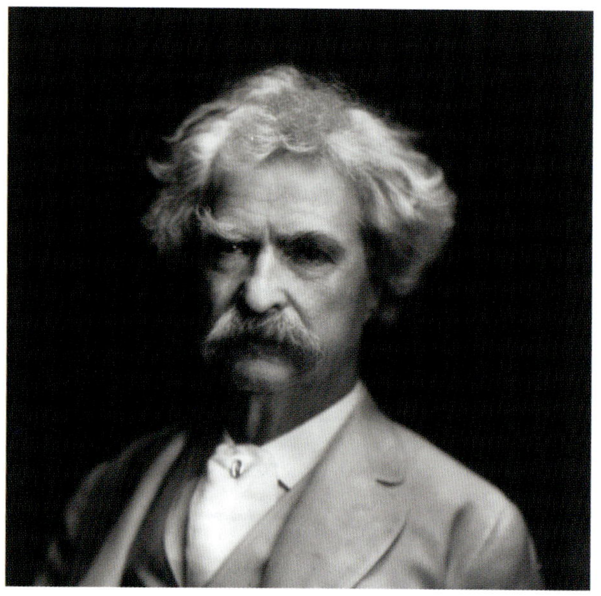

Library of Congress, LC-USZ62-28784

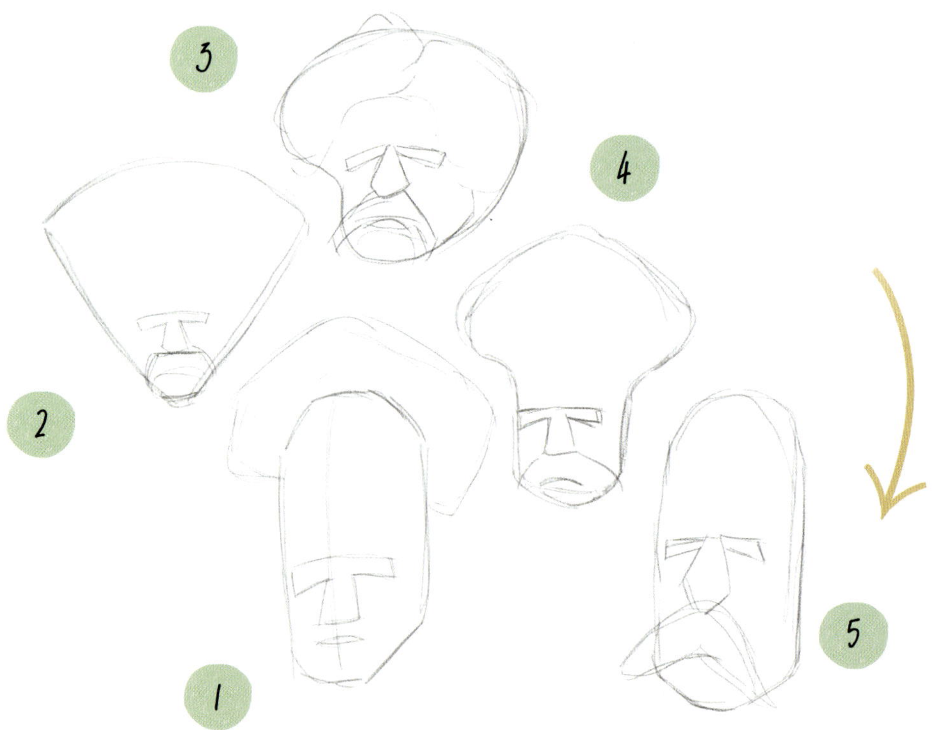

USE THE T-SHAPE

Another way to start is to utilize the T-shape in the face (where the eyes and nose sit) to place the features. As always, focus on the basic shapes first. Simplifying shapes is key to both drawing something accurately and exaggerating it. Ignore the details of the features until you've established those geometric shapes, and then plug in the details within those exaggerated shapes.

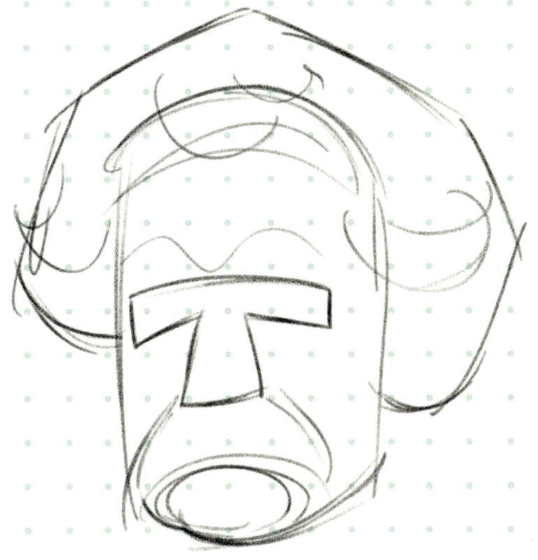

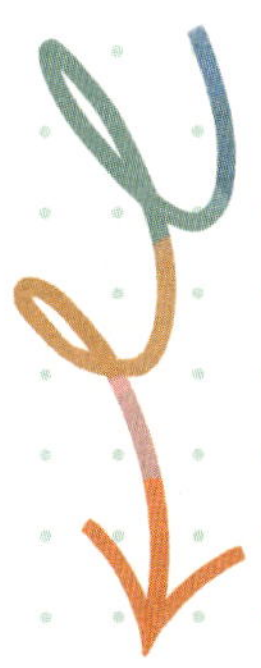

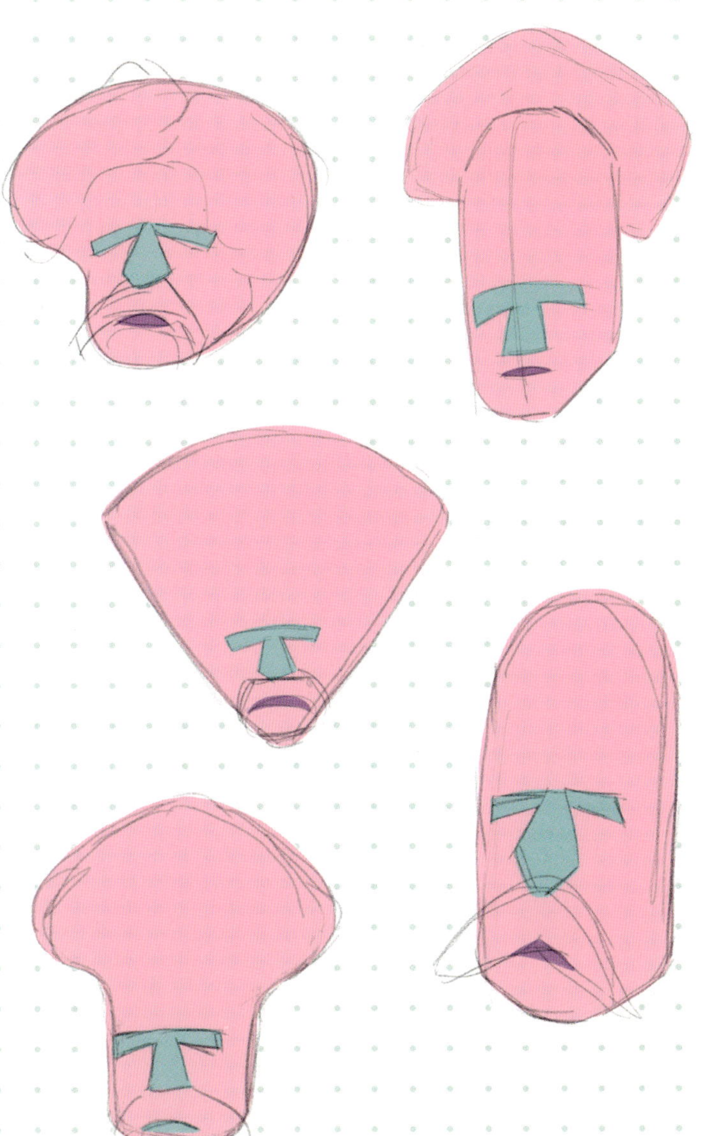

ARTIST INSIGHT

It can be helpful to draw a more accurate version and refer to it when drawing the rest. I'm so used to drawing from life (I majored in studio art in college and took many a figure drawing course!) that I have a tendency to draw proportionally: it's my natural instinct. So I use the more accurate sketch as a reminder of what not to do when drawing both the overall face and the T-shapes.

STEP 2: REFINE YOUR THUMBNAILS

Remember that the individual features deserve more attention in this step; also, this is the time to focus more closely on capturing the subject's likeness.

OBSERVATIONS

- Long, narrow face
- Narrow bridge of nose with wide end
- Nose ball that tilts downward
- Wide-set eyes
- Longer forehead than chin
- Heavy eyebrows and mustache
- Ears set low on his face

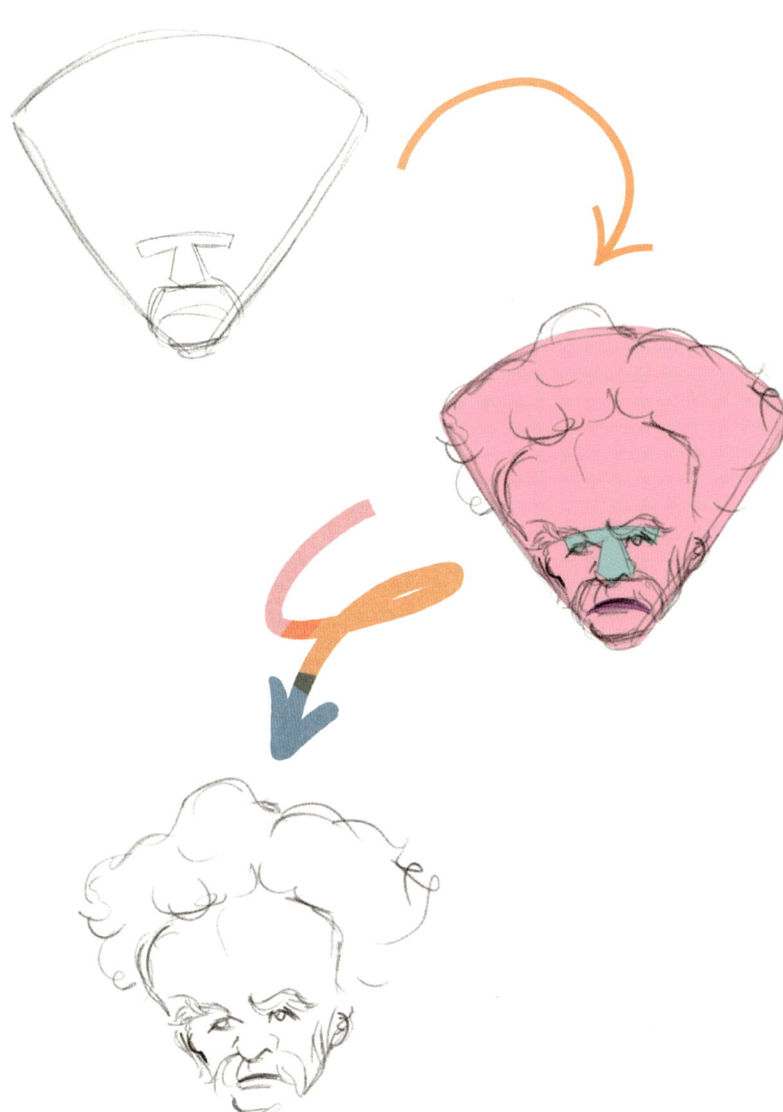

Because he has a prominent nose that is larger than the rest of his facial features, I found the T-shape technique particularly helpful for drawing Mark Twain. I was able to quickly establish his nose shape and build everything else around it with relative ease. It also served as a helpful reminder for the tilt of his eyes as I was drawing them. Anything you can do to remind yourself of your initial observations and the characteristics you want to explore is a good idea.

I learned something new about Mark Twain's face with each thumbnail I drew (right, numbered in the order I drew them), and I think the drawing improved with each consecutive design. The features became more and more specific with each version.

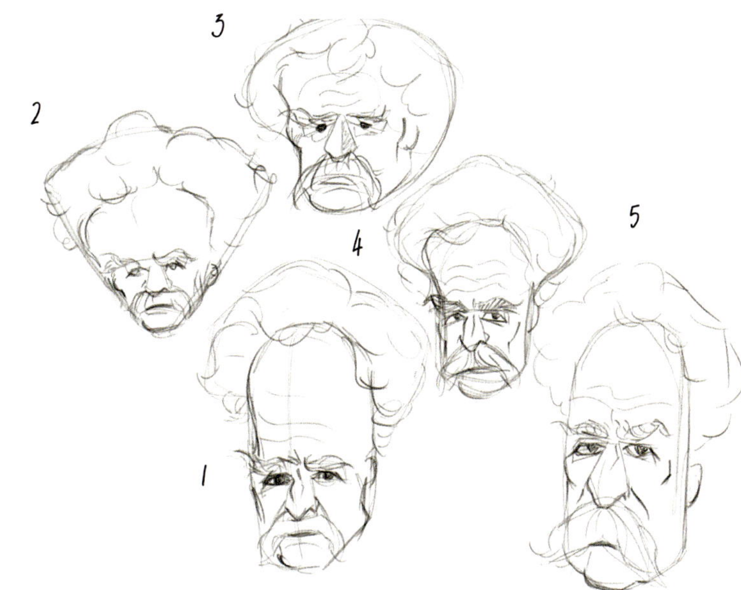

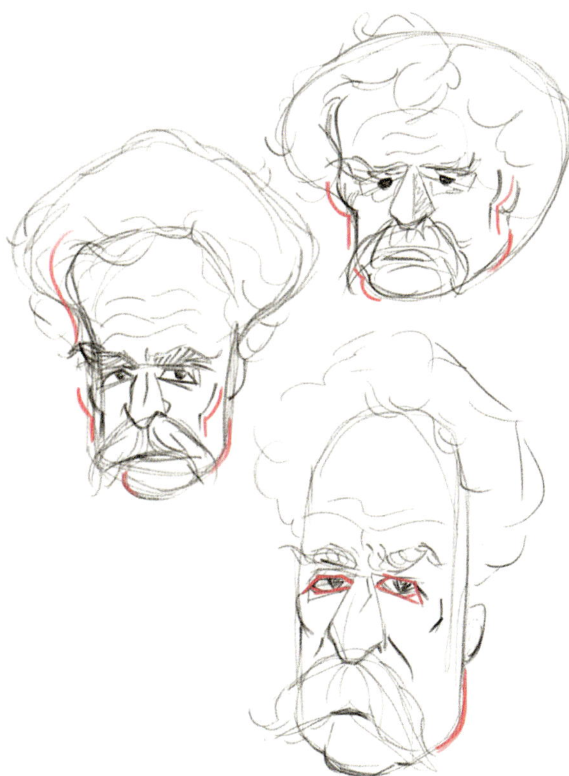

ARTIST INSIGHT

Another drawing illusion regarding the placement of features is that, even when drawn at the same exact width, placing the end of the nose closer to the eyes makes it appear wider than one drawn farther away. In other words, noses with a shorter bridge create the illusion that the end is wider.

Ultimately, I knew I wanted to explore this overall head shape, but just as with my thumbnail drawings of Marilyn Monroe, there were elements of most of these sketches that I liked: eyes from one, cheekbones from another, and so on.

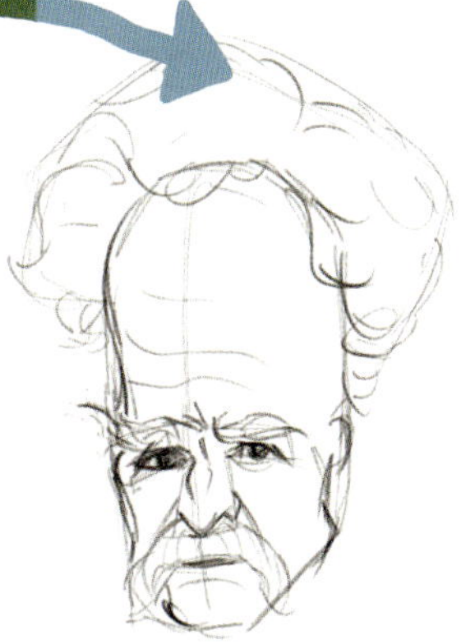

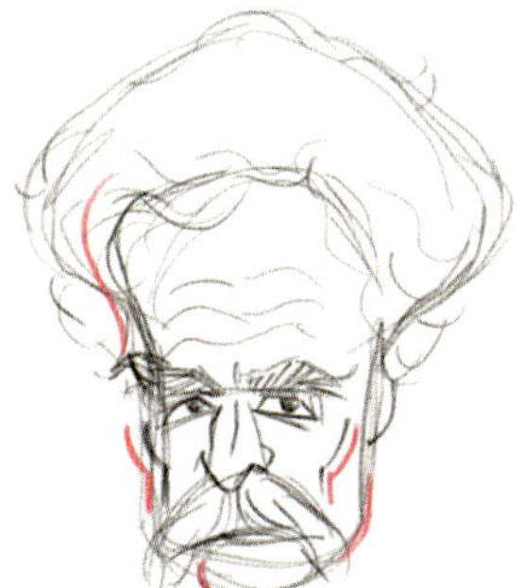

STEP 3: DRAW OVER THE TOP

The next step is to pick your favorite thumbnail and draw over the top of it, continuing to refine it as you work.

It was difficult to decide which thumbnail I wanted to develop further. I think both of these sketches are solid cartoon representations of the subject. Ultimately, I decided to progress with the larger sketch, but I think either could have made for a pretty decent caricature.

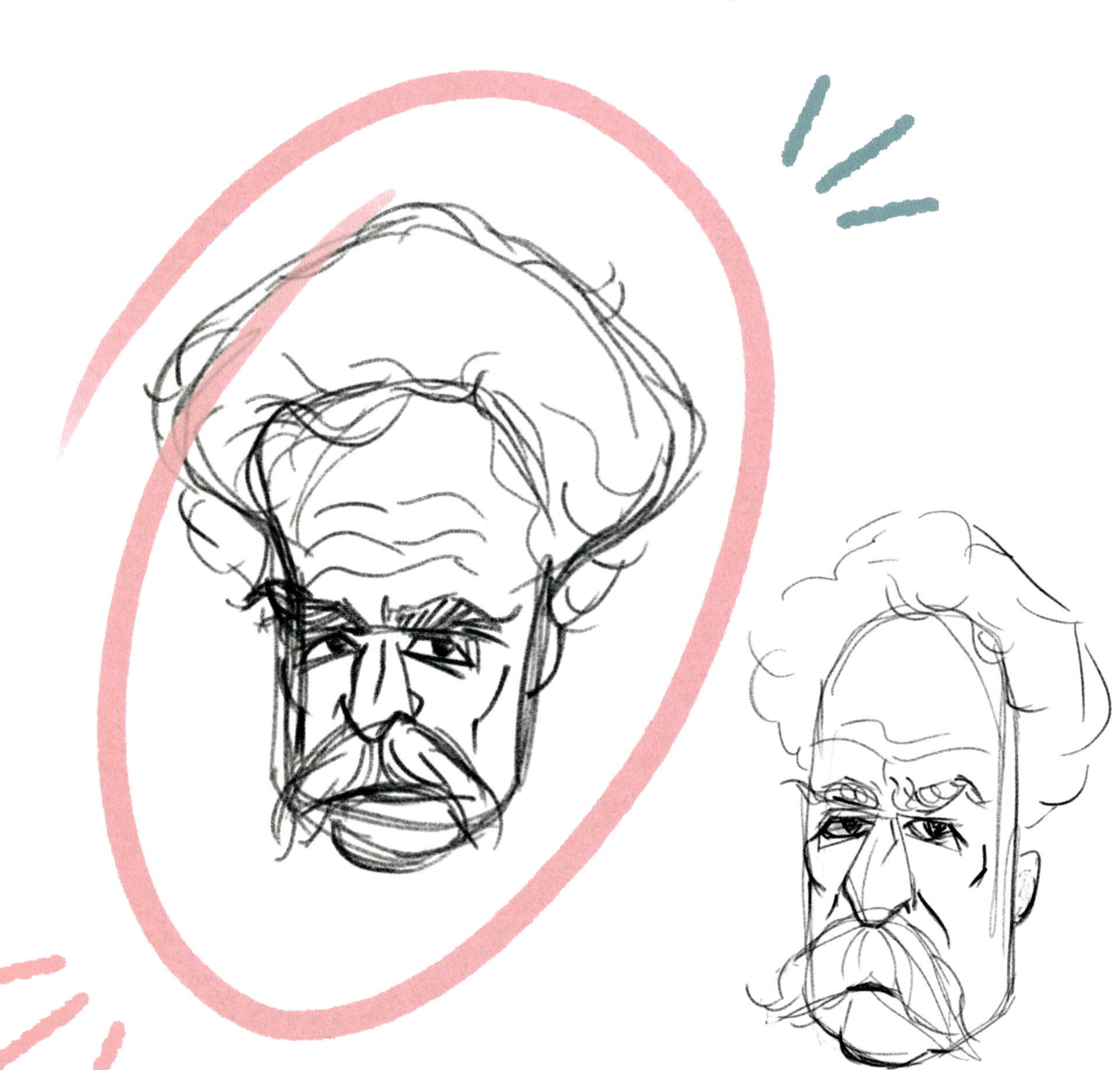

Something magical happens in this cycle of refinement and redrawing. Each time you trace over your work, you're not simply copying; you're making subtle decisions that strengthen the overall design. Plus, with each iteration, your hand becomes more confident, your lines more deliberate, and your exaggerations more purposeful.

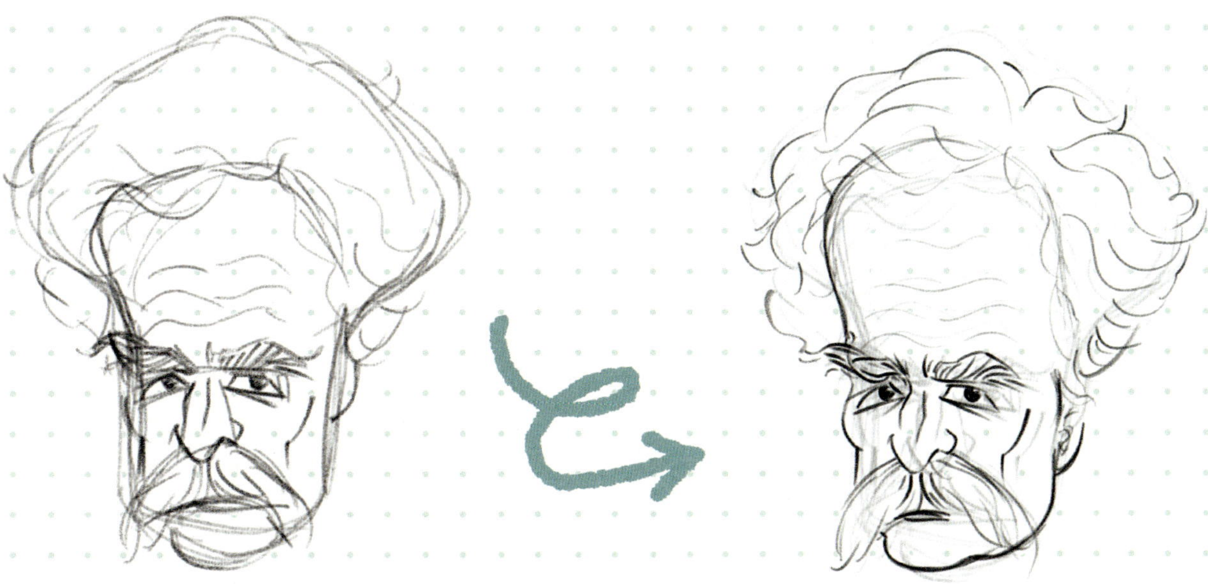

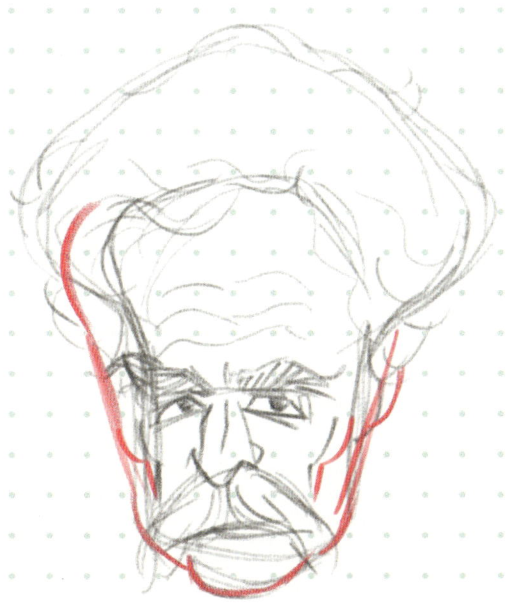

This iterative approach also allows you to gradually improve upon what works while quietly abandoning what doesn't. Unless they're doing live caricature, professional caricaturists and character designers rarely arrive at their strongest work on the first attempt; they understand that creative breakthroughs often come after pushing through resistance.

REDRAW, REDRAW, REDRAW

In my opinion, step 3 is the most tedious part of the process. There was a part of me that really wanted to start rendering a couple of the other thumbnail sketches I did. I was practically champing at the bit to get to that stage, but despite that, I knew deep down that I could push the design even further. I knew that I'd regret spending more time on those other sketches than I should. In my heart, I wasn't yet satisfied, so I made myself redraw it until I was.

The final drawing often appears spontaneous and effortless precisely because you've worked through the awkward stages privately in your earlier sketches. When you feel that urge to stop at "good enough," challenge yourself to redraw just once more.

It can be difficult to know when it's the right time to move forward with an idea, especially if you're a beginner, but the more you do it, the more you start to develop an instinct for it.

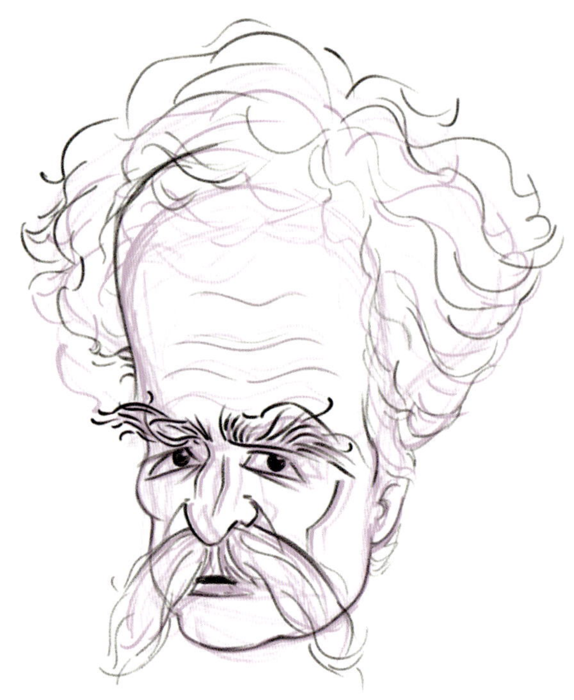

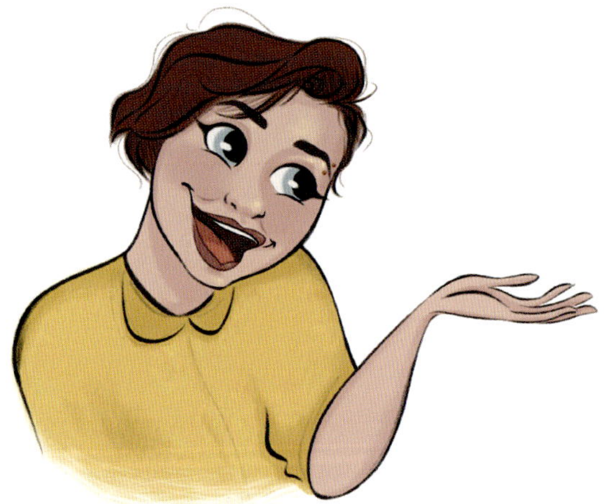

ARTIST INSIGHT

It's best not to tie down your design too quickly. You don't want to miss the opportunity to really explore. I used to jump right into drawing the details, I'd get really precious about my initial drawings, and have a hard time exploring and changing things. I'd also make construction mistakes that I didn't notice, and then I'd work on the detail and realize I had to redraw it, wasting all that time. At this stage, think of your drawings more as scribblings or notes that you're taking.

With each redraw, I raised his forehead higher and higher. It continues to retain his likeness, so I probably could have pushed it even further!

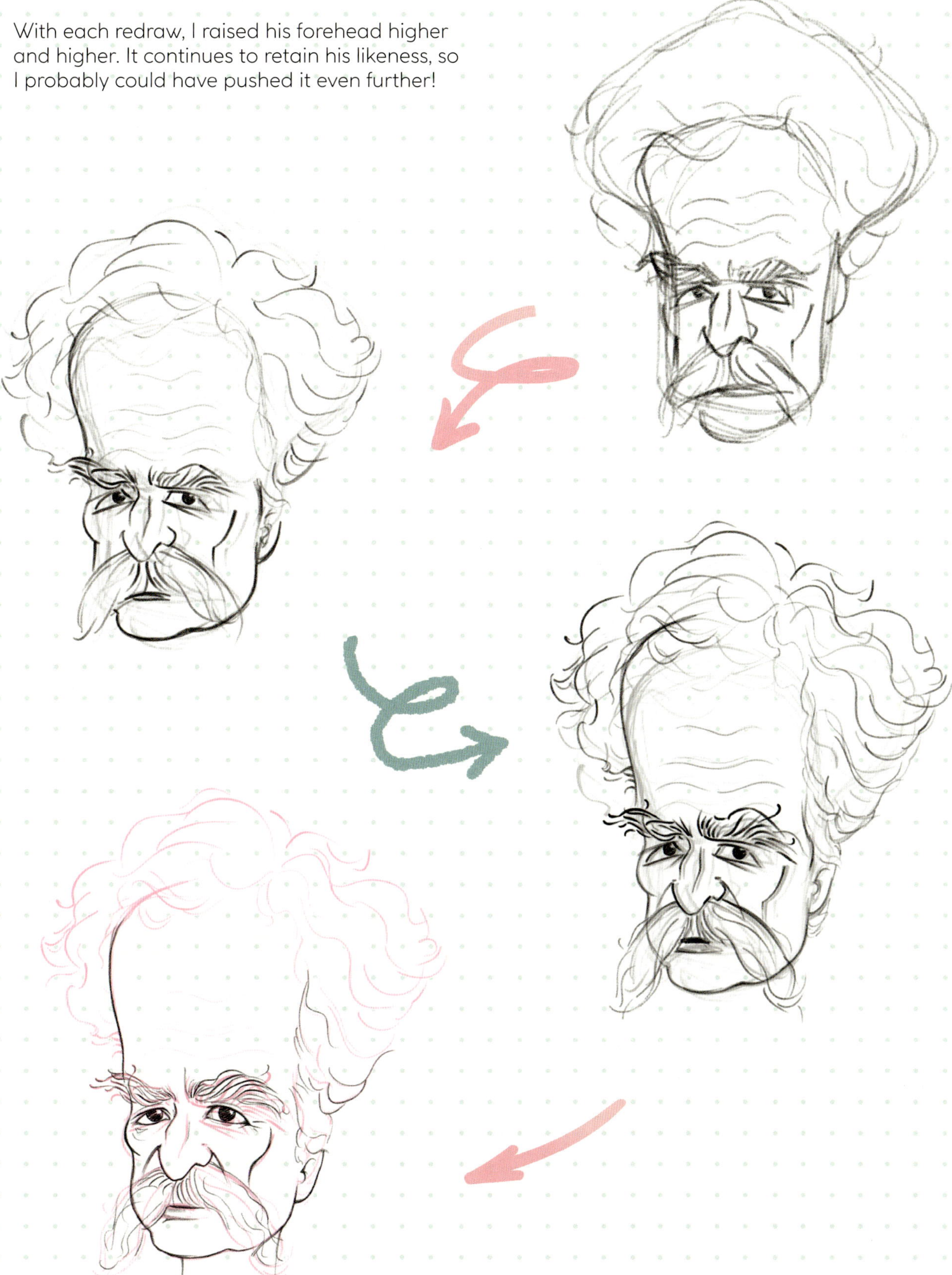

STEP 4: RENDER & REFINE

My final sketch for this caricature is simpler and more stylized than my final sketch of Marilyn Monroe, but funnily enough, I decided to render this one with even more detail and aimed for a higher level of realism.

ANATOMICAL ACCURACY

I decided to challenge myself to build realistically rendered facial features on top of the stylization. I studied my reference and followed the natural contours of the face—around the curve of the cheeks, along the bridge of the nose, and around the spherical form of the eyes—but I did so by also using the stylized shapes of my under drawing as guides.

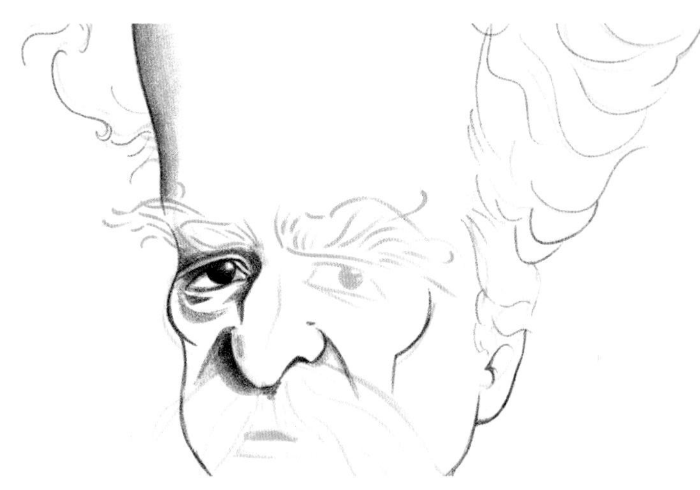

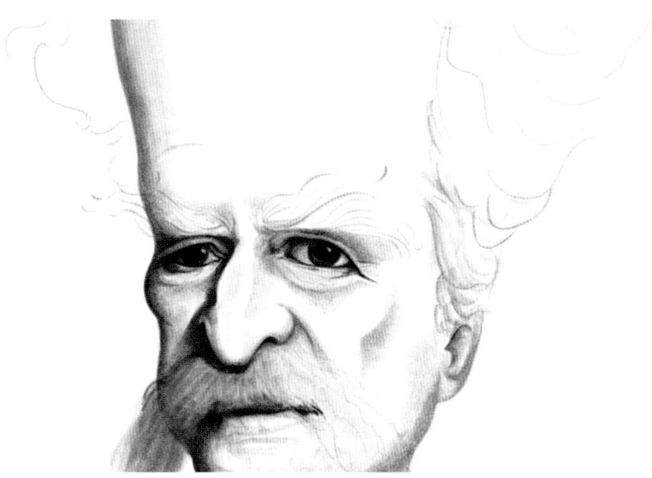

I meticulously followed the anatomical reality of Mark Twain's face, doing my best to capture all of the nuanced details and true-to-life textures (note the wrinkles and freckles) that contribute to its authenticity. The shading follows every contour and plane shift across his features. The proportional distortions convey Twain's essence while the anatomical accuracy grounds the caricature in some level of believability.

EFFECTIVE SHADING

Mastering realistic shading with graphite begins with understanding the full range of values your pencil can create. Start with a light touch, gradually building up layers of graphite rather than immediately pressing hard for dark areas. Layers are everything! Layering your shading creates rich, dimensional shadows with subtle transitions. Work systematically from light to dark, preserving your highlights by leaving the paper untouched in these areas. Most dry media digital brushes, like pencil and charcoal brushes, have transparency built into their functionality, so all of this applies to digital drawing as well.

For smooth blending, you have the option of using tools like blending stumps or tortillons for soft transitions, or simply using your finger for larger areas. If you're working digitally like I am, you can use the smudging tool.

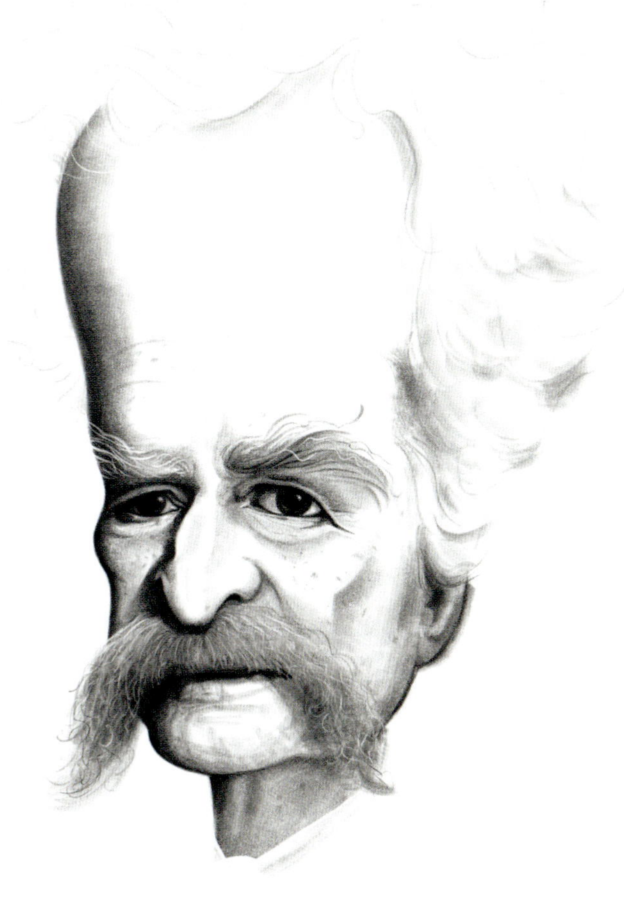

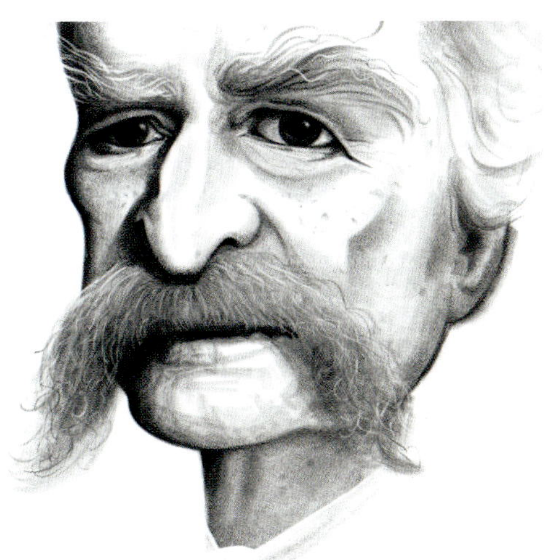

ARTIST INSIGHT

If you're working traditionally with pencil and paper, remember that graphite has a natural shine when heavily applied, so avoid making your darkest areas too dense, or they'll reflect light and appear lighter than intended.

THE FINAL STAGES

I decided to change my background color to a dark gray (I'm working digitally) to make the white of Mark Twain's hair and mustache pop against the dark background. Because of this, I drew in his hair in white and let the background gray filter through the semi-transparent pencil brush I used.

If I had drawn this on a white piece of paper, I would have done what I did with the mustache, which was to draw in the gray first and then use a combination of a white pencil or Conté crayon along with my eraser to draw in or erase white hairs over the gray. I had a lot of fun with drawing details in the hair. I added way more flyaways than I do for more simple caricatures.

The tiny, chaotic lines to represent the frizz of his mustache were particularly fun to draw!

Did this process take a long time? Yes, it did. I spent a good six to eight hours carefully shading this. But was it worth it? Absolutely, yes.

ARTIST INSIGHT

We don't just see the world in outlines; we see it in shapes of light and dark tones. If you squint your eyes and still see a likeness in just the light and dark tones, you know your design is strong.

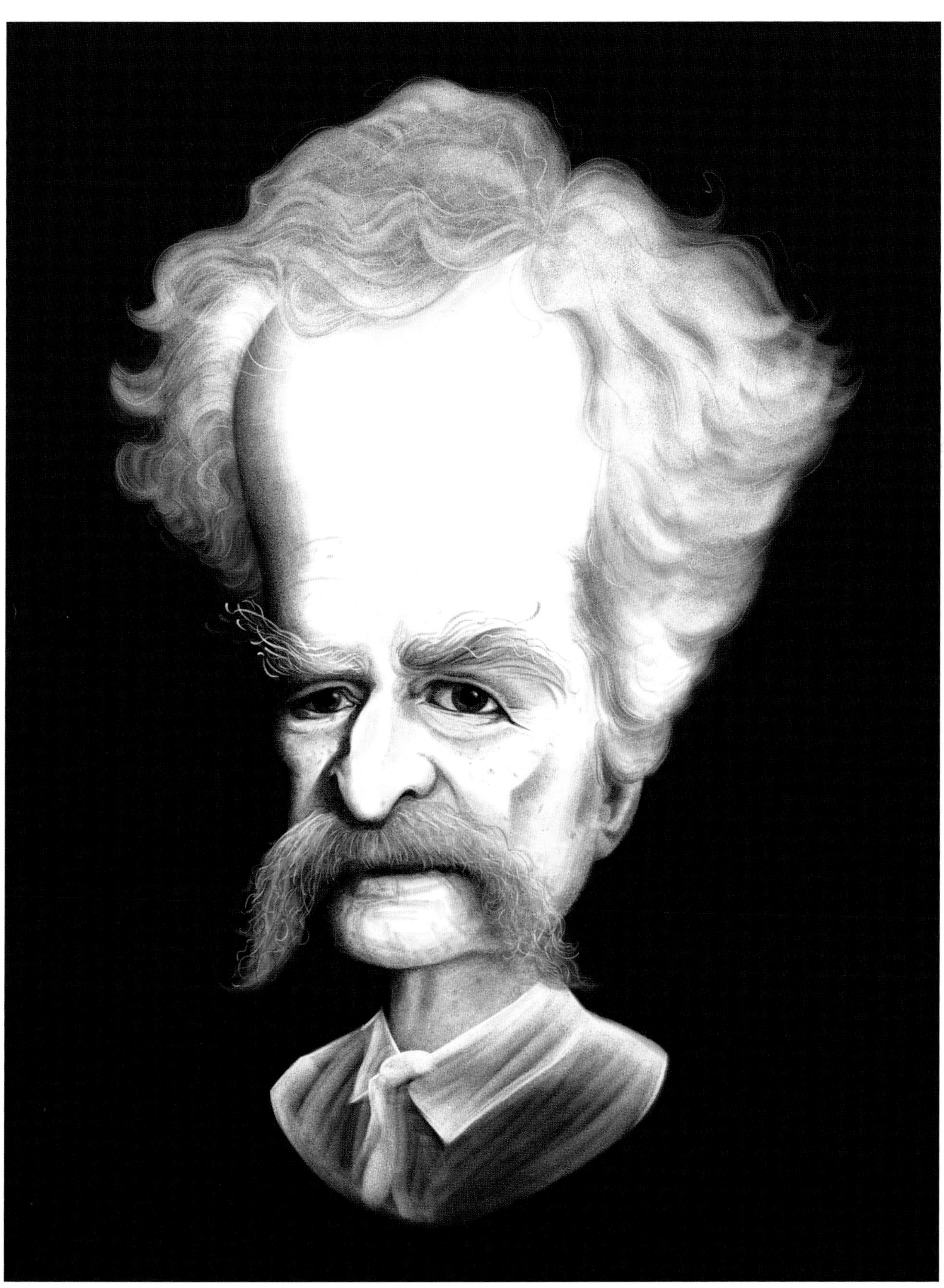

CARICATURE A LIVE ACTION FICTIONAL CHARACTER

In this chapter, we'll look at the intersection of caricature and character design, and I'll be showing you how to cartoon-ify a live-action fictional character and yourself! The secret sauce that makes for great characters is actually pretty similar to what we've been doing with caricature, i.e., identifying key features and capturing personality. In this chapter, I'll break down the fundamentals and walk you through transforming your own likeness into a cartoon character. The cool thing is, once you can cartoon yourself, you can apply these same principles to create all kinds of original characters with personality and impact.

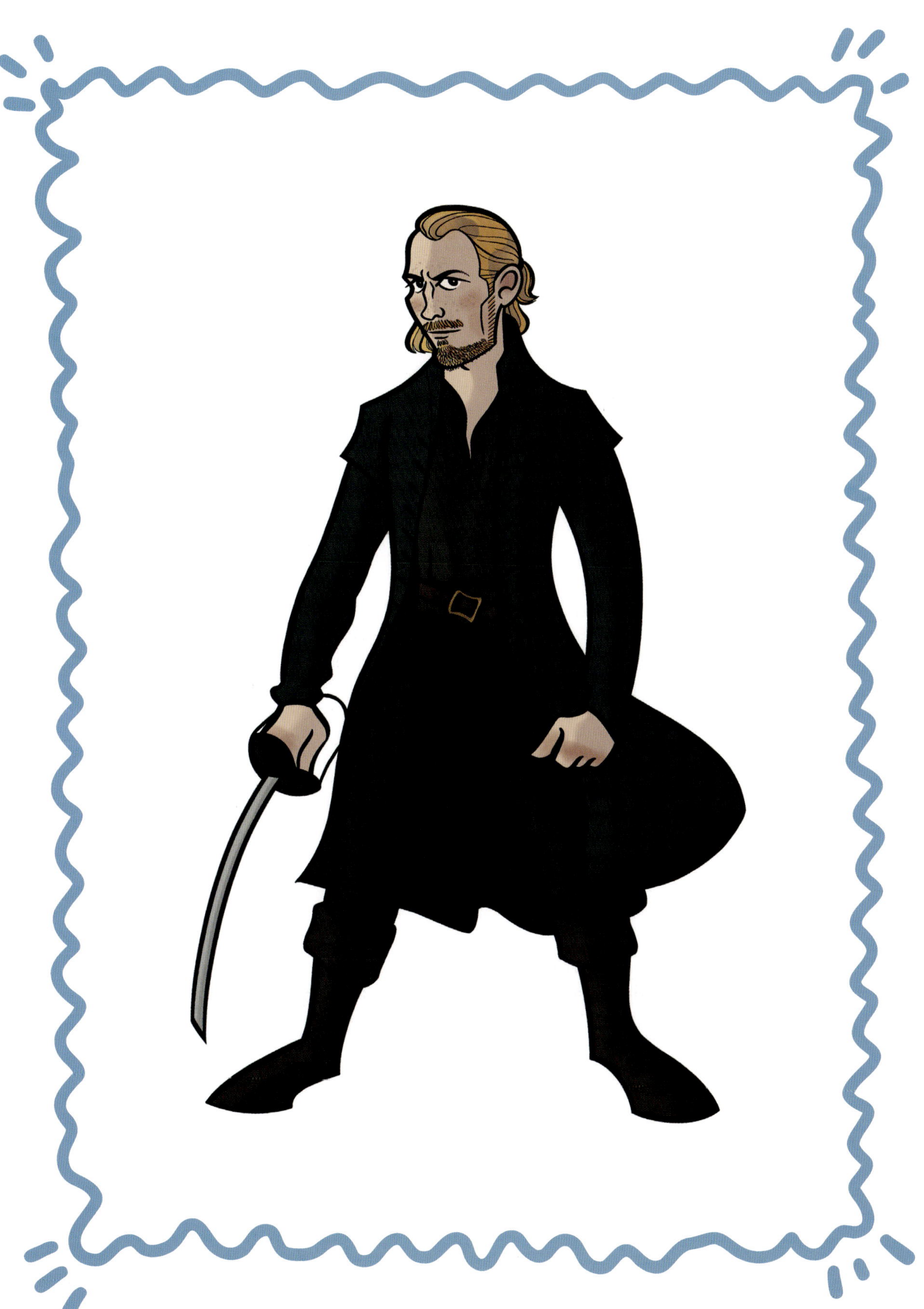

CHARACTER DESIGN FUNDAMENTALS

Naturally, we've focused on faces for the majority of this book. I now want to briefly touch on some of the basic landmarks of the average human body. This will help you understand the construction and proportion of the figure.

The diagram (right) illustrates the proportions of an average adult human figure. When in profile, there are some angles that you may not be aware of that you should keep in mind, particularly the tilt of the rib cage and the hips.

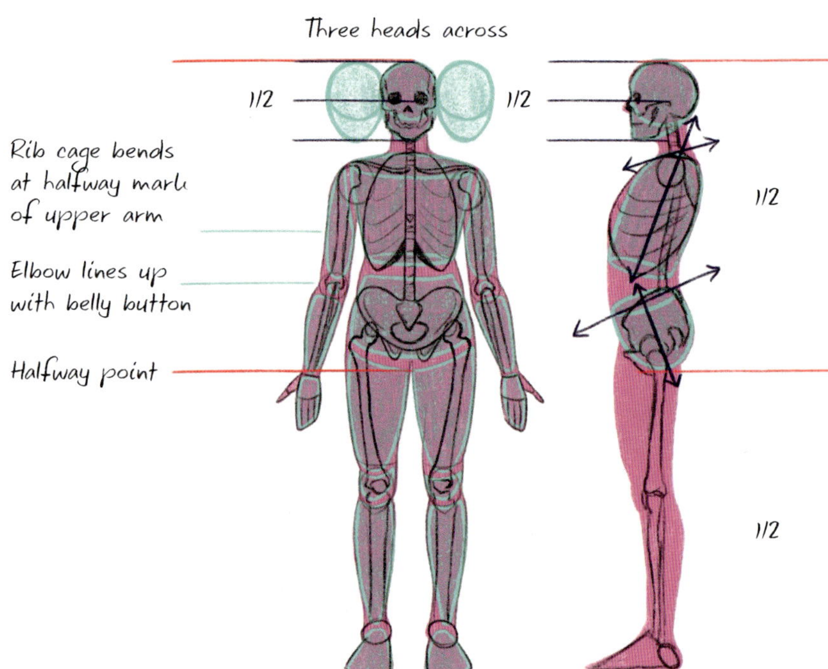

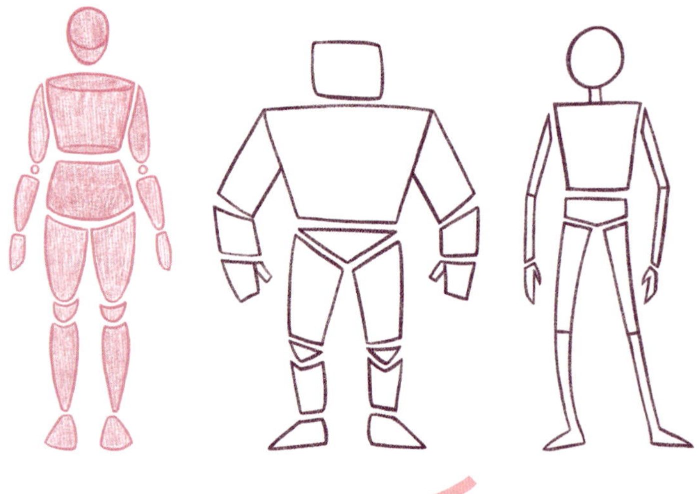

Just like with caricature, when cartooning, you will break a lot of these rules of anatomy, but it's important to keep them in mind. In the illustration (left) the pink figure on the left represents an average, proportionate figure broken down into simple shapes, while the figures on the right are stylized representations based on the first figure. I was able to create them relatively easily by applying my knowledge of proportionate figures to help inform my stylization choices.

SILHOUETTE AND TANGENTS

Drawings need to be clear and easily interpretable and one way to ensure that is to pay close attention to the silhouette. A clear silhouette—the outline or shape of an object or figure—makes your work much easier to understand at a glance, and effective character design makes use of silhouette in a highly readable way. A great example of this is Pokémon. If you search "Pokémon silhouettes," online, you'll see what I mean. If you are at all familiar with these characters, you can probably identify many just from their silhouettes alone. Take Pikachu's distinctive zigzag tail, for example!

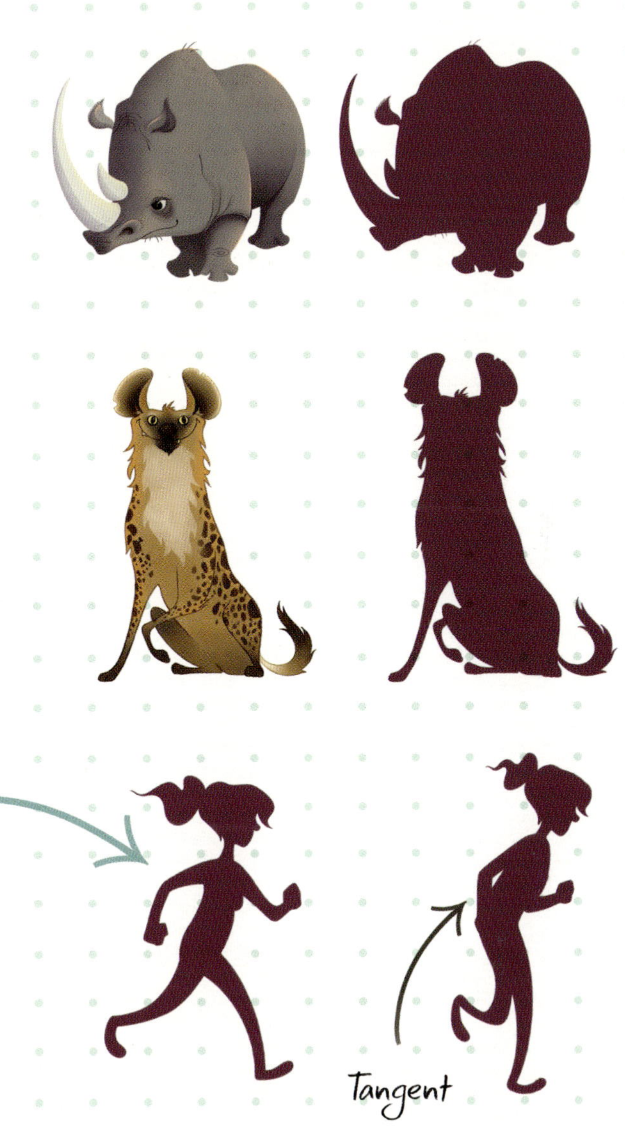

Silhouette also helps with creating successful poses. If the action is clear in the silhouette alone, the pose will automatically be stronger. The silhouette on the left works because there is more negative space. You immediately understand what the character is doing without the need for any other context clues. The silhouette on the right, however, is unclear. The figure's arms and legs are bunched together awkwardly, making it confusing to look at and much less visually appealing.

Tangents occur when two or more shapes or lines touch in a way that is visually bothersome. In the silhouette on the right, the point where the arm meets the lower back is creating a tangent, making it appear as though the arm blends into the thigh. There's a visual tension there, created by the tangent, that you should aim to avoid.

ARTIST INSIGHT

The key is keeping your poses open and easy to read. When the silhouette tells the story, your art is much stronger!

VARIATION

Variation in design is really important, as variety automatically makes things more interesting to look at. The four key elements of variety are size, color, shape, and rhythm.

The top row of sketches on the right are examples of what not to do! Below are some really simple examples of how varying your size and shape can create more visual interest.

Rhythm in design is essentially what makes your eye move across an image. Rhythm is, in part, created by variety, through contrasting angles, straights against curves, wide and narrow, large and small, light and dark, and so on. Contrasting these things builds visual interest and appeal.

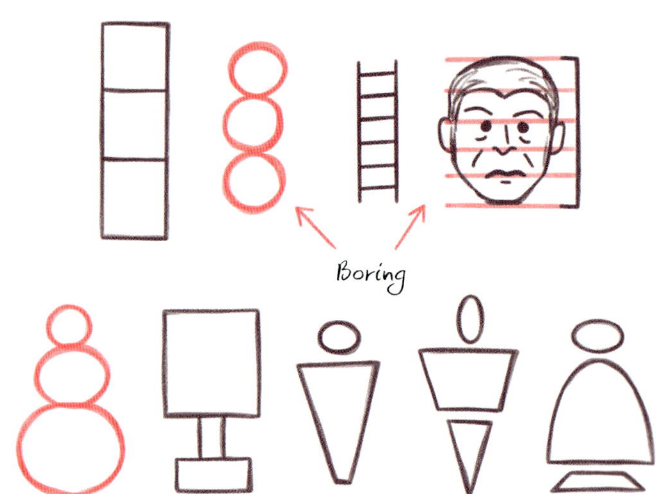

AVOIDING THE BOWLING BALL AND THE LADDER

These are concepts that I learned from Stephen Silver. The bowling ball effect mostly applies to the face and it happens when the features of the head and face are the exact same size and shape and it's, frankly, boring to look at. You can avoid the bowling ball by varying the size and position of the eyes and nose. In the example (right), the first character has big eyes and a small nose, and the second has the opposite. The bear's ears are also small, but the eyes and ears are different shapes, so there's still that appealing variety there.

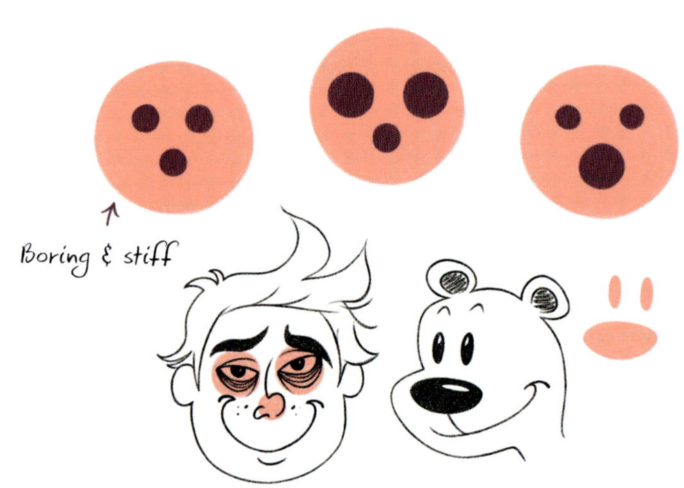

This occurs in nature, too! Mouse lemurs, margays, and tarsier monkeys are a few of my favorite animals with big eyes and teeny tiny noses. Do yourself a favor and image search them! The variety in their little faces is part of what makes them so interesting (and adorable) to look at.

The ladder refers to when everything is parallel, equidistant, and the exact same size. Our bodies actually have a lot of natural rhythm, and you want to try to take advantage of that.

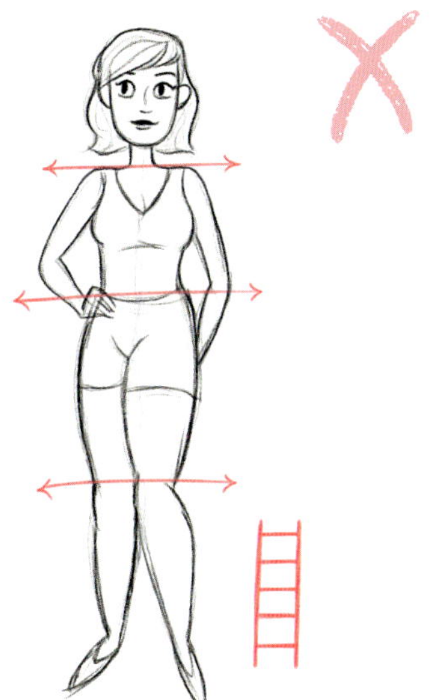

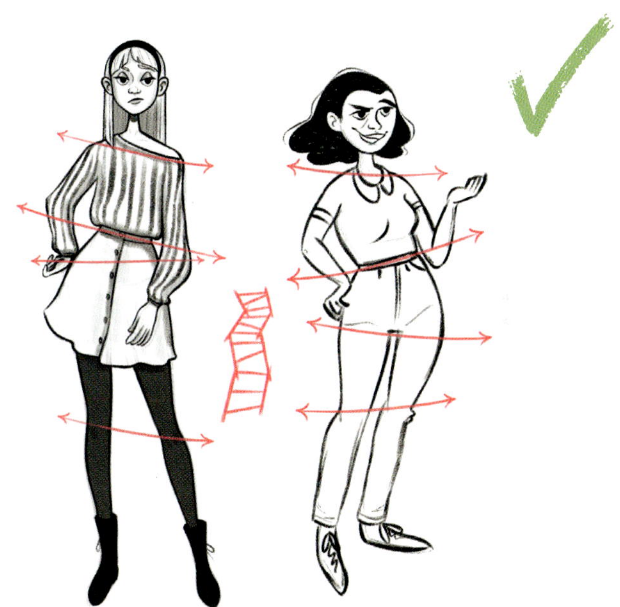

BROOKE GLASER

Brooke Glaser is an artist who is excellent at creating a lot of appealing variety in her work, particularly through her shape language and color choices. Her palette here is thoughtfully limited to just blues, reds, oranges, browns, and yellow-greens, but because she uses a range of tints, tones, and shades of each color, plus a mix of saturated (pure pigment) and desaturated (more gray) hues, there's plenty of contrast, variety, and visual appeal. Her use of contrasting straight and curved lines adds a lot of appeal as well.

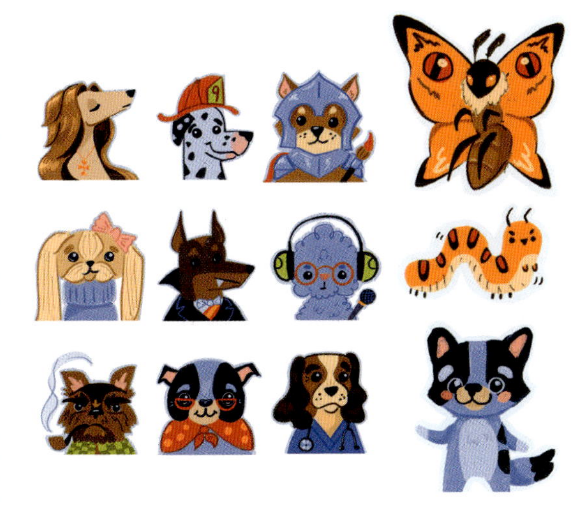

Brooke Glaser (2025, February), video game characters

CONTRASTING STRAIGHT & CURVED LINES

Juxtaposing straight and curved lines and shapes adds a ton of visual appeal to your artwork.

One thing you want to avoid is drawing what I like to call the "Sausage Man," which is what happens when there are too many curves against curves. It ends up looking a bit like the Michelin Man. That's not to say that I think the Michelin Man is bad design; it's not! But that's because it is done with intention. Generally, when it comes to building a character, it's much more visually appealing to juxtapose straight lines adjacent to or across from curves.

As always, though, there are exceptions to the rule. For this little guy, I've ignored it and done just the opposite. I've created little sausage-shaped legs. It's appropriate for a baby because of their adorable, pudgy limbs.

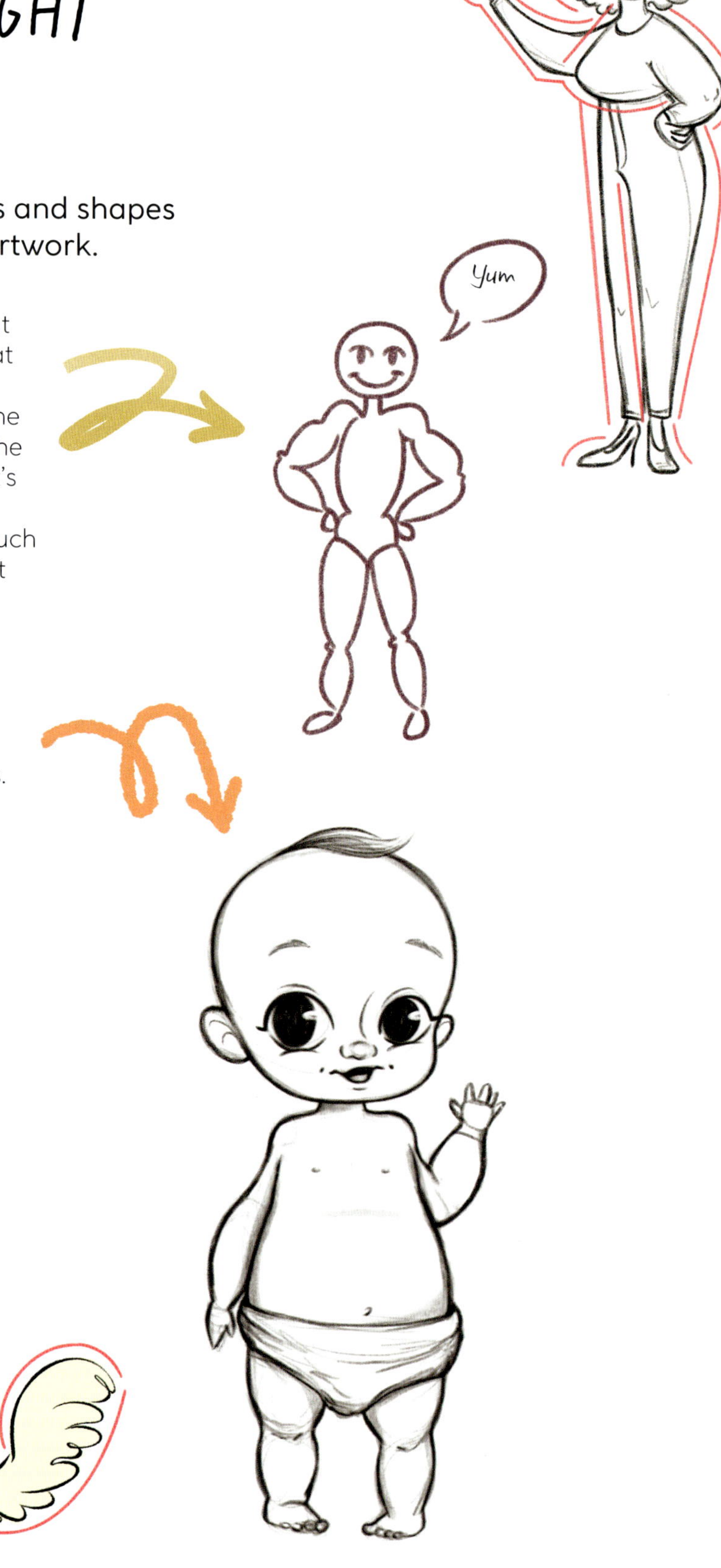

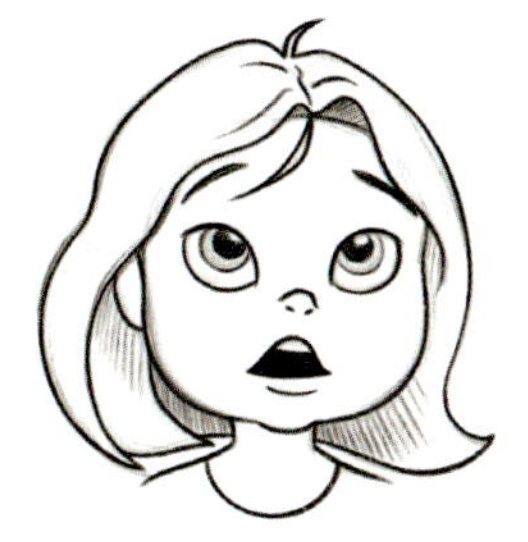

THE EMOTIONAL QUALITY OF SHAPES & LINES

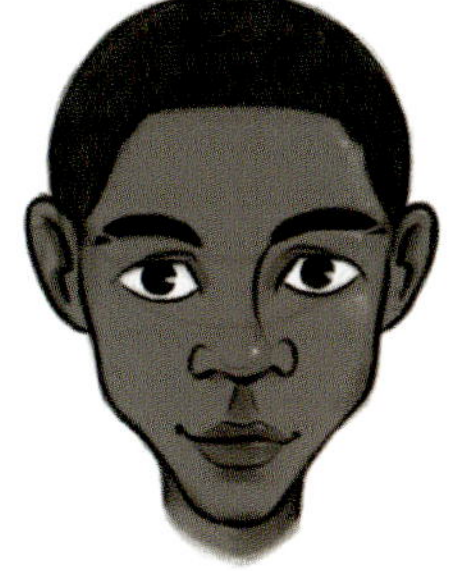

Shapes and lines can evoke a feeling or emotional response. Sharp, harsh lines and shapes can feel intimidating and scary, while rounded, curved shapes tend to feel more harmless, soft, and safe.

For example, we know that sharp, jagged objects like thorns and broken glass can cut and cause pain, so those qualities in drawings automatically convey a sense of danger. This is why cute character design tends to use a lot of rounded shapes. Smooth and fluid lines feel safe and comforting.

Additionally, because our faces become more angular as we grow older and lose our baby fat, soft, rounded features tend to age characters down, while sharper features age characters up.

PROPORTION AND PLACEMENT

The proportions of the shapes you use play a significant role as well. For example, you can instantly age a character up or down by changing their proportions. The younger you want your character to appear, the smaller the head-to-body ratio should be. Part of the reason why the boy on the left looks young is because his head is nearly the same height as his body i.e. his head-to-body ratio is 1⅓.

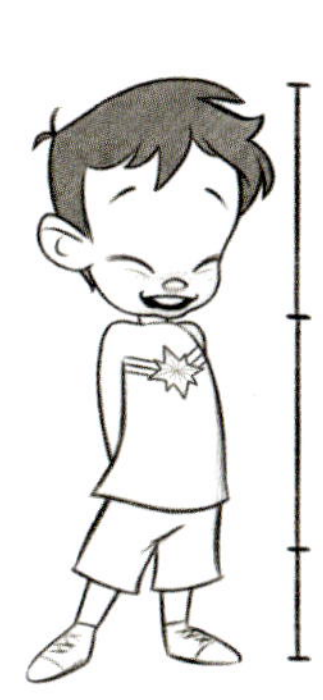

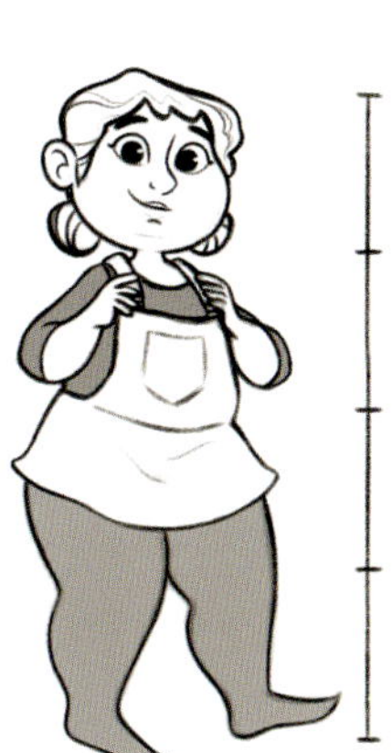

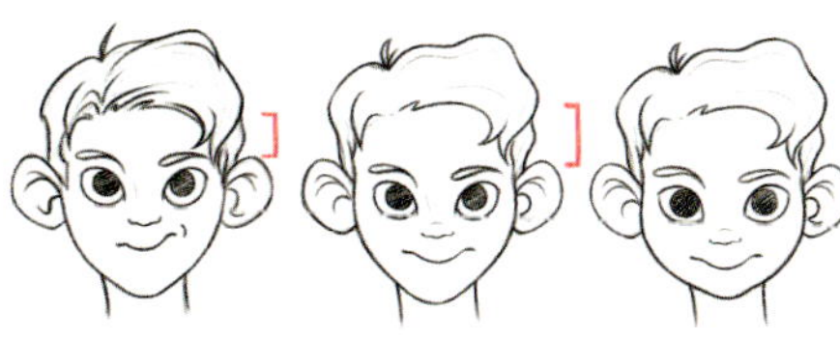

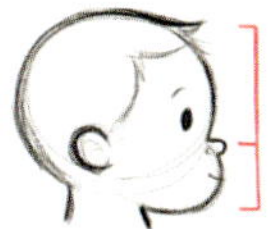
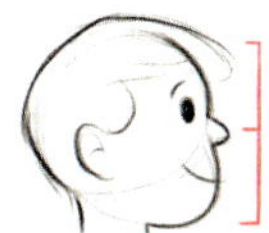
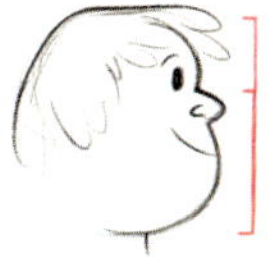

Changes in feature placement can affect a character's perceived age too. Lowering all the facial features, as shown in the two right-hand drawings of the boy, ages a character down. In the third drawing, I also shortened the chin and widened the cheeks, but in the middle drawing, all I did was move the features down. This is because larger foreheads, fuller cheeks, and smaller chins will help make characters look younger. Placement is also important in profile view and works similarly in both complex and simpler design.

CARICATURE YOUR CHOSEN CHARACTER

In this exercise, we will turn a live-action character into a cartoon. I have chosen the character Captain James Flint from my favorite TV show, *Black Sails*. The goal is still to represent their likeness, just in a very stylized, simplified way.

1. I start by creating several quick, rough studies of the character/actor's face, exploring as many angles as I can find reference photos of: profile, front-facing, three-quarter, you name it. The idea is to get a good handle on their features, instead of just going with your first pass. As I've said before, the first attempt is often not the best one.

   Focus on identifying and emphasizing their distinctive features and the shapes that define them. In these studies, I noted a couple of Captain Flint's key features: his eyes slant downward on the outsides; the bridge of his nose is an interesting diamond shape. I took these observations and used them in each consecutive sketch. My final sketch (circled) is my favorite.

   My aim was to achieve a more cartoony look compared to my previous caricatures, so with the final sketches, I made an effort to stick to simpler lines and shapes that are more representational rather than realistic. I was also not overly concerned with exaggeration. This style, while not easier than caricatures, is certainly a lot simpler.

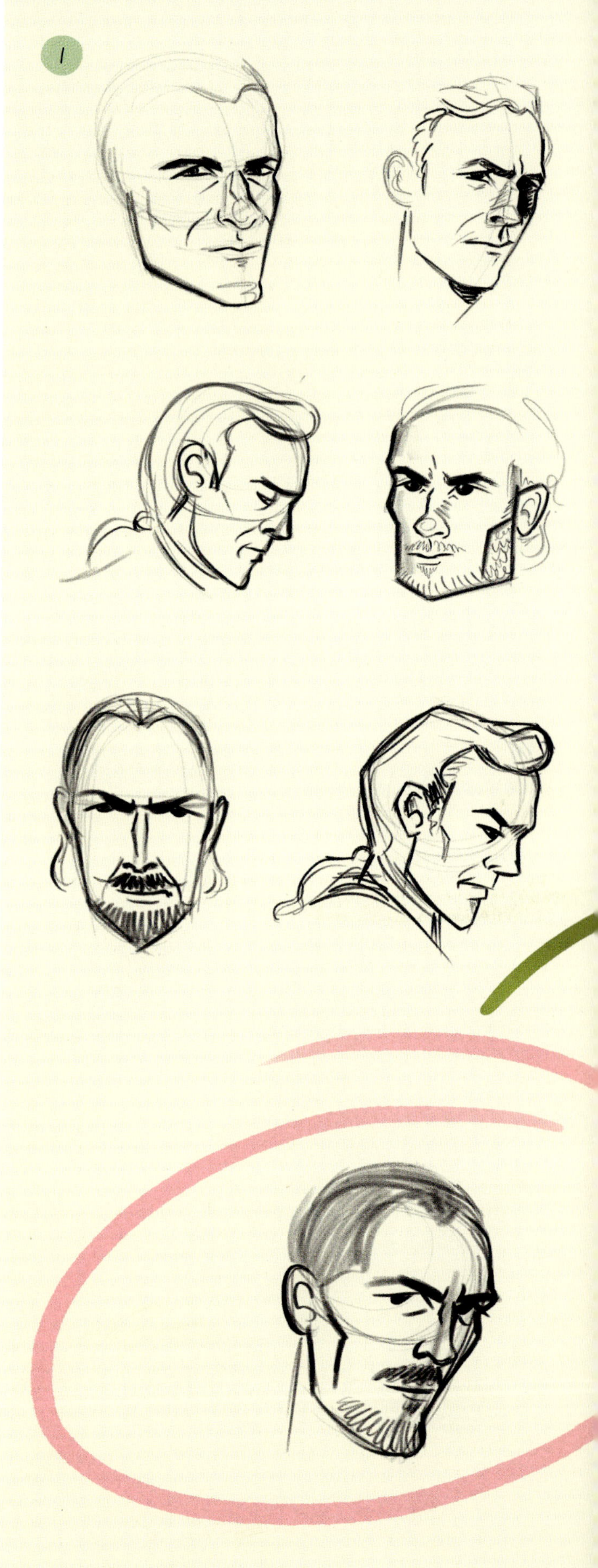

2. Next, draw rough pose sketches. I sometimes start by drawing a series of quick silhouettes then, once I feel satisfied with the direction, I move on to a rough figure sketch. I often have to do a few layers before I feel comfortable moving on to detail and line work. Full disclosure, I still struggle with full-body poses because I don't draw them as often as I draw faces. This design wasn't easy for me to land on, but I pushed through! I've learned to appreciate this struggle because it signifies my improvement. If everything were easy, I wouldn't be growing as much.

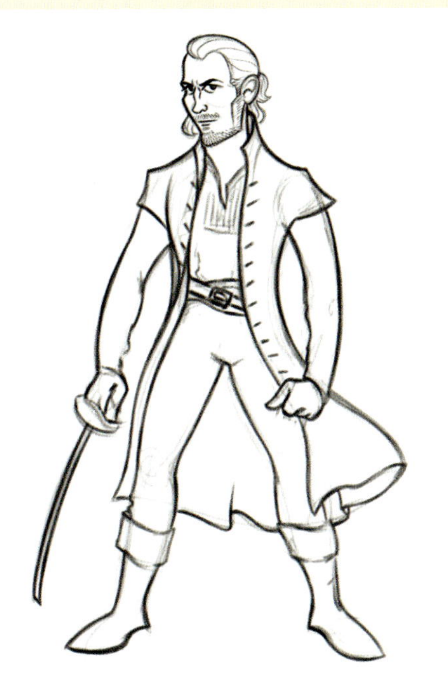

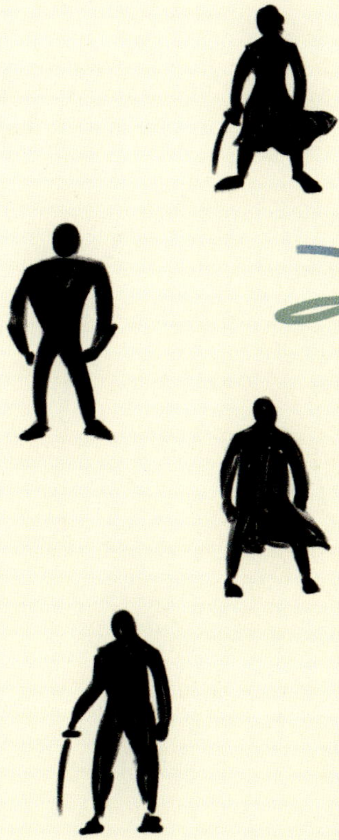

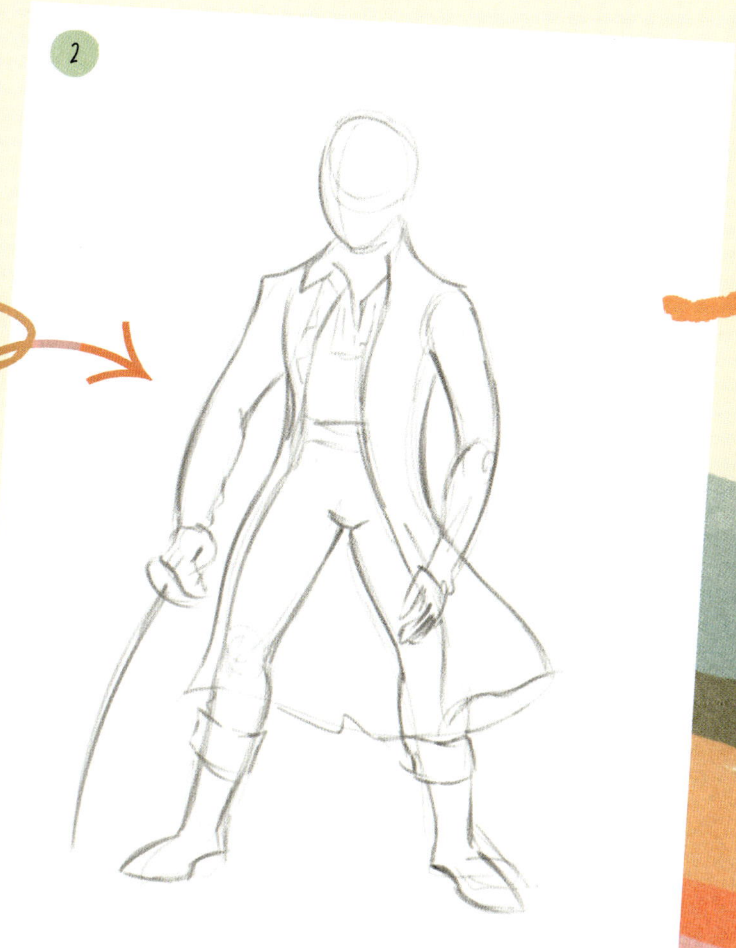

3. It's time for line work! Captain Flint has somewhat sharp features. I decided that I wanted to emphasize that in his cheekbones, brow ridge, nose, and jaw. I pushed the sharpness even further with these clean, solid, angular lines.

   Whether working traditionally or digitally, it's important to maintain a consistent line weight throughout your drawing. Be intentional with your line work and make sure that your lines are either the same width or that they all taper similarly. If you're going to use different thicknesses, they need to make sense within the context of the drawing. For example, detail lines, like the lines in the face and hair, are slightly thinner than the lines that make up the body but they still maintain a consistent thickness within the face and hair. I decided to make the overall outline slightly thicker than the rest because I think it creates a nice effect. If I made just one or two random lines thicker, it would look off.

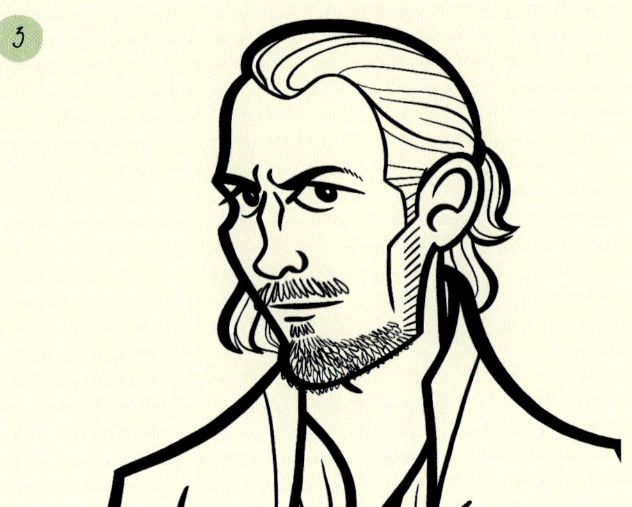

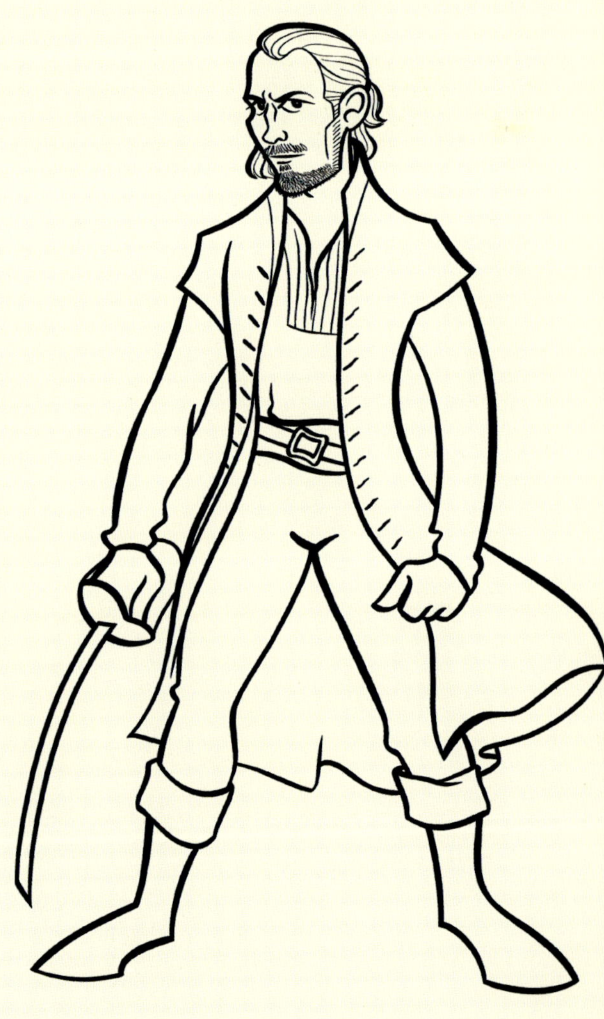

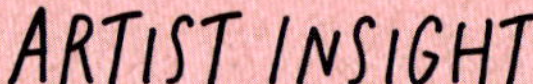

Since this is live-action we're talking about, it's helpful to watch video of the character so that you can better understand their movement, body language, mannerisms, expressions, and personality. After all, you're trying to capture their personality!

4. For the color, I just laid down flat colors pulled from various screen shots of the show and used slightly darker versions of each color for the shading. Ta-da!

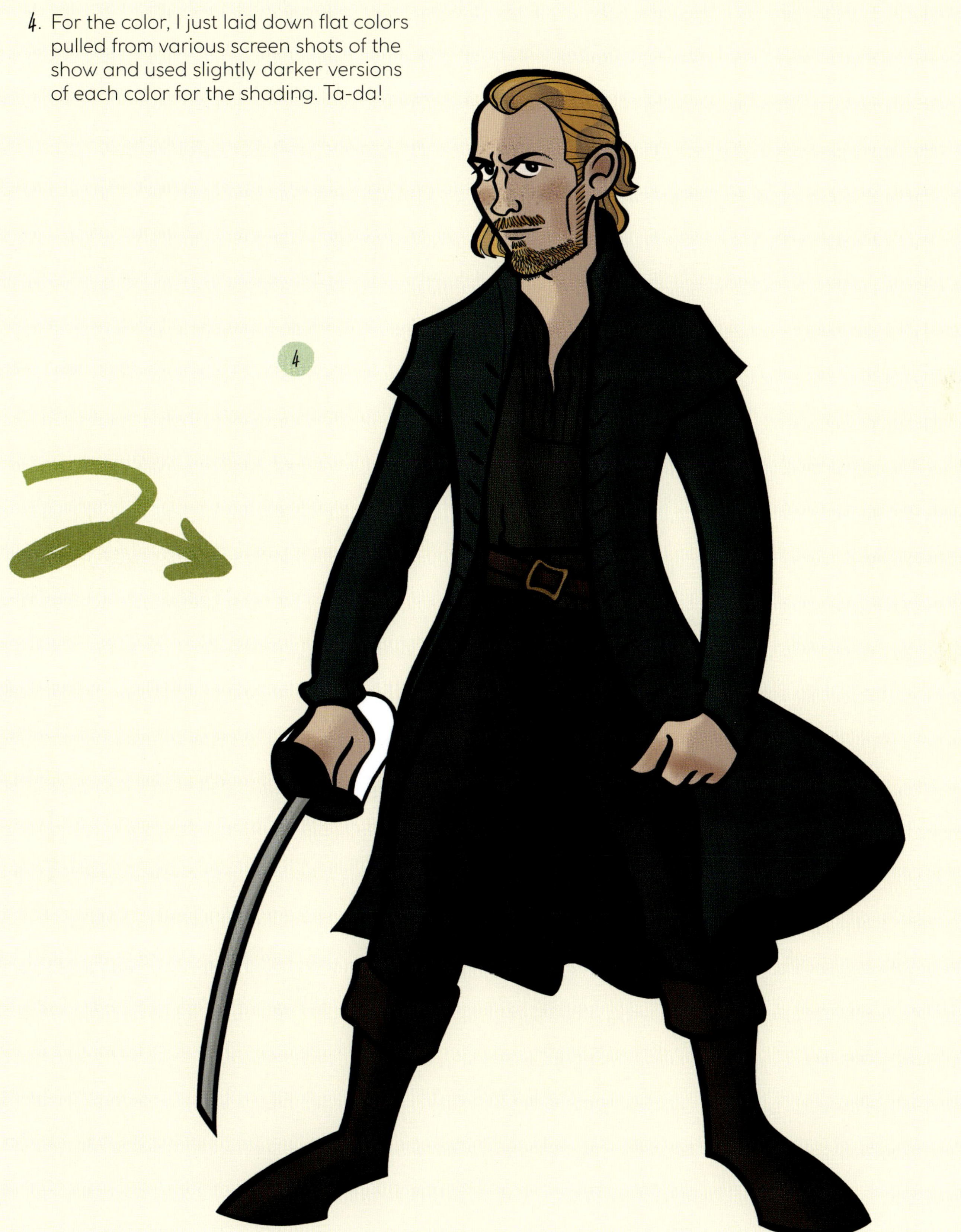

TURN YOURSELF INTO A CARTOON!

In this exercise, I studied and identified the shapes, spacing, and proportion of my own features and the different sections of my face and then experimented with caricaturing and cartooning it.

The drawing on the left could really be pushed more. It's not a bad drawing but it's very safe. I see this as a first or second pass. To be perfectly honest, when I drew this, it had been a little while since I'd done any caricature, so I was timid with my choices.

I have big eyes and a somewhat wide, expressive mouth, so those are the two main features that I chose to exaggerate in these drawings.

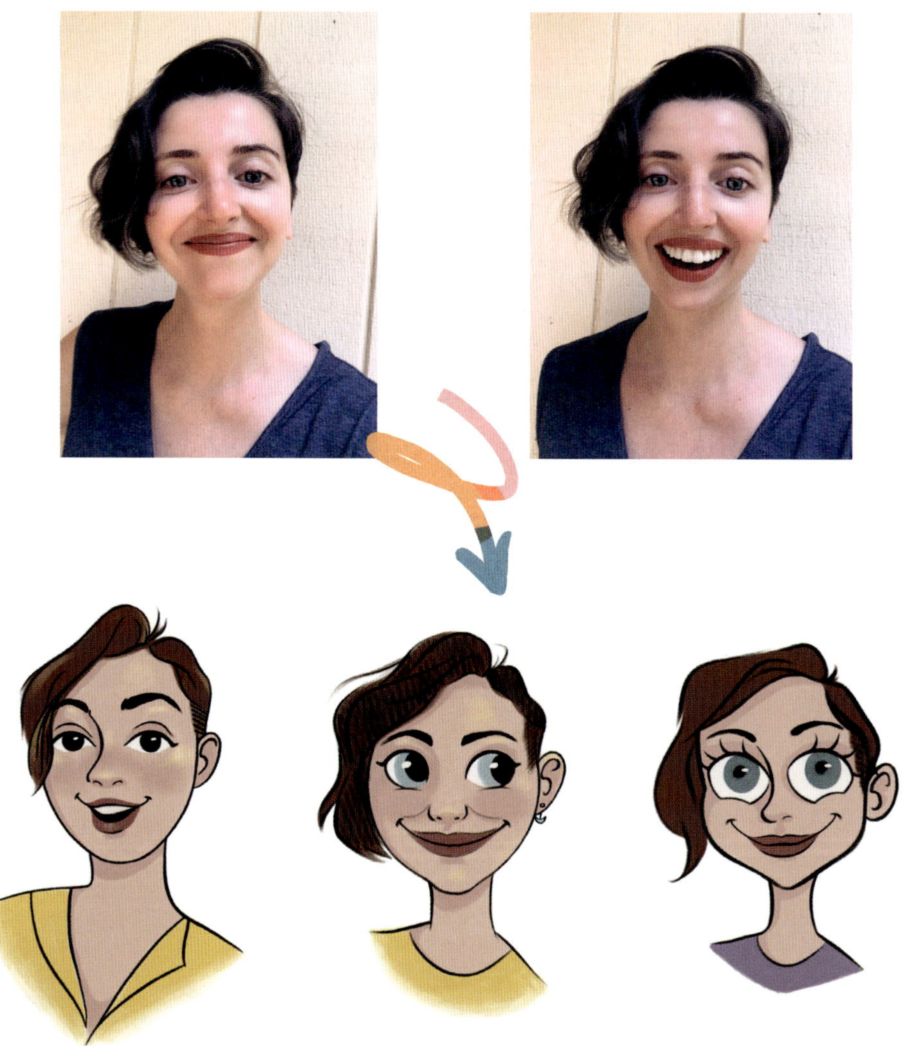

I also have an example here where I put aside those observations I made and deliberately messed around with the spacing and proportions. Notably, I made my eyes smaller and my nose longer. Remember, it's not just about making certain features bigger or smaller. By elongating my nose, I increased the spacing between my eyes and the bottom of my nose, which affects the entire face. This illustration of me is far less successful than the others. While none of those have a super strong resemblance to me, due to their symbolic and cartoony style, they capture more of my essence and spirit. I think that the areas of my face that I chose to exaggerate, and the personality inherent in those choices are what helped me achieve that effect. Likeness can be captured in personality just as much as in accurately portraying features!

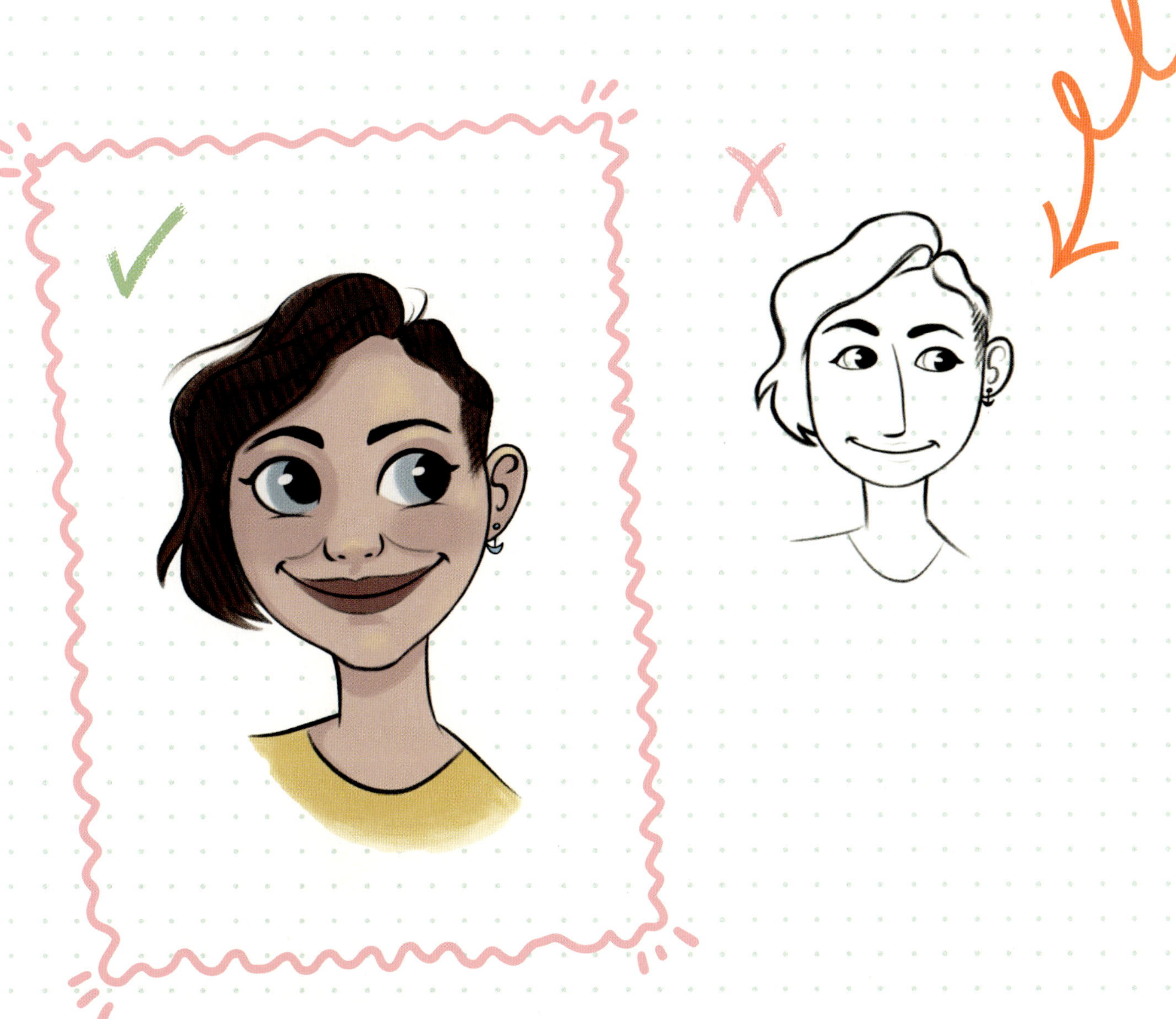

ABOUT THE AUTHOR

Melissa Lee is an illustrator and surface designer living in the hilly forests of Northern California. Alongside freelance illustration, quilting fabric design, art licensing, and selling her own products on Etsy, she's a Top Teacher on Skillshare, providing classes on a wide range of subjects, including surface pattern design, creative entrepreneurship, vector programs, watercolor techniques and, of course, caricature and character design.

For a long time, Melissa thought she wanted to be a character designer, but after interning for a video game company for a couple of years, she learned that she really only wanted to make her own characters. Despite knowing she didn't want to make it a career, she still had such a strong desire to continue learning and honing her character art skills. This is where her love of caricature began. Learning how entwined character design and caricature are led her on a path to consume any and all of the online education she could find (and some in-person workshops, too!). Eventually, she felt confident enough in her skills to start creating online caricature and character design classes of her own!

Melissa loves making repeating patterns, character art, and watercolor paintings, and is endlessly inspired by animals and nature (whether living today or extinct), science fiction and fantasy, space and astrology, witchy things, and bees.

Always bees.

You can follow more of Melissa's creative journey through her Instagram account @melissaleedesign and on her website at melissaleedesign.com.

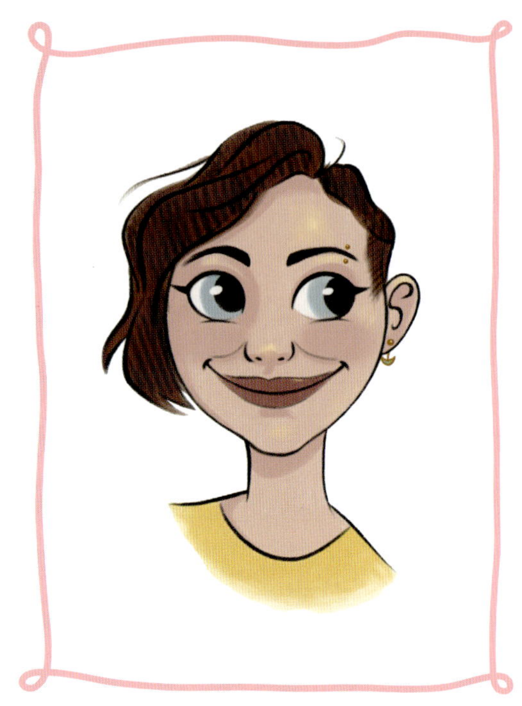

SUPPLIERS

Blick Art Materials

dickblick.com

Traditional media and paper.

Huion

huion.com

Light boxes (as recommended in the book).

Apple

apple.com

Apple iPad and Pencil.

RESOURCES

COURT JONES

Court's online courses are available on the Proko YouTube channel or at: Proko.com.

STEPHEN SILVER

Silver's online courses are available at: Silvertoons.com.

BROOKE GLASER

Brooke Glaser's online art classes are available at: brookeglaser.com.

CARICATURES BY MARIETTA

Specializes in quick caricature services for corporate events, weddings, parties, and festivals throughout the Kansas City area. Learn more at: mdartist.com.

WOMEN IN CARICATURE

An organization that "aims to provide a safe space and community for the development of women in caricature." They are trans-inclusive and offer a variety of resources, including workshops, artist spotlights, community nights, and opportunities to connect with other women in caricature. Learn more at: womenincaricature.com.

THE GAP BY IRA GLASS

A short film by Ira Glass (2023), made by Daniel Sax—inspired by and uses a quote by Ira Glass.

STEAL LIKE AN ARTIST

Book by Austin Kleon (2012), Workman.

ACKNOWLEDGMENTS

Creating this book has been a truly special experience, made possible by the support and encouragement of so many wonderful people along the way.

This book would not exist without the incredible team at David and Charles. Thank you for believing in me and this project. Special thanks to Nigel Browning, Lindsay Kaubi, Jess Cropper, and Clare Ashton for their expert guidance throughout this journey, not to mention their seemingly infinite patience. And a huge thank you to Lucy Ridley, whose brilliant graphic design work elevated this book beyond anything I could have envisioned myself.

To my family, who believed in me every step of the way. I am forever grateful for the countless ways you've enabled me to pursue this path. This book would not have been possible without you. And to my friends, my found family, who offered encouragement, feedback, and understanding during late nights and missed gatherings—your support has meant everything.

Finally, to you, the reader. Thank you for joining me on this caricature adventure. May these pages spark joy and creativity in your artistic journey.

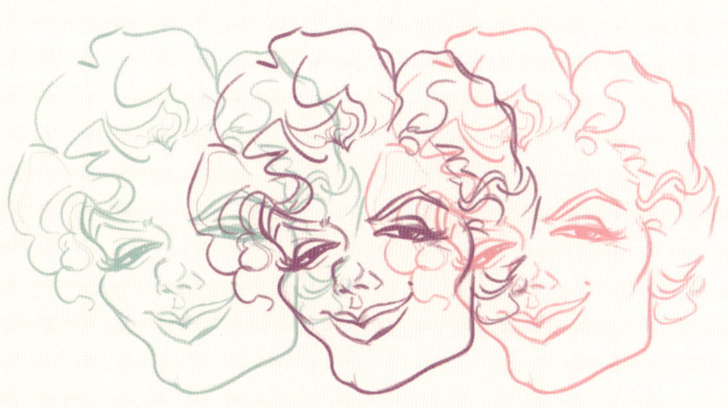

INDEX